THE ATTE  D

THE ATTENTION DEFICIT CHILD

Formerly titled *The Hyperactive Child*

Grant L. Martin, Ph.D.

Chariot Victor Publishing
A Division of Cook Communications

Chariot Victor Publishing,
a division of Cook Communications,
Colorado Springs, Colorado 80918
Cook Communications, Paris, Ontario
Kingsway Communications, Eastbourne, England

Editor: Barbara Williams
Design: Bill Gray
Cover Illustration: Mike Cressy

14 15 16 17 18 19 20 Printing/Year 02 01 00 99

Library of Congress Cataloging-in-Publication Data

Martin, Grant
    [Hyperactive child]
    The attention deficit child: what you need to know about attention-deficit
hyperactive disorder: facts, myths, and treatment/Grant L. Martin
    p. cm.
  Previously published: The hyperactive child. Wheaton, IL: Victor Books, 1992
    Includes bibliographical references (pp. 231-239).
    ISBN 1-56476-720-5
    1. Attention-deficit hyperactivity disorder--Popular works.
I. Title.
RJ506.H9M423   1998
618.92'8589--dc21

CONTENTS

INTRODUCTION

Some children can't sit still. They appear distracted by every little thing and don't seem to learn from their mistakes. These children disregard rules, even when they are punished repeatedly. They also tend to act without thinking, and this results in many accidents and reprimands.

Maybe you know a child like this. Perhaps you have a child who seems "hyper" or distractible. This book is about children who have problems with attention, impulse control, and over-arousal. This collection of problematic features is called Attention-Deficit/Hyperactivity Disorder (ADHD). Here are a few examples of experiences common with ADHD children:

> Whenever we take Fred out in public, we spend all of our time reminding him to sit down or be quiet. He never stops. He's impossible to take to church, so we've about decided not to go anymore. He's always moving ninety miles an hour.

> Sally daydreams constantly. We know she's bright, yet she's flunking several of her classes. The other day her dad and I struggled with her for several hours to get her homework done. At first she said she didn't have any. We checked her notebook and found the assignment sheet. She was tearful, but we finally completed the two pages of math. And would you believe it, the next day we got a call from her teacher telling us Sally hadn't turned in her work.

> I hate to pick Terry up at school. It seems that every day his teacher is telling me about Terry talking out in class, making animal noises, or getting out of his seat. He's only six years old, but I'm afraid he's already beginning to dislike school. I feel it's all my fault.

ADHD is one of the most common reasons children are referred to mental health professionals. It may be one of the most prevalent problems of childhood. The consensus of professional opinion is that approximately 3 to 5 percent of children have

ADHD. This translates to as many as 2 million school-age children. Every classroom in the country averages one ADHD child.

What is the problem here? Why do these children impulsively go from one activity to another? Whatever the reasons, ADHD makes family life very disruptive and stressful. No matter how hard parents of ADHD children try to do the right thing, their children persist in daydreaming, missing homework assignments, and neglecting chores.

Raising any child is difficult. But the burden seems overwhelming when a child fails to respond to normal methods. This "difficult" child continues to struggle with school, can't make or keep friendships, and becomes increasingly discouraged. Notes from the teacher and complaints from other parents about the inattentive and overactive child add to the parents' consternation.

Perhaps you are one of these disheartened parents. You've tried everything, but can't seem to get your child to settle down. This book is written for your aid and comfort.

We know a great deal about attention disorders. Because of extensive research, much has been identified about the prevalence, developmental nature, prognosis, and treatment of ADHD. At this point there is no known cure. However, enough is understood about management to make the life of an ADHD child much less frustrating. And with that help, you as a parent will find your guilt and anxiety reduced. Notice, I didn't say your anxiety would be eliminated. The job of parenting and teaching an attention deficit child is stressful. There will be times when you will want to move to Tasmania. However, I believe the material contained in this book will make your job much more manageable.

I have spent over thirty years working with children and their families. In that time, I have served as a school psychologist, classroom teacher, special education researcher, college professor, and clinician. I have dealt with almost 7,000 children and adolescents. Over the last twenty-four years in private practice as a child psychologist, I have completed hundreds of evaluations concerning the emotional and educational status of elementary and secondary students. Many of these students have had the features of attention deficit, hyperactivity, and related concerns.

It was from this base of experience that I wrote the first edition of this book, entitled *The Hyperactive Child*, in 1992. Now, it is from further experience and understandings that I have prepared this revision. Additional research on ADHD, changes in the official terminology, and refinements in my own experience suggested a revision was needed. With these updates, a more inclusive title for the book has been adopted. While I discussed both the hyperactive and inattentive types of children in *The Hyperactive Child*, the title conveyed that only the hyperactive, impulsive type of child was being described. The current title better conveys my intent to provide information about all aspects of ADHD.

I will be combining the best ideas of known authorities in the field, along with my own experience, to give you a practical resource. There are three parts to this book. In part 1, we will look at the definitions and the process of identifying an ADHD child. The labels for attention-deficit/hyperactivity disorder are confusing. Many children have difficulty with inattention and distractibility, but are not hyperactive. Some children have attentional and motivational problems along with overactive and impulsive behavior patterns. I will explain the different forms that attention disorder can take.

Historically, more boys than girls appear to have ADHD. For this reason I have chosen to use the male designation in many of my descriptions. Girls have been under-identified, partly because they tend to be daydreamers rather than "hyper" or aggressive. Hopefully, this type of discussion will make it possible for more of these youngsters to be identified and get the help they need.

Also in part 1, I will present the current best definitions of ADHD and tools for screening your child. If it appears as if your son or daughter may have some of the characteristics of ADHD, you will find help from the section on how to obtain a multidisciplinary evaluation, as well as the current opinions about the sources of attention disorders. A summary of genetic and environmental factors will help you understand the latest scientific explanations of the causes of attention disorders. Some of the myths of attention disorder will also be identified and explained, along with family reactions to a diagnosis of ADHD.

Part 2 will focus on the multidisciplinary approach to treatment and intervention. A child with attention disorder demands a whole-person approach. Medication alone is seldom sufficient. Those with ADHD need to learn the *skills* of living and learning, not just take the *pills*. Therefore, I will highlight several forms of intervention. Parental styles or deficiencies do not cause ADHD. However, some types of parental reactions can exaggerate or intensify the problems of an ADHD child. Many specific suggestions will be given to help you more effectively manage your high-maintenance son or daughter.

Part 2 will also present ideas for teaching self-control and social skills to the child who struggles with impulsivity and failure to follow rules. The difference between *unable* and *unwilling* is important. We will discuss this difference and how it applies to the ADHD child.

Educational intervention is critical to the success of an attention deficit student. Children with ADHD have chronic problems with distractibility, incomplete assignments, and disorganization. I will suggest ways to help reduce these hassles and help bring about more success at school. It is also true that many ADHD students have learning difficulties of some type. The implications for class placement and instruction of these students will be discussed.

Medication is often recommended for attention deficit children. While research shows medication can be quite helpful for many children, there are many legitimate questions about the use of medication in treating ADHD. We will examine some of the pros and cons of using medication, along with descriptions of treatment protocols, so you can make an informed decision about the possible use of medication for your child. Diet and other nonmedical strategies for the treatment of attention disorder will be briefly described.

An important section highlights the crucial aspects of spiritual issues in dealing with the whole child. In this part, I discuss the importance of prayer, spiritual resources, and keeping your own spiritual balance.

Since many parents of attention deficit children also have ADHD, chapter 10 includes a brief description of ADHD features in adults. This chapter includes an overview of adult characteristics, along with a summary of treatment approaches specific to ADHD adults. References for further study are also included.

Part 3 contains updated resources for the home and school. Educational materials for both the child and parent are listed, as well as names and addresses of various support groups and sources of additional information about ADHD. New resources and materials have been added since the first edition to make this section as relevant and useful as possible.

Attention-deficit/hyperactivity disorder is a very real problem that affects millions of children, adolescents, and adults. Certainly not all disruptive, forgetful, or active children have ADHD. It is important to know the differences. My prayer is that this book will help you become a more informed and confident parent or teacher. God desires a life of abundance for every child. The goal of this book is to help your child or student grow toward that potential.

Grant L. Martin, Ph.D.
Seattle, Washington
1998

PART ONE

Identification of ADHD

"I do not understand what I do. For what I want to do I do not do, but what I hate I do."

Romans 7:15

CHAPTER ONE

DO I HAVE AN ATTENTION DEFICIT CHILD?
Definition and Characteristics of ADHD

The tiger perched silently on the ledge overhanging the earthen trail below. His tail waved fitfully in the thick jungle air. A gray mist partially concealed the images of the adventurers inching their way toward the hungry cat. The bullet hole in his thigh served to intensify his rage and lust for a kill. The humans in expedition gear had no forewarning of the fate that awaited them. Then, just as the intruders passed under the ledge. . .

"Andrew, have you picked up your coat yet?" his mother called from the kitchen. "I told you thirty minutes ago to take your coat to your room. What on earth have you been doing all this time? Turn off that TV and do what I told you this very minute."

"But, Mom," Andrew wailed from the family room, where he was engrossed in the video game his uncle had given him for his birthday. "I'm in the middle of my Forbidden City adventure game. I'm at the third level and I've got 5,000 points. If I quit now, I'll lose!"

"I don't care where you are or how many points you have. Turn off that game and do what I told you or else I'll take it away and you won't play with it until you're twenty-one," Andrew's mother threatened.

Then, turning back to her casserole preparation, Andrew's mother muttered to herself, "I will never understand how he can sit in front of that stupid TV for hours or play silly video games without batting an eye. And yet when I ask him to do something, he can't concentrate for more than two minutes. What is the matter with him?"

Does this sound familiar? For many parents of children with attention disorders, this vignette is a common occurrence. There are over 12 million people, including children and adults, in the United States who have difficulties with attention, impulsivity, and overarousal. The current term for this collection of features is *attention-deficit/hyperactivity disorder* (ADHD). No one seems to know why these individuals can't pay attention. They are accused of being lazy, disobedient, willful, immature, or even demon-possessed. Left untreated, this developmental disorder disrupts a child's life and results in low self-esteem, poor grades, and social and emotional problems. Many of these features will not be outgrown without help. Imagine the impact of this description following a child throughout his school years.

Follow along as some other descriptions of ADHD are provided.

Noah is only five, but he keeps his household in constant turmoil. He throws temper tantrums over the slightest frustration. His moods shift in dramatic fashion. One minute he is lovable and cuddly. The next minute he can be angry beyond words.

Sarah never gets into trouble at school, yet her assignments seldom get completed on time. She dawdles getting ready for school and the constant delays surrounding her bedtime routine drive her parents crazy. She is forgetful and absentminded, but there are times when her insight and intelligence are amazing. Once a popular playmate with her peers, she now seems socially immature and out of step with many of her classmates.

It is only the middle of the school year, but the teacher is already talking about retaining Alex in the first grade. He seems bright enough, but seldom finishes his work. Any distraction at all in the classroom results in his attention shifting away from his assignment. Alex often blurts out answers without being called on, and constantly fidgets with items in his desk.

Karen got good grades through the eighth grade. She had always been a little spacey, and had lost more coats and backpacks than another dozen kids put together, yet had always managed to do just fine. However, in high school she seemed to hit the wall. Her grades dropped, she started hanging out with undesirable kids, and seemed to develop an attitude of indifference and apathy. Her parents were afraid they were losing their daughter.

If your child is having some of these problems at home, in school, and with his or her peers, you are concerned. It's also likely you are frustrated, and even frightened, because you don't know how to make things better for your son or daughter. Friends and family have offered all types of suggestions. You may have tried some of these ideas with limited or no success, and then have blamed yourself for your child's problems. Some family members say you need to be more firm and consistent. Others imply you are spoiling your child. You're told all he needs is a good spanking.

These well-meaning folks don't understand how difficult things are with your child. They don't realize that exclusively punitive methods just make him more aggressive.

It is difficult not to take on some feelings of blame and guilt. You believe you should be able to manage your child more effectively. There must be something wrong with you or your parenting skills to produce such a problem child. It's very natural that you would feel this way. Many parents of children with attention deficits have experienced the same range of emotions.

You also may have felt anger and resentment toward your child. You want him to respect and obey you, and you tend to take some of his misbehavior personally. Why does he always seem to be testing you? Sometimes you think he could embarrass the stripes off a zebra with the errors and accidents you have experienced. It seems this child of yours has a life mission to make you miserable. You bet you have taken these actions personally!

This anger also can become intense and frightening. Your patience is exhausted. The chores still aren't done, and you are nose-to-nose arguing about the status of the hamster cage. In the middle of this, your child calls you a demeaning name and your emotions cut loose. You slap him across the face, and he runs screaming to his room.

Later, you worry about physically or emotionally harming your child. Your tears overflow as feelings of despair and hopelessness overwhelm you. This is not what you wanted from parenthood. The books about parent-child relationships always show pictures of smiling children cuddling up to a beaming parent. Why hasn't this happened for you? Where did you go wrong?

Perhaps your situation is quite different. It may be that you don't have significant problems with angry or aggressive behavior, because your child is usually loving, cooperative, and obedient at home. Her problems revolve around school. She is bright but her grades are average. She either doesn't complete her assignments or fails to turn them in. The teacher thinks she's lazy.

The symptoms are different, but your feelings of frustration, guilt, and anger are constant. You want your child to succeed, but can't come up with a way to ensure her success. The teacher has suggested various ideas with little progress. Something works for a few days or weeks and then the old pattern returns. You wonder if there isn't something wrong with this kid's brain.

Is there hope? I want to assure you that there is help and hope for children with attention problems. It is true that we don't know of any "cure" for this disorder. However, much can be done to restore your faith in yourself and in your ability to care for your child.

Change always has two parts. The first part is *awareness* of the nature of a problem. The balance of this chapter will help you understand the various characteristics of attention disorders, so that you can more clearly identify whether your child has problems of this type.

The second component in bringing about change is appropriate *intervention*. It doesn't do any good to define the existence of a problem and then hope it will get better. There must be specific and relevant procedures that produce changes. The key is to know which interventions will bring about the desired improvements in the behavior of attention deficit children and adolescents. Possible interventions will be the thrust of the remaining chapters. But first, we must return to the task of understanding the nature of ADHD.

Why Should We Be Concerned?

Children with attention disorder are at high risk for school failure. Ninety percent of students with ADHD underachieve in school. As many as one-half are held back a grade at some point. Around 20 percent experience problems in reading. Serious handwriting difficulties occur in a majority of these students. About one-third drop out before high school graduation. Very few, perhaps 5 percent, complete a four-year college degree.

Untreated children with attention disorder of one type or another can experience serious social problems, including difficulty making and keeping friends, along with conflict with family members, resentment by siblings, and frequent scolding and punishment by caretakers. All of this contributes to a further disintegration of the child's attitude and behavior. A high number of the impulsive-hyperactive type develop severe enough behaviors to be later diagnosed as oppositional-defiant or conduct-disordered. Legal problems and substance abuse are two to three times more common in children and adolescents with untreated ADHD. For example, more than 20 percent of children with attention disorder have set serious fires in their communities, and more than 30 percent have engaged in theft. In addition, adolescents with attention disorder have nearly four times as many auto accidents, are more likely to cause bodily injury in these accidents, and will have three times as many citations for speeding than adolescents without ADHD.[1]

Definitions of Attention Disorders

History of terms

Because changes in terminology can be confusing, I will review the history of attention disorders. This will help you see the evolution of thought about the causes of this disorder. Efforts have been made to find a medical basis for problems of attention and overactivity, but the search for causes has been frustrating. New ideas about causation have brought accompanying changes in terms.

One of the earliest descriptions of hyperactive symptoms appeared in 1848 in a children's story written by a German physician about *Fidgety Phil*. The first scientific paper on the subject was written in 1902 by Dr. George Still, who described children who were inattentive, impulsive, and difficult. He referred to these children as having problems with "defects in moral control" and "volitional inhibition." An important feature of Dr. Still's work was his idea that the inattentive and distractible features of these children were not part of normal development. He thought the causes of the problems included heredity, trauma, and learning history. Dr. Still's discussion was helpful, even though he was pessimistic about treatment for these children.

Following a world outbreak of encephalitis in 1917–1918, researchers noted symptoms of restlessness, inattention, overarousal, and hyperactivity in children who had otherwise recovered from encephalitis. These patterns of behavior were thought to stem from some type of brain injury and were called *post-encephalitic disorders.*

In the 1950s, *psychotropic medications* became a very important part of treatment for institutionalized persons. With the help of medication, many of these adults could function in society. This success brought about a renewed interest in the use of stimulant medications for children with attention difficulties. The primary problem was thought to be hyperactivity. Limited attention span and impulsivity were seen as secondary symptoms. The source of hyperactivity was thought to be a brain injury. One of the main terms used during that period was *hyperkinetic impulse disorder.* However, clear evidence of any type of brain damage was still lacking.

Minimal brain dysfunction was the term used in the 1960s. However, much of the research of that decade was focused on the symptoms of the disorder, rather than its causes. By the 1970s, the shift in research resulted in the core problem being seen as *inattention* rather than excessive activity. The idea of some type of actual brain injury being the cause of these problems with inattention fell on hard times because of the lack of any medical support. Further research determined that most children with verifiable brain injuries did not develop hyperactivity. Additionally, hard evidence of structural brain damage was only found in fewer than 5 percent of hyperactive children. Since it could not be shown that there was obvious structural impairment, the term *minimal brain damage* became the diagnostic label of these years. It must have been "minimal" because the researchers couldn't see it. This term persisted, even though there was very little corroborating evidence of central nervous system damage.

A substantial amount of research during the 1970s resulted in the prevailing view that poor attention span and impulse control were of equal importance to hyperactivity. A major shift in views about causation took place during this period. Actual brain damage was thought to have a relatively minor role as the source of these problems. Other brain mechanisms such as underarousal, brain neurotransmitter deficiencies, or neurological immaturity were viewed as possible contributors to the problem. Diet and child-rearing were also seen as possible causative factors.

In the 1980s, investigation on the subject continued, making ADHD the most researched problem of childhood. The disorder was renamed Attention Deficit Disorder, with or without hyperactivity. ADHD and ADD were the letters used to designate the two forms. In 1987 the term was changed slightly to Attention-Deficit Hyperactivity Disorder to reflect the research findings that hyperactivity and impulsiveness found in these children are highly related to each other. By 1990, most professionals viewed ADHD as a developmentally handicapping condition that was usually chronic in nature. In 1994 a slash was added between "deficit" and "hyperactivity." Based on the history of these terms, this is probably not the final form of the label for this cluster of characteristics.

Current Definitions for ADHD

Most professionals now believe that ADHD consists of three primary problems in a person's ability to control behavior: (1) difficulties in sustained attention, (2) impulse control or inhibition, and (3) excessive activity. Some researchers, such as Barkley, would add the additional problems of: (4) difficulty following rules and instructions, and (5) the presence of excessive variability in response to many situations, especially schoolwork.

In short, ADHD is a developmental disorder in a person's ability to regulate his or her behavior, especially in regard to anticipating future actions and decisions. The child with ADHD seems to have a relative inability to keep from responding to whatever seems the most interesting or rewarding at the moment. They just can't wait. The causes are thought to have a strong biological source and are believed to be found in children with a hereditary predisposition.[2]

Impulsive-hyperactivity

Children with hyperactivity exhibit aggressive conduct problems, bizarre behavior, appear guiltless or unpopular, and perform poorly at school. They show less self-control and greater impulsivity. The hyperactive child is more noisy, disruptive, messy, irresponsible, and immature. The "whirling dervish" or

"Dennis the Menace" labels will apply. These children have a higher risk for serious aggressive or oppositional behavior and antisocial or acting-out behavior.[3]

Inattention-distractibility

In contrast, those attention deficit children who are predominantly inattentive tend to be anxious, shy, socially withdrawn, moderately unpopular, poor in sports, and have low school performance. The primarily inattentive student often is seen staring into space or daydreaming, is often forgetful in daily activities, appears to be low in energy, and is sluggish and drowsy. This group seems to have difficulty becoming sufficiently aroused and vigilant at a level that fosters adequate attention to academic tasks.

This student may be described as a "space cadet" or "couch potato" and often seems lost in thought, apathetic, and lethargic. He or she is less aggressive, impulsive, and overactive both at home and school, and has fewer problems in peer relationships.[4]

Combined features

Some children can have a combination of both inattention and hyperactive-impulsive features. This child will have most of the behavioral manifestations of inattention, such as failure to give close attention to details, careless mistakes, and being easily distracted by extraneous stimuli. In addition, the child will have trouble with hyperactive-impulsive features: he or she fidgets with hands or feet, is unable to remain seated, is often on the go, interrupts others, and has difficulty awaiting his or her turn.

All children will sometimes be inattentive, impulsive, or have high energy levels. But with attention deficit children, these symptoms are part of the daily routine rather than the exception. Also, these behaviors tend to occur at school, church, Grandma's house, and the grocery store, as well as at home. The general rule is that these children are consistently inconsistent.

The previous description follows the current official diagnostic criteria found in the *Diagnostic and Statistical Manual of Mental Disorders, Fourth Edition* developed by the American Psychiatric Association. A summary of the criteria of ADHD is presented in the table found on page 24. To qualify for an official diagnosis, a minimum number of these specific symptoms needs to have been a persistent problem for at least six months. These symptoms also need to occur to a degree that is maladaptive and inconsistent with the child's developmental level.

Besides finding six or more of the symptoms within each category that have persisted for six months or longer, these ADHD symptoms must be evident before age seven. We would also look to see that there was some impairment evident in two or more settings of a child's life, such as school, home, or in the community. In addition, there must be clear evidence of clinically significant impairment in a person's social, academic, or occupational functioning. Furthermore, the symptoms must not be a result of another mental disorder, such as schizophrenia, or some type of mood or personality disorder.

Depending on the type and number of symptoms present, a child can be identified as ADHD, predominantly Inattentive Type; ADHD, predominantly Hyperactive-Impulsive Type, or ADHD, Combined Type.

Remember, this is a beginning awareness. Checking off six or more of the above characteristics doesn't automatically mean your child has ADHD. These criteria are intended to be applied by a highly trained professional and combined with many other pieces of information.

There are some problems with using the DSM-IV guidelines. The DSM-IV criteria have no provision for normative comparisons. A five-year-old will have a different level of significance than a ten-year-old. Boys will also have a different profile from girls. The same criteria are supposed to be used with children and adults, yet we know many of the hyperactive symptoms subside in adulthood. Other problems arise when there is disagreement between parent and teacher evaluations. The DSM-IV criteria also require that behavior problems show up in at least two settings, such as home, school, and work. How many eight-year-olds have a work setting?

The DSM-IV list is inadequate by itself to provide an accurate diagnosis. If it is the only factor used in assessment, we would come up with too many children who score high on the checklist who are not really ADHD. There are definite methods and procedures to work around the weaknesses of these criteria. I just want to emphasize how important it is to get a professional opinion based on a thorough evaluation before reaching a firm conclusion or diagnosis of ADHD.

Not all ADHD children look and behave the same way, and we must be sensitive to their differences. The type of intervention chosen should be based on the specific needs of your child. We must not blindly treat all attention deficit students in the same manner. The answer is to use these diagnostic criteria as part of a compre-

DSM-IV
Diagnostic Criteria for ADHD[5]

Symptoms of Inattention:
- ❏ Often fails to give close attention to details or makes careless mistakes in schoolwork, work, or other activities.
- ❏ Often has difficulty sustaining attention in tasks or play activities.
- ❏ Often does not seem to listen when spoken to directly.
- ❏ Often does not follow through on instructions and fails to finish schoolwork, chores, or duties in the workplace (not due to oppositional behavior or failure to understand instructions).
- ❏ Often has difficulty organizing tasks and activities.
- ❏ Often avoids, dislikes, or is reluctant to engage in tasks that require sustained mental effort (such as schoolwork or homework).
- ❏ Often loses things necessary for tasks or activities (e.g., toys, school assignments, pencils, books, or tools).
- ❏ Is often easily distracted by extraneous stimuli.
- ❏ Is often forgetful in daily activities.

Symptoms of Hyperactivity-Impulsivity:
Hyperactivity
- ❏ Often fidgets with hands or feet or squirms in seat.
- ❏ Often leaves seat in classroom or in other situations in which remaining seated is expected.
- ❏ Often runs about or climbs excessively in situations in which it is inappropriate. (In adolescents or adults, may be limited to subjective feelings of restlessness.)
- ❏ Often has difficulty playing or engaging in leisure activities quietly.
- ❏ Is often "on the go" or often acts as if "driven by a motor."
- ❏ Often talks excessively.

Impulsivity
- ❏ Often blurts out answers before questions have been completed.
- ❏ Often has difficulty awaiting turn.
- ❏ Often interrupts or intrudes on others (e.g., butts into conversations or games).

hensive evaluation which draws on several types of objective assessment instruments. I will give more details about the assessment process in chapter 3.

Characteristics of ADHD Children

I will now describe specific ways that children with ADHD act and respond. There are four categories of behavior that most experts report as crucial to identifying the presence of attention disorders. These features go beyond the basic characteristics identified in the DSM-IV listing and give a more complete picture of the various ways attention disorders can manifest themselves in daily life.

Boys versus girls

Some studies have shown boys are three to six times more likely to have ADHD than girls. Other data indicates that when more precise measures of attention are used, the incidence may be more equal. Girls tend to display their ADHD more through attention deficits than through problems with impulsivity and aggression. Girls are often seen as "daydreamers" rather than hyperactive. They tend to have fewer problems with outward conduct, so aren't referred as often. Thus, girls may be seriously underdiagnosed.[6]

No one is sure why ADHD appears to be more common in boys. We do know that boys seem to be more at risk in developing almost any childhood behavioral or emotional problem. For example, three or four times as many boys as girls are referred for reading problems. Current thought about ADHD is that it may be a sex-linked predisposition which causes the condition to show up more frequently in males. More research is needed to complete the explanation. We also need to make sure our definition of ADHD does not bias our search in the direction of overactivity and leave out the less active girls.

Inattention and distractibility

Children with ADHD commonly have difficulty with *inattention and distractibility*. An attention deficit child may have difficulty remaining with a task and focusing his attention, in comparison to other children of the same age. He may daydream or become easily distracted. One minute he is listening to the teacher; then he may switch his focus to the bug on the wall or the bird flying around outside the window. This means he will have difficulty concentrating on schoolwork or anything that requires sustained attention. Completing tasks or following through on instructions will be difficult. This is especially hard if the instructions involve multiple steps. This child gives the impression of not listening, and often loses or forgets things because he is inattentive and distracted.

Just as surprising, and often frustrating to the parent, is the remarkable ability of many ADHD children to pay attention under certain circumstances. An example is watching TV or playing video games. The child may also attend well when he is in the doctor's office or when he is interacting one-on-one with an adult. This variable ability can add to the problem. When parents and teachers see the child attending in one situation, they may conclude that he simply does not try to pay attention at excluded times when he is asked to do chores or listen to instructions.

We assume a child is able to choose to ignore or respond to a stimulus presented to the brain. When a teacher starts talking, for example, a child should consciously shift his concentration from the book he is reading to the teacher's voice. To understand attention disorders, we need to know how much of the attentional choosing is under conscious control and how much is biochemically determined.

In summary, these children have difficulty *beginning* activities, *sustaining* attention until the activity is completed successfully, and *focusing* attention on two stimuli at the same time. Focusing includes tasks such as taking notes in the classroom and watching the teacher write on the board at the same time. Finally, they have trouble being *vigilant* or ready to respond to the next important cue or prompt necessary for instruction or direction.

These children tend to have problems *selecting and screening* the important from the unimportant features of their immediate surroundings in their attempt to attend to a task. ADHD students may also be distracted *internally* by their own thoughts. These difficulties in inattention and distractibility create a dual problem which yields poor and inconsistent performance in many school, home, and social situations.[7]

Hyperactivity

The second major characteristic is *overarousal* or *hyperactivity*. Some ADHD children are excessively restless, overactive, and easily aroused. This feature can affect body movement and/or emotions. We will look at these areas separately. It is also important to remember that while hyperactivity used to be the primary descriptive feature in attention disorders, it actually occurs in less than 30 percent of children who have ADHD. Most ADHD children are not hyperactive. The terminology has been confusing here. Sometimes *hyperactivity* is used to refer to the entire syndrome of ADHD. Other times the term is intended to describe only the specific characteristic of overarousal. Keep these different uses in mind as you read various books and articles about attention deficit disorders.

Children who are *hyperactive* have difficulty controlling their body movements, especially when they are required to sit still for a long time. This hyperactive aspect of ADHD can range from minor fidgeting to perpetual motion. A child can have difficulty sitting still in class or can be in constant motion from morning till night. Some hyperactive children also have short and restless sleep patterns.

Because the hyperactive behavior pattern is rarely focused, the child moves from one item to the next with very little purpose. This activity level can rise with increased stimulation in the environment. A trip to the grocery store can be an adventure with a hyperactive child. However, a journey to the shopping mall with a stop at the toy store can be an absolute disaster.

The second component of overarousal is the *emotional variation*. What is obvious here are the extremes of the children's emotions and the quickness with which they go to those extremes. This variation is greater and more intense than in the same features of their peers. Whether happy or sad, their feelings are expressed ever so clearly for everyone to notice. They become frustrated very quickly, often over minor incidents. However, they will forget an upsetting event just as quickly. This can be frustrating to a parent who is still bothered by the outburst and can't understand why the child no longer is agitated. Because of this quick turnaround, the assumption is often made that these children are lacking in conscience. This is usually not true. They have moved on to other thoughts and feelings, and have put the outburst behind them. It's hard to believe sometimes, but it's true.

Impulsivity

The third major characteristic of ADHD is *impulsivity*. These children appear to not think before they act. Due to their concentration problems, they have trouble weighing the consequences of their choices and planning future actions.

In young children, impulsivity may result in frequent injuries. The child often literally leaps before he looks. He may jump off of the back of the couch because it looks like fun, but not have the coordination to land safely. He may also have frequent fights with his friends because of his impulsive words and actions.

This impulsive quality makes these children want to be in charge of all social interactions. As a result, they annoy their peers by their attempts to dominate. Impulsive-hyperactive children seek to take charge because this dominance allows them to move quickly from one interaction to another so they won't become bored. They may also aggravate others because of their aggressiveness.

In the classroom they may constantly interrupt the teacher, jumping up to answer a question before it is even asked. They are prone to work impulsively on paper, jotting down answers without thinking problems through or reading the complete question.

When you reason one-to-one with children who have attention deficit, they can often logically analyze the consequences of their actions. Put them back in a group, however, and they seem to be overwhelmed and continue to act first and think later.

Problems in inhibition and following rules

A major characteristic of an ADHD child is his trouble following rule-governed behavior. He may know the rule and be able to explain it to you. But ten minutes later, when the parent is not looking, that same child is unable to control his behavior. The need for immediate gratification and an inability to stop and think, results in repeated offenses. This leads to more impetuous, non-thinking behavior. And from all appearances, the child does not learn from his experience. The parent may often label this behavior as willfully disobedient, inconsiderate, and oppositional. This child is frustrating because of his inability to benefit from experience.

One way to understand the essence of ADHD is to imagine *a thick barrier*. This barrier stands firmly between the child and the attempts of the outside world to control his behavior. The rewards, punishments, and consequences that usually make it through the child's skull and influence behavior seem to bounce off the ADHD child's thick barrier. It is like a giant callus that overlays the brain, keeping instructions and consequences out. Even when the message gets through, its impact doesn't last for very long.

Several years ago, a leading researcher and proponent of the thick-barrier hypothesis was Dr. Russell Barkley. He summarized the core problems as deficits in: (1) the ability to cope with routine rules; (2) the ability to sustain appropriate behavior in the absence of clear, frequent, and immediate consequences; and (3) the long-term effects of rewards and punishments.[8]

These deficits concern the ADHD child's inherent difficulties in being appropriately regulated by his environment. An ADHD child falters when confronted by rules. He has problems completing tasks unless there are very clear limits and immediate consequences to the behavior. Reinforcements must also be interesting and meaningful to have any effect. This last characteristic takes us to the next unique feature.

Most children with attention deficits have *difficulty with rewards*. ADHD children have problems working toward a long-term goal. They often want brief, repeated payoffs, rather than a single, delayed reward. They want what they want right away and are less patient than we would expect children of that age to be. Even with repeated rewards, ADHD children do not respond as well as other children to incentive systems. They often learn to work to avoid aversive or negative consequences (negative reinforcement), rather than to earn positive consequences. Also, once the reward system and structure are removed, the ADHD child is more likely to regress.

Punishments also seem to have limited effect on the child's behavior. A scolding might keep a non-ADHD child well behaved for most of a day. It will usually work on the ADHD child only for a few minutes before the misbehavior resumes.

More recently Barkley has suggested that the problems experienced by those with ADHD arise from a core deficit in *behavioral inhibition*. They have a developmental delay in impulse control. This is a problem of putting on the brakes or having reliable control of one's behavior. In this view, all of the defining characteristics of ADHD reflect a serious problem in controlling, regulating, or executing behavior. Those with attention disorder don't suffer from a lack of skill; rather, they have a deficiency in their ability to control themselves.[9]

Dr. Barkley's theory proposes that ADHD is a disorder of self-control, willpower, and the organizing and directing of behavior toward the future. Due to developmental/neurological problems affecting the frontal part of the brain, a person with attention disorder has an impairment in the basic mental process which allows him to inhibit his behavior. It's kind of like driving a car and intending to stop for a light, only to find that when you step on the brake pedal, the car doesn't respond to your command and just keeps on going.

One way to differentiate between the ADHD child and the

child who looks hyperactive but is not is the "can't versus won't" dimension. The ADHD child can intentionally be disobedient. Yet he often has trouble with self-control, sustained attention, and organization, even when he wants to do well. You have a sense that sometimes the ADHD child cannot pay attention or follow the rules, in spite of his best efforts.

To illustrate, I would like to share a short essay written by an ADHD student. The essay was assigned after an act of disobedience. (It was one of many such failures.) The topic was "Following Rules," and I think this fourth-grade boy's statements show how he really wants to be obedient but often fails. (I corrected his spelling to make it easier to get his poignant message.)

"It's good to follow the rules because if you don't you could get hurt, die, break a bone, or have a bad injury. I should follow the rules too. I try to, but it's hard for me because I'm too hyper. If you don't follow the rules, you will get a lot of referrals. Too many referrals means suspension from school. If you don't follow the rules you'll end up like me, a low-down scumbucket. I am a very bad kid in school.

"I like school. The only problem is I always have trouble. I'll do anything if you don't tell my mom about this. Also if you don't follow the rules, you'll never grow up right and nobody will like you. You might become a robber and steal jewelry. You'll be rich but it was stupid of you to steal in the first place. You never learn anything if you don't follow the rules. I barely ever follow the rules. I never learn anything.

"If you don't follow the rules, when you're grown up you might turn out like a bum. And you'll never ever be smart unless you go back to school and start from the third grade. I get bad grades because I don't follow the rules that much. Always follow the rules and you'll never ever be a bad person."

You get the feeling from this boy's letter that he really wants to follow the rules and do well in school. At the same time he is very discouraged because he can't do a better job.

In contrast, the disobedient child who is not ADHD often shows the capacity for self-control. You get the feeling from such a child that he chooses, either consciously or otherwise, to resist following the rules. If you know this capable but noncompliant child well enough, you begin to get a sense of willfulness or "won't" that tells you the capability to behave correctly is there. However, the child chooses otherwise.

In the chapters on various forms of intervention, I will highlight the importance of *discerning between unwilling* and *unable*. Sometimes, with an ADHD child, expecting him to follow certain rules consistently is similar to asking a blind person to read the evening newspaper. The difference is that a blind person will consistently be unable to see, while an ADHD child can sometimes follow the rules and sometimes not. Life isn't easy for the ADHD child or for his parents.

Hyperfocus
Although not a part of the official criteria, some people appear to have a tendency to hyperfocus. They become so absorbed and pre-occupied with an activity that they tune out everything around them. It appears a bomb could go off in the same room and they wouldn't deviate from the TV program they were watching, the book they were reading, or the model they were building.

There have also been a few people who seem to be the extreme opposite of hyperactive. They are said to be *hypoactive*. They move like cold molasses on a winter morning. Lethargy, apparent indifference, apathy, and slow motion are their way of life. At the same time, projects or school assignments don't get completed because it takes so long to get things done.

Individual uniqueness and creative potential
Remember, no ADHD child will have all of the features described. Like snowflakes, no two persons are alike. Attention disorders covers a large collection of traits and behaviors. Some children may have dozens of those traits, while other children will have only a few. Even if two children have an equal number of traits, each set of features can be quite different.

I would like to emphasize a couple of important points to remember about attention disorder. First, ADHD is not a single dimensional characteristic. At this time, we use one general term to describe the cluster of problems associated with attention-deficit/hyperactive disorder. This term actually encompasses a series of related, but different, characteristics. As has been described, some children (and adults) are seen as primarily inattentive and are more likely to be seen as "out of touch," "in a fog," or not quite "in gear" when it comes to many aspects of thinking and doing their schoolwork. Other students fit the ADHD profile, primarily the hyperactive-impulsive category, and are more active, aggressive, and likely to have social and behavior problems. Then there are those who have both sets of features and are identified as ADHD, combined type. All three types can be challenging to parents and teachers. Yet each category has different needs that require unique forms of intervention.

The second important point to remember is that ADHD occurs along a continuum of severity. The DSM-IV uses the designations *mild, moderate,* and *severe,* although there is no objective threshold for any of these descriptors. If your child suffers a broken arm and requires a cast, it is reasonably clear what his limitations are going to be for a few weeks. It is not as obvious with attention disorders. Not all students will require the same degree of accommodation or environmental modification. To further complicate the picture, many students with ADHD are consistently inconsistent. On Monday, Betty gets ready for school with minimal fussing. However, on Tuesday she has several hissy fits before she even gets her teeth brushed. The structure and routine appear the same on both days. What accounts for the variation in Betty's behavior? We don't really know. The same could be said about the fact that Harold seems to know his multiplication tables well on Wednesday, and on Thursday acts as if he's never seen them before.

It is true that most ADHD students perform best when there is close supervision. They also do best when the activity contains frequent and intense reinforcement. They attend better when the task at hand only requires short-term participation or contains material that is novel, interesting, or highly entertaining. If, on the other hand, the assignment requires diligent concentration, sustained effort, and has minimal supervision, the probability of successful completion is very low.

There are common features that allow us to identify students with attention disorder as opposed to something like depression. However, we must never lose sight of these individual differences and the implications for treatment. It is a tremendous injustice to lump all special-needs students into the same box and respond to them in the same manner. Each child is unique, and we need to account for all of those individual aspects as we plan and care for them.

I wish to also emphasize the importance of focusing on the positive and not on the negative features of ADHD. There are many positive qualities to attention disorder. Many characteristics of these children are quite appropriate and desirable. Their spontaneity, zest, tirelessness, enthusiasm, intensity, curiosity, stimulating brashness, and life-of-the-party energy have their useful moments. The inattentive child can be thoughtful and deliberate, kind to others, often doesn't make waves, and is easier to have around the home or classroom.

Also, there may be some link between ADHD and giftedness and creativity. These children have rich imaginations and can quickly generate new and different ideas. They can pick up on emotional nuances that other people miss. Many of them can combine ideas in creative ways through art and written forms that no one else has tried.

Dr. Lynn Weiss has described teens and adults with ADD in another format. While not an "official" or research-based model, her observation is that the core characteristics of ADD seem to surface in three distinct ways. There is the Outwardly Expressed ADD, the Inwardly Directed ADD, and the Highly Structured ADD.[10]

Outwardly Expressed types or *active entertainers* tend to be honest, forthright, expressive, and often have a positive attitude toward their goals. Their feelings are expressed openly and actively. They tend to be quite spontaneous and have a keen awareness of their environment. They can be good at problem-solving, often excel in sports, and have a great sense of humor. This type of person can be successful in sales, entertainment, entrepreneurship, or any other field which requires quickness and high energy. The teenager or adult with Outwardly Expressed ADD will often have a number of close friends instead of just one, and thrives on change and the challenge of new situations.

Inwardly Directed types of ADD could also be called *restless dreamers*. Their feelings and behavior are not overtly displayed, but are stuffed inside. They tend to keep their feelings to themselves. Their impulsivity and impatience is more subtly expressed. They can be good friends, are not judgmental, and are sensitive to other people's needs. They spend a lot of time with their friends or talking on the phone. This type of person excels at work that requires being a supporter or helper rather than a leader. They are cooperative and make excellent team members. The Inwardly Directed type can find success in fields utilizing creativity, mechanical, technical, and computer skills, along with service-oriented careers.

The third type described by Dr. Weiss is the Highly Structured ADD or the *conscientious controller*. These people prefer structure. They feel out of control if their structure is changed. They can work hard, attend to their school assignments, and are detail-oriented perfectionists. Their impulsivity and impatience are often expressed as judgments. They tend to be anxious and demanding. They often are good debaters, have strongly held opinions about most things, and can usually do a good job of communicating their point of view. These people can make effective leaders and project managers because of their attention to detail. Career possibilities include the military, accounting, and other fields which demand attention to detail and precision.

Each of these types also has its areas of difficulty. For example, the person with Outwardly Expressed ADD takes too many risks, may suffer wide mood swings, and may spread himself too thin. The person with Inwardly Directed ADD may not set appropriate boundaries, may have trouble making decisions, and may be inefficient in the approach to tasks. Finally, the person with Highly Structured ADD may be too demanding, have problems with anger, and be overly controlling.

The point here, again, is to remember that your child is unique. He or she has strengths and characteristics that can be tremendous assets for life. We just need to find ways to focus those abilities in the most positive way possible. ADHD ends with the word "disorder." Some would choose to change that to "different." ADD doesn't have to be seen as a disability. With proper direction, many of the qualities of attention differences can be used in beneficial ways.

The great need is to bring their problem behaviors under control so that their abilities can be harnessed for good. Some of the most creative persons in history, such as Thomas Edison and Albert Einstein, may have had ADHD.

Try to remain optimistic and hopeful. Even though the future will hold times of discouragement, the ADHD child and his or her family can experience joy and success. The purpose of the following chapters is to help you move closer to that goal.

Developmental Profile of ADHD

Now we will look at ADHD characteristics from a developmental perspective. The major categories of inattention, overarousal, impulsivity, and difficulty with rewards will be present at each age. This discussion will help identify how these major symptoms present themselves at each of the developmental stages.

• *Infants.* Some children who are later identified as attention deficit may show the following behaviors at an early age. They are high maintenance from day one. They often have sleeping and eating problems. Colic is common, as are food allergies and ear infections. Sharp mood swings may be apparent and many ADHD babies are fussy, difficult to comfort, and resist being held or cuddled. This can feel like rejection to the new parent and can even lead to difficulties with bonding between parent and infant. Many of these same infants may also be highly sensitive to stimuli, ranging from sounds or light, to types of clothing. These same babies also appear to be very alert, active, and curious. In addition, they can display amazing strength as evidenced by holding their head up or turning over in the first few weeks.

Keep in mind that these symptoms do not necessarily mean your child has attention deficit disorder. However, some of these features do identify babies who are at risk, especially if either of the parents has been diagnosed with ADHD.

Another concern is for children who have been adopted. Estimates of the incidence of ADHD in these children have ranged from 25 to 40 percent. Prospective adoptive parents should get as much medical and educational background as possible in order to weigh the risks before making a final decision.

• *Preschool children.* At some point most parents will describe their preschooler as inattentive and overactive. Eventually these qualities will level out. As a result, these descriptions alone will not help identify young ADHD children. It is recommended that any of the symptoms of ADHD have at least a one-year duration before being considered a stable condition.

Young children with a durable pattern of ADHD, impulsive-hyperactive type, are restless, always on the go, acting as if driven by a motor. They can be like a walking tornado. They move into a room pulling toys off shelves, dumping out baskets of crayons, and knocking over the dolls and blocks. If an object is not nailed down, it will be picked up or pushed over. They frequently climb on and get into things. They are more likely to have injuries as a result of their overactive, inattentive, and fearless behavior. This type of child takes risks that most children would not take. They are forever getting hurt but never learning from the experience. They don't know why they jump out of open windows—it just seems like a good idea at the time.

Childproofing your home is a good idea to help prevent accidents and injuries. It also is necessary to protect family valuables, such as your grandmother's Tiffany lamp, from the vigorous and destructive pattern of play often seen in these children. They are persistent in their wants, demanding of attention, and have an insatiable curiosity about the world in which they live.

It is at this preschool stage that we begin to see the child's ability to focus and concentrate is impaired. She may watch TV for five minutes, get distracted, and color for five minutes. Then she sees a friend outside and wants to play, even though it is nearly bedtime and her mother has just told her to get in the bathtub.

In a one-on-one situation, the child can sustain attention for longer periods, although there will still be a lack of ability in this area. Also, exposure to a group usually results in more distractibility and higher activity levels. Many parents have told me birthday parties and family gatherings spell disaster for their oversensitive child.

Sometimes, even in a group, an ADHD preschool child will focus on an activity by blocking out the rest of the world. Then she may concentrate for long periods watching a television program, digging in the sand, or playing with Legos. When a child's focus is locked on an activity, it can be difficult to distract her. You may need to go to the child and touch her on the shoulder in order to get her attention. This will work much better than yelling. While focusing on her program, she really doesn't see or hear what is going on around her. It is frustrating to work with a child when you think she is ignoring you. You need to remember that the child with an attention deficit has to tune everything else out in order to concentrate. She isn't making a conscious choice to ignore you. She probably doesn't hear you at all.

The child may not have this tuning-out ability all the time, and it usually doesn't happen in a group setting. You do need to recognize this "blocking out" process does occur from time to time, and then treat your child with understanding.[11]

All of this presents a major challenge to parents. Patterns of family disruption are established quite early. Negative cycles of tell-remind-yell-spank become established. It becomes easy to see the child as a negative influence on the whole family.

Some ADHD preschoolers also exhibit excessive moodiness, quickness to anger, and low adaptability. Temper tantrums are common for all preschoolers, but the frequency and intensity is greater in ADHD children. Also, some ADHD preschool children may show rhythmic patterns, such as head banging or rocking. This may first show up in their crib or bed, but it can also happen while they are playing or trying to focus.

Stomach problems are common in ADHD children. Lack of coordination in large or small muscle group activities is also noticeable. They will produce sloppy or messy seatwork at preschool, Sunday School, or kindergarten. On the other hand, many ADHD children are quite coordinated and athletic, so this feature is not a firm characteristic for attention disorder.

There can be a great deal of off-task behavior. The child will wander away from his seat or table at school. While the teacher is instructing other children on a certain task, this child will be doing something else. He requires greater amounts of adult attention and supervision than do most other preschool children.

Preschool ADHD children, particularly of the impulsive-hyperactive type, begin a pattern of intrusiveness. They bother others by talking to them, touching them, or intruding on their projects and play. They also seek attention through inappropriate or excessive ways such as making animal noises, teasing, or clowning.

At times these children do slow down enough to interact, and then we find they can be very loving and caring. We see that they want very much to please and have a hard time understanding why everyone is so frustrated with them. When they break something in their relentless pursuit of activity, they truly are remorseful. They fail to learn from these experiences, though, and as other acts of aggression increase, they begin to alienate their peers and teachers.

• *School-age children.* Once an ADHD child enters school, a major social burden is placed upon him that will last for at least the next twelve years. School makes the greatest demands on his areas of disability and can create a large amount of distress for the child and his family. The abilities to sit still, attend, listen, obey, inhibit impulsive behavior, cooperate, organize actions, and be pleasant with other children are essential to negotiating a successful school career. These skills go beyond the cognitive and achievement skills needed to master the curriculum itself. Also, if there are any types of learning disabilities in addition to ADHD, the burden is multiplied. Because of these demands, identification of ADHD often takes place after entry into the full-time classroom.

The school may raise the issue of retaining the child in either kindergarten or first grade because of immature behavior and/or low academic achievement. Homework requirements become a focus of concern because of the ADHD child's inability to complete them or turn in his assignments. Daydreaming, talking out, and out-of-seat behavior are frequently reported by the teachers of ADHD elementary students.

It is common to hear parents complain that their perfectly

bright child can get all of her spelling words the night before the test. However, at exam time the ADHD child acts as though she'd been raised in Madagascar and had never seen an English spelling list in her life. The student sincerely wants to do her best, but the schoolwork doesn't improve.

This child will be listening to the teacher one minute, then a classmate will sneeze or drop a pencil and her attention will be lost. Then she can't redirect herself back to the original focus. Her distractibility makes it hard to complete an assignment. She starts out with a strong effort, but loses her train of thought and ends up on a whole different track. She may not even get past putting a heading on the paper before she completely forgets the assigned task.

Free flight of ideas is a constant problem for young school children with attention deficit. Their minds may wander so extensively that they actually spend a large portion of their school day in a world of imagination. While they think about birthday parties and baseball games, they look like they are concentrating on what the teacher is saying. In reality, their minds are miles away.

Impulsivity can seriously affect schoolwork. The ADHD child may not take the time to think through what he is doing in regard to a written assignment. He may work quickly and carelessly, making frequent spelling errors by leaving out letters. The child may make many mistakes on simple math problems by putting numbers in the wrong columns or using an incorrect procedure, such as subtracting instead of adding.

Disorganization is very common in the ADHD student. Inevitably, the child will bring home the wrong book or forget the dentist appointment right after school. He will fail to turn in the homework he spent an hour completing with his parents the night before. The same applies to chores around the home. The child with attention deficit fully intends to cut the lawn. He just got distracted by the neighborhood football game and forgot to finish the lawn, leaving the lawn mower, rake, and garbage bags right in the middle of the yard. The end result is that children with ADHD need more supervision and assistance with daily chores and self-help activities such as dressing and bathing.

The ADHD child is forgetful when it comes to her belongings. She continually misplaces articles of clothing, shoes, toys, and books. Parents may have a terrible time getting the child off to school on time with matching shoes and socks, jacket, lunch, textbooks, and homework. She will have no idea where the missing items are. Homework papers will turn up in the clothes hamper, and the lost lunch is eventually found in the toy box.

Social rejection is common with many attention deficit children, particularly if they are impulsive and hyperactive. Even when an ADHD child displays appropriate behavior toward others, it may be at such a high rate or intensity that it elicits rejection. Vocal noisiness, and a tendency to touch and manipulate objects more than is normal for this age, combine to make the ADHD child overwhelming, intrusive, and aversive to others. It is common to find these children developing feelings of low self-esteem about school and peers. Yet many will blame their problems on their teachers, classmates, or parents because of their limited self-awareness. As they grow, temper tantrums will decline, as happens with most children, but ADHD children will still have more temper outbursts than non-ADHD children.

Relationships with siblings may be filled with tension and conflict. Some brothers and sisters will develop resentment over the greater burden they often carry compared to their hyperactive siblings. They may also become jealous over the amount of time an ADHD brother or sister demands from their parents.

Most children become active in extracurricular community activities such as sports teams, clubs, scouts, and church groups. ADHD children may find themselves barely tolerated or even

---

Things to Do with an Eraser—
If You're ADHD

1. Use it as a substitute for gum.
2. Throw it toward the wastebasket like a basketball.
3. Build an igloo with tiny pieces.
4. Bounce it on the floor.
5. Use pieces of it in a peashooter.
6. Break it into small pieces and use as confetti.
7. Share parts of it with your neighbors.
8. Feed it to the class guinea pig.
9. Use it to level the legs of your desk.
10. Lose it or use it, so you can borrow another one (while the teacher is giving the class spelling words).

rejected. Parents then have to come to the rescue, explain or apologize to leaders, and try to negotiate the child's reentry into the group.

Many of these attention deficit characteristics sound like normal childhood traits. Most children are distractible, forgetful, impulsive, and moody at times. All children daydream occasionally and have trouble concentrating on reading material or the words of a speaker. What makes these characteristics significant is their severity and persistence. The frequency with which these features present themselves, and the degree to which they interfere with adequate functioning, reflect their importance in distinguishing the child who has attention deficit.

• *Adolescents.* Even under "normal" circumstances, adolescence is a challenging developmental period for families. The teenager is undergoing major physiological, cognitive, behavioral, and emotional changes. However, the normal problems of this phase are magnified greatly for the individual with ADHD. This happens because the features of attention deficit interfere with successfully mastering the developmental tasks of adolescence. The emerging issues of independence, identity, peer group acceptance, dating, and appearance erupt as new sources of demands and distress with which the ADHD adolescent and his family must cope. As a result, ADHD teens encounter academic failure, social isolation, diminished hopes about future success, depression, and low self-esteem. They also become embroiled in many unpleasant conflicts with their families. Many of the problems relate to noncompliance around the house and to school-related issues such as homework.

Many studies have dispelled the notion that ADHD is typically outgrown by the adolescent years. Most children diagnosed as hyperactive in childhood continue to display their symptoms to a significant degree in adolescence and young adulthood. The symptoms of ADHD that present themselves in adolescence are the very same as found in childhood. The characteristics in the DSM-IV list continue to apply, although they may be difficult to separate from normal features of adolescence such as impulsiveness and moodiness.

There may be two distinct groups of ADHD adolescents. The first is the student who has some type of learning disability along with his attention deficit. Children with a mild form of attention deficit, but who are well motivated and who are receiving help for their learning problems, can sometimes overcome their concentration problems without need for additional help. They may never be identified as ADHD because they were thought to have only learning problems that needed attention. However, if the learning disability is accompanied by ADHD, the increasing demands of junior high and high school may overload the coping or compensation system the child was using to offset either problem. The combination of ADHD and learning disabilities will prove too much, and a dramatic deterioration in academic performance will result.

The second type of adolescent diagnosed with attention deficit has above-average intelligence and a very involved, motivated family. In the early years of school, there might have been indicators of ADHD, often without hyperactivity. However, because the child had the skills to cope, and/or a strong support system, the problem did not become serious enough for recognition until he or she hit secondary school. Because the student was bright, it took longer for his coping techniques to be overwhelmed.

Closely related is the child with some ADHD features who had a very supportive school and home environment which provided needed assistance along the way. Tutoring help, private school, or parental assistance with homework may have carried the student until the increased demands of high school overcame the ability of the student and his family to compensate.

The diagnosis of attention deficit in older students can come as a tremendous relief and can help explain why school has been so difficult. I have had students who came to me during their high school years feeling stupid and depressed. They knew they were capable of doing most of the work and couldn't understand why the organization, memory work, or note-taking was so difficult. Often a comprehensive assessment helped to separate any learning disabilities from ADHD symptoms and we could systematically work on the respective problems. Some of these students have come back with enthusiastic thankfulness for determining they were not stupid and for pointing the way to dealing with their problems.

An excellent book by Chris Zeigler Dendy, entitled *Teenagers with ADD: A Parent's Guide,* describes most of the common behaviors of teenagers with attention deficit disorder. These behaviors include: seeking independence and freedom, disobedience and conflict with adults, immaturity, impulsivity, difficulty paying attention, forgetfulness, disorganization, lack of time awareness, difficulty planning ahead, hard to discipline, low frustration tolerance, argumentativeness, irresponsibility, difficulty with family events, difficulty with team sports, restlessness, and boredom. These adolescents typically seek material possessions, are self-centered, accident-prone, thrill-seeking or daredevils, have sleep disturbances, can't wake up, find the morning routine difficult, prefer peers with similar problems, are apathetic and indifferent, absentminded, exhibit slow mental processing, are attention seekers, intrusive, and have difficulty relating to others.[12]

• *Adults.* Because as many as one-half of the parents of attention deficit children and adolescents also have ADHD, it is highly advisable for each parent to take a close look at himself or herself. It is often the case that after I have completed an evaluation of the child, one of the parents will ask whether it's possible he or she might also have attention deficit disorder. Frequently, we find this to be true.

I recall a parent who asked to have his son evaluated for ADHD. We completed the initial history interview with the father and scheduled the next appointment to begin the formal evaluation of his son. At that next appointment, I greeted the father in the waiting room, but did not see his son. I asked where he was, and the father gave me this puzzled-panicked-embarrassed expression. He had forgotten to bring his son! I had a clue right away that we needed to take a look at Dad at the first opportunity to see if he was ADHD. We did, and he was.

Adults with ADHD may display some of the following characteristics: problems with self-control as seen in excessive debt, eating disorders, substance abuse, and other addictions; more speeding tickets and accidents than average; trouble organizing and maintaining family life; frequent interpersonal conflicts; poor school performance; difficulty with follow-through and completion of projects or tasks in spite of good intentions; easily bored; chronic lateness; and inconsistent employment and work performance.[13]

Rather than extend this chapter, I have added an entire section at the end of the book on adults with ADHD. Be sure to take a look at chapter 10 to see if anything might apply to you or someone you know.

This concludes our general discussion of the definition and nature of ADHD. You should have a pretty good idea of the various features of attention deficits. These characteristics include: inattention, impulsivity, overactivity, difficulty with rule-governed behavior, inability to wait, and difficulty "putting on the brakes." You may also have some strong impressions about

whether your child has ADHD, but don't make any final judgments yet. You need more information. In the next chapter we
will look at the causes of ADHD. This will include a discussion
of several false beliefs about parental and environmental influences. I think you will find it helpful.

References

1. R. Barkley, M. Fisher, C.S. Edelbrock, & L. Smallish, "The
Adolescent Outcome of Hyperactive Children Diagnosed by Research
Criteria: An 8-Year Prospective Follow-up Study, *Journal of Child
Psychology and Psychiatry*, 29, 1990, 546–57; R.A. Barkley, *Taking
Charge of ADHD* (New York: Guilford Press, 1995), 18–19.

2. R.A. Barkley, *Attention-Deficit Hyperactivity Disorder: A Handbook
for Diagnosis and Treatment* (New York: Guilford Press, 1990), 3–38;
R.A. Barkley, *Taking Charge of ADHD* (New York: Guilford Press,
1995), 29; Goldstein, S., & Goldstein, M., *Managing Attention Disorders
in Children* (New York: John Wiley & Sons, 1990), 7–9.

3. R.A. Barkley, G.J. DuPaul, & M.B. McMurray, "Comprehensive
Evaluation of Attention Deficit Disorder with and without Hyperactivity
as Defined by Research Criteria," *Journal of Consulting and Clinical
Psychology*, 58, 1990, 775–89; T.E. Brown, "Attention Deficit Disorders
without Hyperactivity," *CHADDER*, 7, 1993, 7–10.

4. R.A. Barkley, "An Update on Draft of DSM-IV Criteria for ADHD,"
The ADHD Report, 1 (1), 1993, 7–8; Barkley, "The Latest on the DSM-
IV and the Disruptive Behavior Disorders," 3–4.

5. Reprinted with permission from *Diagnostic and Statistical Manual of
Mental Disorders, Fourth Edition* (Washington, D.C.: American
Psychiatric Association, 1994).

6. Sam Goldstein, *Managing Attention and Learning Disorders in Late
Adolescence & Adulthood: A Guide for Practitioners* (New York: John
Wiley & Sons, 1997, 54–55); M. Gordon, *ADHD/Hyperactivity: A
Consumer's Guide* (DeWitt, N.Y.: GSI Publications, 1991), 57–58.

7. Sam Goldstein & Michael Goldstein, *Managing Attention Disorders
in Children* (New York: John Wiley & Sons, 1990), 7–9.

8. Russell A. Barkley, *Attention-Deficit Hyperactivity Disorder. A
Handbook for Diagnosis and Treatment* (New York: Guilford Press,
1990), 71–73.

9.   Russell A. Barkley, *Taking Charge of ADHD*, 29–54; "Attention-Deficit/Hyperactivity Disorder, Self-regulation and Time: Toward a More Comprehensive Theory," *Journal of Developmental & Behavorial Pediatrics*, 18(4), August, 1997, 271–79.

10.   Lynn Weiss, *Give Your ADD Teen A Chance* (Colorado Springs: Pinon Press, 1996), 73–78.

11.   Robert A. Moss, *Why Johnny Can't Concentrate: Coping with Attention-Deficit Problems* (New York: Bantam Books, 1990), 44–45.

12.   Chris Zeigler Dendy, *Teenagers with ADD: A Parent's Guide* (Rockville, Md.: Woodbine House, 1995), 159–62.

13.   William L. Hathaway, "ADHD and the Military," *The ADHD Report*, 5 (5), October, 1997, 3.

CHAPTER TWO

WHY DOES MY CHILD HAVE ATTENTION DEFICIT?
Causes and Sources of ADHD

"**W**hy does my child have these problems?"
"Is his ADHD caused by something we did as parents?"
"Could this have been prevented?"

As you toss in your sleep at night, you may have wondered about the causes of your child's attention disorders. In this chapter, I will give you the best answers scientific research has been able to provide about the origins of these problems. The most accurate general statement I can make is that we don't really know for sure what causes ADHD. There are many pet theories, some more promising than others. I'll give a summary of each of the main areas of exploration.

ADHD continues to be one of the most thoroughly researched conditions of childhood. Yet the exact causes are still not known. Neurochemical abnormalities which might underlie this disorder are difficult to document. The research appears to be moving toward a consensus that ADHD has a biological base. The data points to a genetically endowed predisposition, along with a common neurological mechanism. In other words, many

ADHD children seem to arrive in the world with temperaments that leave them difficult to manage. Part of the basis for this pre-disposition may be inherited. Very often I will hear parents describe their child as "a chip off the old block," or say, "I acted the same way when I was a kid." They may tell me about relatives who appeared to have a history of inattentive and overactive behavior. All of this suggests a genetic basis for the problem. I'll describe some of the details shortly.

Environmental conditions may play a role also. However, factors like diet show up on an individual basis, rather than in large numbers. For example, sugar has not been shown to be a consistent source of overactive behavior. Yet parents continue to report that children have dramatic negative reactions to excessive sugar in their diet.

Parenting and ADHD

The symptoms of ADHD are not externally created by parents. It is extremely important for you as a parent not to blame yourself. You did not cause your child's attention problems through faulty discipline. It is true that parental frustration and negative reactions toward your child can aggravate the problem. Your guilt, anger, and resentment can contaminate the relationship with your child and interfere with effective treatment. Your behavior can have a substantial effect on your child in both positive and negative ways, but your actions alone did not create ADHD in your child. Research studies have shown the negative behavior of parents is most often a response to the difficult behavior of these high-maintenance children and not the cause of the behavior.

Family dysfunction, divorce, abuse, and faulty parenting can certainly produce behavior patterns that resemble ADHD. However, these types of negative family influences are most like-ly to contribute to aggressive and defiant behavior in children, rather than typical ADHD characteristics.

Children with ADHD can have other problems such as learning disabilities, depression, obsessive-compulsive behavior, or even bipolar disorder. That is one reason why an accurate diagnosis is needed. More will be said about that in the next chapter. For now, realize your influence as a parent is indeed crucial to the overall emotional health of your child. A nurturing home with clear and consistent structure is crucial to the treatment of ADHD children. However, your actions did not bring about the attention deficit.

Theories about the Cause of ADHD

Let's look at some of the ideas that have been propagated to explain the causes of ADHD. I will first describe some factors which appear to play a minor role in the origin of attention deficit and hyperactivity.

• *Brain injury.* ADHD was thought to occur as a result of brain infections, trauma, or other injuries or complications taking place during pregnancy or delivery. Brain damage can result in symptoms of hyperactivity, inattentiveness, and impulsivity. It was the association of these symptoms with brain injury and brain infection that led to the disorder being called *minimal brain damage*. Because of this association, inattention and hyperactivity were thought to be signs that brain damage had occurred. Researchers then attempted to identify the possible causes of brain damage.

One such source is brain damage that may occur as a result of an *infection* in the mother or from *drugs* taken by the mother. The latter include prescription drugs as well as substances such as alcohol and cocaine. Babies born with fetal alcohol syndrome are known to suffer from severe behavioral problems which can include hyperactivity. Data collected several years ago from maternity hospitals showed that 375,000 babies are born each year with drugs in their systems. It is estimated that 20 percent of all newborns have been exposed to drugs in the womb. The National Institute on Drug Abuse estimates that 4 to 5 percent of all newborns are exposed to cocaine in the womb.[1]

A study was done of 1,900 infants born with cocaine in their systems at New York City's Harlem Hospital. Of these babies, over one-third were premature, and 15 percent had lifetime handicaps, such as mental retardation, cerebral palsy, or blindness due to strokes in the womb. Nearly all the remaining children had less serious afflictions that emerged later, including hyperactivity, impaired motor skills, and delays in language use.

Some of these children have symptoms of ADHD, but the connection is still not clear. More studies are needed to clarify the exact influence of drugs and toxins on infants. So far, the reviews of the evidence suggest that only 5 to 10 percent of ADHD children have hard neurological findings indicative of actual brain damage.[2]

• *Smoking.* Research has shown that the risk for ADHD increases significantly in the offspring of women who smoke during their pregnancies. It is possible that a mother who smokes is reflective of a person with attention disorder, and thus the increased ADHD in her offspring could be more related to genetic influences than to smoking. However, recent studies have helped clarify this issue. The association of ADHD with maternal smoking remains significant even after controlling for such confounding variables as socioeconomic status, parental IQ, and parental ADHD status. The evidence is fairly clear that maternal smoking during pregnancy is a significant risk factor for attention disorder in the children of those pregnancies.[3]

• *Birth injury.* This has long been suspected to be a major cause of ADHD and other neurological problems of childhood. Researchers studied 66,000 pregnancies in the Collaborative Perinatal Project, keeping detailed records of all aspects of pregnancy, labor, and delivery. Psychological, neurological, and medical follow-up examinations were conducted during the child's development after birth. The Apgar score was used to measure the health of the infant. This consists of a five-part rating system of a newborn based on movement, tone, color, respiratory effort, and heart rate. The Apgar score did not correlate with subsequent development of ADHD symptoms. This indicates that on an individual basis, a difficult pregnancy or delivery is not sufficient to establish birth injury as the cause of ADHD.[4] While certain types of trauma, infection, or disease of the central brain may contribute to the development of ADHD, these causes account for very few ADHD children.

• *Delayed brain maturation.* This idea would appear to have merit, given the immature social behavior of ADHD children. There are also frequent findings of maturational delay on neurological exams, and there is a similarity between the ADHD child's deficits in attention, impulse control, and self-regulation and that of younger normal children. At this time, there is no direct neurological evidence available to support this theory, so it remains hypothetical.

• *Lead poisoning.* Lead is a strong neurotoxin that can be found in the peeling and chipping paint of older homes. It was also found in the solder used in years past to weld water pipes. Gasoline containing lead has contributed to high levels of airborne lead in some polluted areas.

There is evidence to indicate that lead in the body can be associated with hyperactivity and inattention in a general population. Some studies have measured the amount of lead in the blood, hair, or the dentine of children's teeth. When teachers were asked to rate the level of hyperactivity and inattention in those same children, some studies did show significant relationships between higher lead levels and attention ratings. Other studies have indicated a low correlation between blood lead levels and hyperactivity. The problem is that ADHD children often show little or no increase in their body lead indicators. The present opinion is that lead may be a contributor to attention and learning problems in some children. However, it is unlikely to be a major cause of ADHD, even though it is a major health problem for the public at large.[5]

• *Food additives.* Additives such as salicylates, food dyes, and preservatives were highly publicized causes of ADHD during the 1970s and early 1980s. In 1974 Dr. Benjamin Feingold, a pediatric allergist, claimed that over half of all hyperactivity was caused by artificial colors and flavors. Dr. Feingold suspected the apparent increase in hyperactivity over the past several decades coincided with increased use of artificial flavors, colors, and preservatives in our food supply. It was the artificial colors which he most suspected because they have a certain chemical similarity to substances known to produce allergic responses.

Dr. Feingold then proposed a complex diet to eliminate these substances, and cited anecdotal evidence to support his theory. He never conducted a controlled study of the problem. However, a substantial amount of research since that time has been unable to support these claims. A few preschool children may have shown a small increase in activity or inattentiveness when consuming these additives. But no evidence has been presented that shows normal children can acquire ADHD symptoms by consuming such substances. Nor has it been shown that ADHD children are made worse by them. Any improvement in behavior when a diet was introduced was primarily a placebo effect. Most formal studies did not show clear evidence implicating artificial salicylates and food additives as a substantial cause of ADHD.[6]

The artificial sweetener *aspartame* (trade names "Equal" and "NutraSweet") has also come under scrutiny as a possible cause of ADHD. From a theoretical standpoint, aspartame does look like a suspicious candidate. It is made up of two amino acids, phenylalanine and aspartic acid, that play important roles in the brain's synthesis of neurotransmitters. Aspartame was extensively studied for cancer-causing potential before it was approved by the Food and Drug Administration. However, it was not researched for its effects on behavior.

A few children appear to suffer extreme reactions to aspartame, including behavior problems, seizures, and headaches. In the studies reported so far, no consistent problems or connection to attention deficits have been identified. Some people may be especially sensitive to aspartame, but the effects otherwise appear to be subtle. The recommendation at this time is to observe your child closely for reactions, and restrict the diet if your observations suggest any problems.

It may be prudent to avoid many such products as much as possible. The possibilities of harm are too great to take a risk with something like aspartame, which has no nutritional value. At the same time, parents need to teach their children how to monitor their reactions to foods. Children must learn that it is important to manage their diet as it relates to mental health, in the same way it is necessary to brush their teeth and practice good hygiene.

• *Food intolerance.* In spite of the early lack of results, recent studies have been more positive about diet and food intolerances. For example, investigators have eliminated multiple food offenders, instead of single foods, with some success. They have eliminated not only artificial colors and flavors, but also chocolate, monosodium glutamate, preservatives, caffeine, and many substances that families reported might affect their specific child. The suggested diet was also low in simple sugars and was even milk-free if the family reported a history of possible problems with cow's milk. More than half of the children were reported to improve on the diet, but not on the placebo. The authors believed their diet had a stronger effect than previous studies because they eliminated many offending agents, not just one. Only further research will determine if this approach has any relevance to the daily lives of most ADHD children.[7]

Toxic environmental influences must have some kind of effect on children. Many children with ADHD and/or learning problems seem to have numerous *allergies.* For example, 94 percent of ADHD children have had three or more ear infections. This compares to a 50 percent incidence for normal children. Sixty-nine percent of ADHD children have had ten or more ear infections, compared to only 20 percent of normal children who have had that many infections.[8] This strongly suggests some type of allergy relationship.

Some children definitely have food intolerances. Dairy products, for example, are frequent offenders. We don't know how all of this fits together in relation to attention deficit. Foods significantly affect the way children behave, learn, and feel. However, it is important to resist the temptation to jump to conclusions without careful safeguards and controlled studies.

It is essential to keep a balance between healthy skepticism and open-mindedness when it comes to suspecting foods as a cause for the aberrant behavior of children. We need additional rigorous scientific investigation to help us understand these possible connections. An example is Dr. Conners' research, which suggests a link between *when* certain foods are eaten and the effect on behavior. Sugar and carbohydrates eaten alone for breakfast can cause problems. However, these same foods can be tolerated if eaten with protein.[9] I guess you can have a cinnamon roll for breakfast, but you need to eat a lean steak, beans, or an egg along with it to avoid becoming a Fidgety Phil.

• *Refined sugar.* Sugar has also been a popular explanation for ADHD. Anecdotes regarding sugar and hyperactivity appeared in the scientific literature as early as 1929. It is legitimate to question the effects of sugar in our diet, since the average person in the United States consumes almost 132 pounds of sugar per year. Some would argue that sugar acts like a stimulant to speed us up. Others would say it makes us depressed. So we have theories which range from a "buzz effect" to "sugar blues."

Despite widespread attention by the general public about the negative effects of sugar, there have been few or no scientific studies actually conducted by those who propose to eliminate sugar. Their evidence is mostly anecdotal. In the controlled studies of sugar which have been conducted over the years, researchers have approached the topic in two ways. One approach is to correlate dietary sugar intake with behavior. The second is to give large amounts of sugar to children and observe their reactions. These studies have generally shown no negative outcome across groups of children. Some individual children certainly experience ADHD symptoms with ingestion of refined sugar and/or other additives. However, there has been no documented effects for significant numbers of children.

While controlled studies have failed to prove a direct sugar connection, the number of anecdotes from parents that suggest it are too numerous to discount. Rather than ask, "Is sugar bad for children?" researchers such as Dr. Conners have suggested it may be better to ask, "Under what circumstances is sugar beneficial or harmful?" Sugar can be either negative or positive for children, depending on their age, diet, and biology. There is a good possibility that a child's changing brain may leave him or her vulnerable to sugar and carbohydrates at certain ages. There may be a vulnerability to either too little or too much. Protein seems to have an important protective role when sugars or other carbohydrates are eaten. This argues for generous amounts of protein in a child's diet. No findings justify eliminating sugar from a child's diet; nor should the desirable features of protein mean that a child should load up on meat, cheese, or fish exclusively. The principle to follow is balance. Carbohydrates, including sugar, are essential ingredients in a normal diet. A varied, well-balanced diet is still the best protection against adverse physical and mental consequences related to food. A nutritionist, dietitian, or knowledgeable physician can help you tailor a program for the needs of your child.[10]

• *Medical illness.* Illness can cause poor attention in many nonspecific ways. There is disagreement about whether attention problems that emerge from illness should even be called ADHD. Specific illnesses which have been linked to ADHD symptoms include iron deficiency, anemia, hyperthyroidism, pinworms, rheumatic chorea, hypoglycemia, and petit mal epilepsy. These are uncommon causes for ADHD, but they should be considered in any complete medical evaluation.

• *Medications.* Medicine taken to treat other illnesses can also trigger ADHD symptoms. Examples include anticonvulsants, such as phenobarbital and Dilantin, and medications which tend to be sedating and can reduce attentiveness and concentration. Also, various medications given to treat asthma, colds, or allergies can act as stimulants.

It is unlikely that these medications are a major cause of ADHD. However, if your child is taking medication for epilepsy, for example, you should be alert to the possibility of the anticonvulsants worsening a preexisting condition. Likewise, medications taken for an allergy can produce inattention, and you should be aware of that connection.

Hereditary and Neurological Factors

Heredity is the single factor shown to be a common denominator among ADHD children. Children with ADHD are four times more likely to have siblings and parents with ADHD than are normal children. Also, children with ADHD raised by an adoptive family are four times more likely to have ADHD in their natural parents than adopted children without ADHD.

A number of studies have evaluated the heritability of hyperactivity among various groups of identical and fraternal twins. The results have consistently shown that if one identical twin develops ADHD, the other one carries a significantly increased risk of developing attention deficit. In addition, identical twins have a higher incidence of ADHD than do fraternal twins. The findings from a variety of studies substantiate a strong genetic component to the presence of attention disorder.[11] Studies in molecular biology also support the idea that attention disorder is an inherited condition.

Let's take a brief look at some aspects of brain function which relate to attention disorders. *Thinking functions* of the brain are localized within the cerebral hemisphere. When a child reads a math problem, information is transmitted from the eyes through the visual pathways to a part of the brain called the occipital lobes. This visual image has no meaning until it is coordinated with the parietal lobe region. The child now is able to comprehend the nature of the question and the answer is prepared. Information is then sent to the frontal region of the brain where the response is translated into a verbal or written answer. If a child has problems with attention and distractibility, we would expect this frontal region of the brain to at least be partially involved. Some studies in recent years have begun to clarify the dynamics of how ADHD might be related to problems with this part of the brain.

One of the landmark studies traced ADHD to a specific metabolic abnormality in the brain. In this study, researchers used a sophisticated brain-imaging technique known as positron-emission tomography (PET), and scanned to measure sugar metabolism in the brain cells of adults who had been hyperactive since childhood and had at least one child with the same problem. The results were striking. The overall brain metabolism was 8 percent lower in hyperactive subjects than in a control group; the largest differences were found in two regions of the brain—the premotor cortex and the superior prefrontal cortex. These are parts of the brain known to be involved in regulating attention and motor control. It was not clear what causes these metabolic differences, but the link between brain chemistry and behavior was more clearly established.[12]

A number of recent studies have offered evidence to support the idea that the core deficit in ADHD is the failure to inhibit or delay behavioral responses. Furthermore, research is supporting the finding that the prefrontal cortex and frontal striatal circuits are implicated in this dysfunction.[13]

Thus far I have described how cognitive functioning can be identified with specific locations in the brain. There is no neurological marker presently understood for ADHD. No single part of the brain is underdeveloped or injured, as far as we know. No particular part of the brain, when removed, produces ADHD symptoms. This means ADHD is *more of a system problem than a component dysfunction*. It might be analogous to the brake fluid in your car's braking system. The mechanical components of the brake system work OK, but the fluid itself is either absent or decomposed to the point that it can't send the message from your brake pedal to the wheels. Consequently, the wheels don't get the information telling them to slow down. As a result, the car runs right through a stop sign, ending up in a collision.

What causes the brain's executive system to fail? The following description is the best opinion we have at this time. The brainstem centers contain the cell bodies which produce chemicals such as norepinephrine, serotonin, and dopamine. These chemicals are then sent through the axons to all areas of the brain. At this time, research suggests the dysfunction of the *dopamine system* is an important contributor to ADHD.

Let's picture how the brain functions in regard to attention, and how the dopamine system fits into that picture. When a brain cell is stimulated, it releases a neurotransmitter that carries the message to the next cell. The neurotransmitter attaches itself to the cell, causing that cell to be stimulated. Then another messenger is released. It's kind of like playing tag. The person who is "it" runs and touches the first person he can catch. That second person becomes "it" and runs to catch somebody else.

The message travels quickly from one cell to the next one, along little highways called neuropathways. There are thousands of these pathways that carry messages to specialized areas of the brain. It's comparable to a network of highways that lead to different regions or cities.

At any point in time, several stimuli may be competing for your attention. You are able to see, hear, touch, smell, and taste all at the same time. This often means you have to make a concentrated effort to select the important from the unimportant stimuli around you. At this moment you are attending to the words and ideas on the pages of this book. At the same time, there may be a radio playing in the background, your body is pressing against the chair, the smell of coffee emanates from the kitchen, and children are talking in the other room. Concentration requires that all of these background stimuli be suppressed so you can make sense out of the ideas in this book. You may even have a light cold, but are still able to focus on your reading.

When you make extra effort to concentrate, your brain releases added neurotransmitters. These additional messengers cause the messages to travel a little more quickly and enable you to focus. You are able to concentrate on one stimulus source and block out the others.

Children and adults with attention deficits do not seem to manufacture extra neurotransmitters. The absence of sufficient dopamine appears to be responsible for this inability to produce sufficient neurotransmitters. As a result, all messages come in at once with equal impact. The person is not able to suppress one and focus on the most important element. The result is like a gridlock on a freeway system when everyone is trying to get to the same place at the same time. The system can't handle it and traffic comes to a halt. Radiators boil over, tempers flare, and apparently random reactions ensue.

The neurophysiological explanation of attention deficit helps us to understand how stimulant medication works. Stimulant medication increases the production or release of neurotransmitters, allowing the person to focus on the most important message being sent.

Now let's look at the *dopamine* connection in a little more detail. Studies of cerebrospinal fluid in ADHD and normal children have shown there is decreased brain dopamine in ADHD children. Some studies show that when ADHD is treated with medication, there is improvement in the metabolic changes of dopamine seen in the spinal fluid. With what has been published so far, the evidence seems to say that ADHD children have a selective deficiency in the availability of dopamine.

Additional support for the dopamine hypothesis comes from the encephalitis epidemic of 1918. This disease produced parkinsonism in adults and ADHD symptoms in children. Research has shown that parkinsonism results from dysfunction of the dopamine system. This close association between ADHD and parkinsonism suggests a common cause may be in the dysfunction of the dopamine pathways.

Animal studies have also shown that increased activity and difficulty with certain kinds of learning are not produced by damage to a specific location of the brain. Rather, the ADHD-like symptoms are a result of damage to the nerve cell endings that deliver dopamine throughout the entire brain. When the dopamine-containing nerve endings in rats were destroyed, they could not utilize the dopamine system throughout the brain. The resulting symptoms were just like ADHD symptoms in humans. Further, when the rats were given methylphenidate (Ritalin), their behavior improved.

From this research it appears that persons with attention deficit are born with a shortage of neurotransmitters or a dopamine deficiency. The frontal lobe of the brain is the area most responsible for controlling attention, activity, and the ability to plan ahead. It is assumed there is a connection between ADHD and the shortage of neurotransmitters that affects primarily the frontal lobe.

Attention Center Model

Several researchers have proposed a brain-based model of ADHD to try to bring all the above information together. We start with the idea of an *attention center,* or executive function, within the brain that utilizes dopamine. This center has input from other areas of the brain, such as the frontal lobe. After this attention center gets a message, it communicates with the rest of the brain to regulate the degree of attention and concentration, much like a captain of a ship directs the speed and course of his ship. If the child is trying to understand a concept in the classroom, the center could be set for intense concentration. Or, this center could be set to allow the child to be easily distracted, as would be more appropriate on the school playground.

Perhaps we could think of a hearing aid as an example. I recall a man in our church who frequently had to adjust his hearing aid. If he was engaged in a conversation with you one-on-one, he would turn up the volume so he could catch all of what you had to say. However, if he was in a group of people, say in the fellowship time after a service, he would turn down his hearing aid so that the background noise and multiple conversations didn't overload his system.

This same idea might apply to our attention center. When we need to focus, the system turns up the concentration level through a biochemical reaction. When we need to be more aware of everything around us, the system turns down the concentration level. Children who have ADHD are unable to utilize the normal brainstem attention center to adjust levels of attention and concentration in the manner available to normal children.[14]

Summary of Probable Causes of ADHD

The major evidence points to diminished activity in certain brain regions and heredity as the most likely cause of most forms of attention disorder. From the available research on the brain, ADHD is essentially a problem with "putting on the brakes." When you step on the brake pedal of your car, that action is transmitted, by means of brake fluid flowing through the brake lines, to each of the wheels of your car. The increased pressure of the brake fluid then activates the braking mechanism on the wheels, and you begin to slow down. However, if you are low on brake fluid, or have a leak in the system, the brakes may not respond precisely the way you want. You may want to stop or slow down, and you step on the brakes, but nothing happens. This is roughly what happens in the brain of a person with ADHD.

The cause of ADHD is understood to be *dysregulation* of certain neurotransmitters in the brain which make it harder for a person to sort out or regulate certain internal and external stimuli. These deficits in brain neurochemistry make it harder to concentrate and focus. Several neurotransmitters, including dopamine and norepinephrine, probably affect the production, use, and regulation of other neurotransmitters, as well as the functioning of some brain structures. These problems with regulation of certain brain functions seem to be centralized in the frontal lobes, which makes it more difficult for an ADHD person to control input from other parts of the brain. The frontal region of the brain, which is just behind the forehead, is said to control the "executive functions" of our behavior. The executive function is responsible for memory, organization, inhibiting behavior, sustaining attention, initiating self-control, and planning for the future. Without enough dopamine and related neurotransmitters, the frontal lobes are understimulated and unable to perform their complex functions effectively.

Distractibility and inattention, from a brain-function perspective, are the failure to "stop" or tune out unwanted internal thoughts or outside stimuli, such as a voice in the other room, or a bird outside the window. Rapid mood changes and hypersensitivity are the results of the brain having more difficulty moderating those parts of the brain which regulate motor movements and emotional responses.

Finally, an ADHD person's difficulty with hyperactivity and impulsive behavior may stem from frontal lobe deficiencies which make it hard to wait, delay gratification, and inhibit actions. All of these characteristics can then interfere with a person's memory and ability to learn and efficiently process information.

Children without this genetic predisposition can develop ADHD through illness or injury, but this rarely happens. At this time, there is very little evidence that ADHD can arise purely out of social or environmental factors, such as family dysfunction, diet, toxins, or faulty parenting.

References

1. P. Anderson, "Schools Brace for 'Crack Kids,'" *The Seattle Times/Seattle Post-Intelligencer,* 4 August 1991:A2.

2. H.B. Ferguson & J.L. Rapoport, "Nosological Issues and Biological Variation," *Developmental Neuropsychiatry,* ed. Rutter, M. (New York: Guilford Press, 1983), 369–84.

3. S. Milberger, J. Biederman, S. Faroane, L. Chen, & J. Jones, "Is Maternal Smoking During Pregnancy a Risk Factor for Attention Deficit Hyperactivity Disorder?" *American Journal of Psychiatry,* 153, 1996, 1138–142.

4. K.B. Nelson & J.H. Ellenburg, "Apgar Scores and Long-Term Neurological Handicap," *Annals of Neurology,* 6, 1982 (1979): (Abstract).

5. R.A. Barkley, *Attention-Deficit Hyperactivity Disorder. A Handbook for Diagnosis and Treatment* (New York: Guilford Press, 1990); E.A. Taylor, "Childhood Hyperactivity," *British Journal of Psychiatry* 149 (1986):562–73.

6. C.K. Conners, *Food Additives and Hyperactive Children* (New York: Plenum, 1980); *Feeding the Brain: How Foods Affect Children* (New York: Plenum Press, 1989), 157–85; R.A. Barkley, *Taking Charge of ADHD* (New York: Guilford Press, 1995), 66–68.

7. B.J. Kaplan, et al., "Dietary Replacement in Preschool-Aged Hyperactive Boys," *Pediatrics,* 83, 1989, 7–17.

8. R.J. Hagerman & A.R. Falkenstein, "An Association Between Recurrent Otitis Media in Infancy and Later Hyperactivity," *Clinical Pediatrics,* 5, 1987, 253–57.

9. C.K. Conners, *Feeding the Brain: How Foods Affect Children,* 73.

10. Ibid., 75–100.

11. J. Silberg, et al., "Genetic and Environmental Influences on the Covariation between Hyperactivity and Conduct Disturbance in Juvenile Twins," *Journal of Child Psychology and Psychiatry*, 37, 1996, 803–16; E. van den Oord, F. Verhulst, & D. Boomsma, "A Genetic Study of Maternal and Paternal Ratings of Problem Behavior in 3-year-old Twins," *Journal of Abnormal Child Psychology*, 105, 1996, 349–57; L. Hechtman, "Families of Children with Attention Deficit Hyperactivity Disorder: A Review," *Canadian Journal of Psychiatry*, 41, 1996, 350–60.

12. A.J. Zametkin, et al., "Cerebral Glucose Metabolism in Adults with Hyperactivity of Childhood Onset," *New England Journal of Medicine*, 323, 1990, 1361–366.

13. B. Casey, et al., "Implication of Right Frontalstriatal Circuitry in Response Inhibition and Attention-Deficit/Hyperactivity Disorder," *Journal of the American Academy of Child and Adolescent Psychiatry*, 36(3), 1997, 374–83; D.G. Amen & B.D. Carmichael, "High-resolution SPECT Imaging in ADHD," *Annals of Clinical Psychiatry*, 9(2), 1997, 81–86.

14. S. Goldstein & M. Goldstein, *Managing Attention Disorders in Children* (New York: John Wiley & Sons, 1990), 41–48.

CHAPTER THREE

HOW DO I FIND HELP?
The Assessment of ADHD

"Honey, have you finished that book about attention disorders?" Julie asked her husband, Jeff, after the kids had left the dinner table.

"Yes," he responded. "I thought it pretty much hit the nail on the head as far as describing things with Danny."

"That's what I thought." Julie sighed. "I couldn't believe it when the author started describing how kids with attention deficit act. It was like every page was a day out of Danny's life. I cried the whole time I was reading it."

"Yeah, it hit me kind of hard too. I guess the next question is what do we do now," Jeff pondered. "I know his teacher has been telling us something is wrong. In fact, didn't she give us that book?"

"She did," Julie answered, becoming a bit more agitated. "Remember, we have a conference with her next week. Maybe she will give us some ideas about how to get help. I know I need it. If something isn't done to calm him down, I'm going to run away and live in a mountain shack in the Siskiyous!"

ADHD is a real and dramatic part of the lives of many families. I assume such conversations have taken place around thousands of dinner tables. Countless concerned and frustrated parents have struggled with the question of where to turn for help.

After reading the earlier chapters, you may believe your child has attention deficit and/or hyperactivity. Maybe a teacher or friend has suggested that your child might have ADHD. Whatever the reasons for your suspicions, you are now wondering where to turn for help. In this chapter, I will discuss when you should consider seeking a professional evaluation for your child, what to expect from the assessment and treatment process, and how to find the right professional.

When to Seek an Evaluation

It's quite difficult and somewhat humbling to contemplate the fact your that child may have ADHD. Denial is understandable, and you certainly should not rush out and obtain an evaluation without careful consideration. Take the time to read several articles or books on ADHD. Talk to other parents who have already been through the process. Prayerfully evaluate what you have learned about attention disorder and compare the information to the consistent behavior of your child. If the descriptions seem to match up, an evaluation may be appropriate. Here are some conditions or characteristics that might suggest an evaluation is necessary:

❑ If a majority of the symptoms of inattention, distractibility, or hyperactivity/impulsivity listed in chapter 1 have persisted for at least six months;

❑ If the extended descriptions of the infant, preschool, school-age, or adolescent child contain features that are very prominent in the day-to-day life of your child;

❑ If other parents or relatives have suggested to you that there might be something out of the ordinary going on with your son or daughter;

❑ If a teacher or caretaker has told you of frequent problems with inattention, distractibility, forgetfulness, noncompliance, daydreaming, impulsivity, problems with peers, underachievement, or incomplete assignments;

❑ If, as a parent, especially the mother, you have had a nagging concern for some time that there might be some type of problem based on the high-maintenance requirements of your child;

❑ There are too many days when you find yourself getting continually frustrated and angry with your child, even to the point of not liking him or her very much;

❑ You see the self-esteem of your child get lower and lower because of problems with self-control, social or school failure, or inability to sustain an interest in activities that occupy most children.

These conditions or events are telling you something. This list of features is not exclusive to attention disorders. However, these enduring characteristics are indicative of some kind of problematic situation. It would certainly be wise to seek professional help in determining the causes and pointing you in the direction of treatment and help.

Expectations of Treatment

Before you proceed to look for a care provider, you need to consider what you expect out of treatment. Then you can select an approach that will be most appropriate for your goals.

ADHD is managed, not cured

Treating ADHD will not make it go away. Your child's inattention, overarousal, distractibility, and difficulty in obeying rules are inborn behavioral and temperamental characteristics. They are part of his very nature. These qualities will stay with him throughout his life to one degree or another. Treatment can improve a child's chances for avoiding many of the long-term problems associated with ADHD. There is every reason to believe your son or daughter can have a very productive life. At the same time, you need to remember this objective will require long-term help. Both you and your child will need to commit to the continuous effort of managing the situation in the best possible manner.

Treatment of ADHD does not consist only of correcting a problem within your child

The child is not the only one who has to change in the process of dealing with ADHD, although he is certainly the focal point. Self-management and self-control are crucial objectives for your child. However, family members and teachers must also be willing to look at how their actions impact the child's difficulties with impulsivity and inattention. Managing the ADHD child involves both modifying his behaviors and altering his environment to obtain a better fit.

For example, a student may have difficulty attending to instructions and turning in assignments. Treatment must focus on the child's inattention. At the same time, the child's teachers will need to find ways of encouraging the child, providing structure, and pacing requirements to his abilities. Parents must learn to use positive, rather than negative, reinforcement. The family climate will need to be altered from constant tension and frustration to clear structure, but with reason and tolerance. This may require an adjustment in your expectations so that your child can meet them. Parents need tools for dealing with conflict and problem-solving, as well as help in self-care and avoidance of burnout. In short, the entire system for the ADHD child will need some adjustments.

Each ADHD child requires a different plan
Children with ADHD are more different than they are alike, even though we use a common term like attention deficit or hyperactivity. Your child has unique strengths and weaknesses that must be considered when designing a program that will help him achieve his full potential. Treatment must also be customized to the needs of your family. A family with only one child has a much different dynamic than one with four children. A diagnosis of ADHD for a family in financial crisis will demand a different kind of support system than for a family that has financial security.

Treatment must be multidimensional
Usually treatment will need to be multifaceted. For example, medication may be used to help control some of the child's inattention and overarousal. Yet medication does not give the child the skills to organize note cards for a term paper, or to make friends. These skills must be addressed by a coordinated effort of teachers, mental health professionals, and family.

A multidimensional approach to treatment is also suggested by the limited long-term effects of medication alone. Medication can have modest long-term beneficial effects on overactivity and impulsivity, but very little on the social and academic aspects. Research has shown that children who receive multimodal treatment have a better long-term outcome than do children who are treated with medication alone.[1]

Multidimensional treatment has another advantage over medication alone. It allows the child to have more of a sense of ownership and control by being less dependent on medication. It can reinforce a feeling of mastery in the child. An example would be the feelings of accomplishment in a child who has worked hard on his social skills. When friends finally start to invite him to spend the night, he knows it is a result of behavioral changes he has made in himself, and not the medication alone. A treatment effort that draws on all aspects of the person builds on this sense of personal accomplishment and self-esteem. It truly is skills as well as pills.

An evaluation should be comprehensive

One reason an evaluation is so important is that you need to determine accurately why your child is having trouble with inattentiveness, impulsiveness, and overarousal. Treatment will vary depending on the underlying problem. Other problems can masquerade as ADHD. For example, an anxious, worried, or even depressed child can be inattentive and fidgety in the classroom. An abused child can be very distractible and disorganized. Students with learning disabilities can appear inattentive when their underlying problem is difficulty with language processing. Treatment for each of these problem areas is quite different, making a comprehensive evaluation very necessary.

A proper diagnosis orients the child, parents, and other caregivers to the general nature of the child's difficulties. In doing so, it provides information about a child's strengths and weaknesses. Assessment procedures help identify which situations are particularly troublesome for a child and which situations are more comfortable. The assessment should also identify the child's particular academic strengths and weaknesses so that the educational program can achieve maximum results.

A complete and thorough evaluation is important for another reason. The severity of ADHD itself is not the crucial predictor of long-term adjustment. Coexisting problems such as learning disabilities, conduct disorder, poor peer relationships, and disruptive family relationships play a key role in determining future health. A comprehensive assessment is needed to determine if some of these additional factors are present, along with the ADHD. Treatment will then be needed, as appropriate, for each problem area.

Where to Find Help

There are several considerations in selecting an appropriate professional to coordinate your child's care. First, you want that person to be competent in assessing and treating ADHD. This person should also be experienced in working with children, and should have up-to-date knowledge about attention deficit.

Second, you want to know if the professional is able to oversee a multidimensional approach to treatment. A key ingredient in this approach is a close tie with the child's school. Teachers are a crucial source of information about many of the areas associated with attention deficits. A teacher can report on how the student attends in class, relates to peers, responds to structure, handles transition periods, and acquires academic skills. Information from the teacher is needed for both diagnosis and treatment. Yet some clinicians initiate very little contact with the school. Many times, as I am talking with a child's teacher or other school personnel, they will tell me how unusual it is to hear directly from the child's primary therapist. If the professional you choose does not invite close communication with the school, your child will not be well served.

Most clinicians have a general theoretical orientation to the management of mental health problems, and a competent mental health professional or physician will fit the treatment to the problem. However, some professionals have a rather fixed approach to managing nearly all mental health problems. Some will deal with childhood problems as manifestations of family disturbances. They tend to work with the entire family right from the beginning and spend no time evaluating the child.

Other professionals see symptoms of ADHD as mostly a by-product of inner psychological conflicts and sexual or aggressive impulses. Their focus is aimed at resolving internal conflict through self-awareness. Finally, some professionals take a strictly medical or neurological approach to ADHD and minimize the importance of school-based intervention.

Each of these approaches can be a legitimate way to deal with some mental health problems. They can even be a part of the total effort for ADHD children and their families. The important point is for the professional to have sufficient perspective to include all aspects of diagnosis and treatment in the management plan.

ADHD is a complex disorder which works its way into all levels of a child's life. It represents more than any one of the orientations mentioned earlier. Therefore, *the most helpful professional is one who will gather information from multiple sources and arrive at a diagnostic decision based on a reasonable integration of the data.* For a problem this chronic and multifaceted, you need someone who is willing to get involved with the diversity of issues that arise at home, in school, and within the community.[2] This person may be a psychologist, psychiatrist, pediatrician, neurologist, or child therapist. The critical factors in your selection are a willingness to work with community agencies such as the school, and specific training and experience in the area of ADHD.

As the primary advocate for your child, you must take the initiative to secure the best help available. Ask questions, become informed, and read everything you can get your hands on. This allows you to challenge and ask about those things that don't make sense to you. Your goal here is to be an active collaborator in the process. When you call or meet with a professional, ask if he or she has had specific training in the diagnosis and treatment of ADHD. What kind of professional workshops has s/he attended? How

---

Checklist for Selecting ADHD Professional

❑ Has appropriate professional degree and licensing—Ph.D., Psy.D., Ed.D., M.D., M.S., M.S.W., etc.
❑ Has experience working with ADHD children.
❑ Has specific training in assessment and treatment of ADHD.
❑ Is able to manage a multidisciplinary or multimodal approach to assessment and treatment.
❑ Is able and willing to work closely with your child's school and teacher.
❑ Seems to appreciate complex nature of ADHD and is able to draw on many community resources to help your child.
❑ Has balanced perspective on ADHD. Recognizes the long-term nature of the problem, but is encouraging about degree of help available.
❑ Makes no promises of instant cures and proposes no unorthodox procedures.
❑ Was recommended by satisfied client or some other professional familiar with their work.
❑ Has a sensitivity and ability to deal with spiritual issues. Is a Christian who can relate faith and practice to your needs.

many children has s/he evaluated? How involved does the professional become in the monitoring of treatment? If you or your child has a problem, how available is the doctor to respond?

You need to feel comfortable and confident with the practitioner. If s/he won't answer your questions or gives unclear answers, look elsewhere. When you are uncomfortable with a practitioner's personality or professional approach, confront the issue or find someone else. This is too important an issue to tolerate incompetence or unprofessional conduct.

At the same time, let me remind you there are no immediate cures or quick answers to the problem of ADHD. If you go looking for a doctor to immediately eliminate all stress and strain from your life, you will always be disappointed. Likewise, if a professional promises you quick fixes, charges unusual fees, and offers unorthodox methods, you should get out of there right away.

The checklist on page 67 summarizes our discussion. Use it as you review your contact with various professionals.

How to find help

With these characteristics and objectives in mind, you are now ready to set out to find a coordinating professional. Many referrals of this type are made through former clients. Talk to other parents who may have had similar problems with their children. See if they have any recommendations. Parent support groups such as the local chapter of Children and Adults with Attention Deficit Disorder (CH.A.D.D.), often keep track of qualified and responsive clinicians. In part 3 I have included national offices for several such groups that can direct you to your state or regional chapters. Your child's teacher or school personnel may be able to give you a list of respected professionals in your area.

Sometimes there is a well-regarded specialty clinic or individual practitioner in your area with a reputation for working with ADHD. Look up Christian counseling centers and ask if they have a person on staff who specializes in learning problems and/or attention disorders. Your pastor could also be a source of information for Christian professionals and counseling centers. Your family doctor or pediatrician can probably refer you to outside help, as well as be a place for you to begin your inquiry.

If your area has a medical center or university, you might call the child psychology or psychiatry department and ask where such services can be obtained. Some cities have medical and mental health referral bureaus that list various practitioners and specialties. You can call or write these agencies and get several names.

You may live in an area where there isn't anyone with specific expertise in handling referrals for ADHD. In that case, you might have to travel to the closest available specialist. Most large cities will have someone who can provide the help you need. Write or call the person or agency and arrange to go in for an evaluation. Some of the preliminary work can be done by mail. Forms can be sent to you to complete and distribute to teachers; these are then returned prior to your initial visit. The interviews, family history, and testing can often be completed in one or two days, if a concentrated schedule is needed. Make sure you have exhausted your local resources before traveling outside your area. It's best if there is a professional close by who can easily be consulted and who is familiar with the local resources and schools. An opinion 200 miles away is no more accurate than competent help from someone close at hand.

Your first choice might be your family physician or pediatrician. If so, you can ask your doctor about his willingness and competency to coordinate the efforts for your child. He may refer you to someone more knowledgeable or recommend an outside consultation. Some developmental pediatricians are very conversant with ADHD and have a treatment plan they utilize. Many physicians, while they can prescribe medication, may not be familiar with the schools and specifics of educational and personal intervention techniques. In that case, they would need an additional resource, such as a psychologist or child therapist.

Sometimes a physician will refer patients with suspected ADHD to a child neurologist. A neurologist can rule out other possible medical problems, but usually does not have access to the behavioral and educational strategies. However, neurologists are useful when there is suspicion of seizures, brain damage, or Tourette's syndrome. For most ADHD children, extensive neurological tests, such as an EEG, and CAT and PET scans, are not necessary. Seldom do they turn up anything, unless there are strong or suspicious neurological or medical symptoms.

Child psychologists are often the professionals most familiar with ADHD. They are usually the most comfortable with behavioral, educational, and social approaches to treatment. Psychologists cannot prescribe medicine and would need to work with the attending physician to get the medical assessment. A psychologist can usually provide the necessary forms to help evaluate the outcomes of the various types of intervention, including the medication trials.

Child psychiatrists have the medical degree that allows them to prescribe medication. They should have the orientation toward management of ADHD and working with other professionals.

Both a psychologist and a psychiatrist would be able to work with the child and the family on issues of stress, anger management, depression, and conflict resolution.

Resources through your local school district

Before looking elsewhere, you should be aware of free evaluations through your local school district. Intelligence, achievement, speech, language, and motor development evaluations are available under Public Law 94-142. ADHD has been determined by the U.S. Office of Education to be eligible for special services.[3] Your local school has an obligation to meet your child's needs to the extent its resources allow. Even if your child is in a private school or is being home-schooled, an educational needs assessment should be available through the public school. Since you pay taxes, you are entitled to receive these services. I have described the process for obtaining services in chapter 7. You might want to jump ahead and look at the first part of that chapter.

Since the school needs to be part of the total planning for your child, it is a very good idea to get them involved as early as possible. Whether or not you utilize the resources of your local school district at the beginning, your child's teacher will still be a vital part of the treatment plan. As I have said, part of choosing an outside professional is selecting someone who is skilled and able to work closely with the school. The communication loop *must* include the teacher. You can start with the school and eventually involve medical and mental health professionals from outside the school. If you start with an outside professional, he or she will subsequently need to work with the classroom teacher. It doesn't matter so much where you begin the process; just make sure all the necessary resources are included.

A major reason for starting the process within your local school is the issue of cost. However, you might want a second opinion, or might not want to wait the ninety days or more that the process often takes in the schools. Perhaps you desire a Christian evaluator to be involved in the process. You are always free to do whatever you think is best for your child. I just want you to know and fully consider all of your options.

Also ask about costs

A basic evaluation will cost several hundred dollars, with five to seven hundred dollars being quite common. Complicated cases requiring extensive specialized equipment and expertise may cost several thousand dollars. Ask what services are covered, including school visits, phone conferences, testing supplies, report preparation, and summary conferences. Most clinicians simply charge for the time spent working on the case, with an hourly charge for all of the services provided. Ask about reduced fees and scholarship or grant programs. You will have to complete some financial disclosure information, but it may allow you to qualify for various forms of financial aid.

Be sure to ask your insurance carrier if they will cover the testing. Specifically ask if insurance will cover a diagnosis of ADHD and/or learning disabilities. Some policies specifically exclude this diagnosis. It's not appropriate and doesn't make sense, but it is still a frequently excluded coverage. If the company does not cover attention disorders, but you do have coverage for other mental disorders, such as depression, you might want to pursue with your insurance company why they are discriminating against ADHD. Since ADHD has been recognized by the Office of Civil Rights as a legitimate disability, it could be argued that your company is discriminating against those with ADHD. If your company will not reconsider their position, you may wish to take legal action or file a complaint with the Office of Civil Rights.

If you are a member of a managed care program, check to see if you need an authorization or referral from you primary care physician in order to initiate the evaluation process. Also ask if any specific procedures are excluded from coverage. The evaluation process usually includes some type of psychological testing and written report. Make sure the details of authorization and coverage are clear in your own mind, and then make sure the process is acceptable to the evaluator.

You should also explore whether the school district could pay for the independent evaluation. If you have had an evaluation completed by the school, but are not satisfied, it might be possible for the school to pay for a second opinion or an Independent Educational Evaluation (IEE). The school may have a specific list of people they want you to use if they are going to pay for the whole evaluation. The school may only pay a portion of the total fee if you choose someone outside of their network. The school district may contest your request for an IEE and ask for a due process hearing to show that its evaluation was appropriate. If the final decision is that the local school district evaluation is appropriate, you still have the right to an IEE, but not at public expense. In any case, it may be worth your while to check out the options before assuming you have to pay for all of an independent evaluation.

What to Tell the Child about the Testing

Honesty and a calm presentation are the key ingredients in communicating to a school-age child about the prospect of testing. I tell parents to inform the child that s/he and the doctor are going to complete some activities that will help the family and the teacher determine how to make it easier for the student to succeed in school. Acknowledge with your child that s/he is having trouble paying attention and getting his/her work done, or is frequently getting into trouble. Your child knows what kind of problems s/he has been having, so it won't be telling the child anything s/he doesn't already know.

Tell the student s/he will not be receiving a grade on these tests, and that other students will not see any of the results. The whole purpose is to help make his or her schooling more successful by finding out how s/he learns and how his/her brain works. Give the child some idea of the kind of changes that s/he might expect as a result of the test data. For example, the approach to homework might be different. Or extra help could be given to strengthen the weak areas of the learning process. Above all, emphasize your unconditional love and support for your child.

Your attitude will set the stage. If you are calm and optimistic about the process, your child will probably mirror the same attitude. You probably won't be allowed in the same room once the formal testing starts. Inform your child that the examiner will be really nice, that most of the activities are fun, and that there will be bathroom breaks when needed. Also be very clear that this kind of doctor doesn't give shots or pull teeth.

Make sure the child has a good night's rest before the testing, and inform the evaluator if there have been any major changes or trauma in recent days that might affect the child's performance. For example, I was scheduled to evaluate a young child who was suspected to have an attention deficit disorder. The picture the parents painted of this child was that of a perpetual motion machine. However, the child had come down with a bad cold and an ear infection. The mother had given the boy some medicine that morning and by the time they arrived at my office, he was sound asleep. I made an attempt to talk to the child, but he was barely able to walk down the hall, let alone produce accurate results in the testing situation. We rescheduled the evaluation for when the lad was feeling better.

Give the child a good breakfast or lunch, and avoid any foods that you suspect have a negative affect on your child's performance. After the sessions, don't ask lots of questions about how the testing went. The child may not be given specific feedback about specific responses s/he made during the testing, so might not know how it really went. A general inquiry is understandable, but don't probe.

Assessment Procedures for ADHD

Regardless of who directs the process, a proper diagnosis of ADHD must include observations and data representing all aspects of a child's life. The coordinating clinician will obtain detailed information from the parents. This will include both current descriptions of the problem and developmental information about the child and family. The clinician will also need objective observations provided by the child's teacher(s) and a physician's medical evaluation. Finally, there will be a clinical interview of the child, and the completion of formal diagnostic testing. I will describe each of these components so you have an idea of what to expect. Then we will look at how it is all put together for confirming a diagnosis of ADHD.

Parent information

The assessment process usually begins with an intake interview with one or both parents of the child during which the clinician asks you to give an overview of the child's problem. This will lead to a discussion of your own history to determine if you experienced similar problems when you were young. Many other aspects of the child's developmental history, disciplinary methods, and prior professional contact will be covered.

Feel free to take along your child's report cards, progress reports, teacher comments, and previous test scores or evaluations. These records can be very useful to the evaluator. Many parents find it helpful to write out ahead of time their concerns, important developmental events, and any questions they may have for the evaluator.

You may receive various questionnaires and rating scales either prior to or during your first session with the clinician. If completed prior to the first interview, these can save time and increase the accuracy of recall during your appointment. Together, the detailed interview and the history form should give the counselor an accurate picture of the child's developmental patterns.

Observation of your interaction with your child is important. The counselor may have you spend some time together in a play-room setting or interview all of you together. Sometimes the clinician may even want to make a home and/or school visit.

The parent interviews and background information forms need to be accompanied by objective parent report questionnaires. I will give a brief summary of the most common forms. Not all clinicians use the same instruments. However, this listing will give you a fairly accurate summary of the procedures used by the respected authorities in the field. The most widely used and best-researched forms are the *Conners' Rating Scale—Revised (CRS-R)* and the *Child Behavior Checklist (CBC)*.

The CRS-R Parent Rating Scale is scored on a four-point scale which includes: Not at all, Just a little, Pretty much, and Very much. A number of subscales, such as Hyperactive-Impulsive, DSM-IV Symptoms, ADHD Index, and Oppositional Behavior, are derived from the parents' responses to the items.

The Child Behavior Checklist—Parent Form (CBC) was developed by Achenbach to record behavioral problems and competencies of children ages two through sixteen. In the CBC, the parent or caretaker rates behavioral descriptions as: Not true, as far as you know, Somewhat or sometimes true, or Very true or often true.

The CBC also contains questions concerning the child's social activities and social interaction. Information from these items is used to calculate age- and sex-referenced social competence scales.

To assess the impact of the child's possible attention disorder upon home and community situations, the *Home Situation Questionnaire—Revised (HSQ-R)* is often used. You are asked if your child has problems paying attention or concentrating in a number of home situations, such as playing alone, getting dressed, at the store, in the car, and when asked to do homework.

If you indicate a problem, then you are asked to rate how severe the problem is on a scale of one to nine. The HSQ-R yields scores for the number of problem settings and the average severity of the problem.

For adolescents, clinicians sometimes use an *Issues Checklist for Parents and Teenagers*. The *Issues Checklist (IC)* assesses self-reports of specific disputes between parents and teenagers. It consists of issues that can lead to disagreements between parents and their teenage children, such as chores, friends, and homework.

The *Conflict Behavior Questionnaire (CBQ)* is another self-report inventory that can be used to assess perceived communication and conflict between parents and adolescents. The separate versions for each parent and teen contain true-false items that reflect general arguments, misunderstandings, the inability to resolve disputes, and specific verbal and nonverbal deficits.

The information from the IC and CBQ can be helpful in tailoring a family therapy program, particularly in the areas of communication skills, problem-solving, and conflict resolution. Repeated administration can monitor progress and assess change.

Another form used by both schools and clinicians is the *Behavior Assessment System for Children (BASC)*. Parent, teacher, and student self-report versions of this rating scale are available, and provide several scales measuring inattentive and impulsive behavior patterns.

Teacher reports and school functioning

A careful and detailed school history is essential to obtain a clear diagnosis of ADHD. The clinician will need to understand any progression or continuance of concentration and attention problems. Earlier report cards, teacher comments, and periodic achievement tests, along with previous testing reports, need to be reviewed. If you have copies of these items, take them along for the counselor to evaluate. It will save time if you make copies to leave with the counselor. It also insures that your originals won't be lost.

Descriptions from various school situations and teachers are also needed. Most ADHD children do not have equal behavioral difficulties in all school situations. If we can get a picture of where the child is more successful, it gives us an initial understanding of his coping skills. This data not only helps confirm the ADHD diagnosis, but also gives the counselor ideas for setting up a treatment plan.

The *CRS-R Teacher Rating Scale* has become a widely used

and researched questionnaire for teacher rating of attention disorder behaviors. The format is identical to the Parent version described earlier, and includes the same subscales.

Another form is the *ADD-H Comprehensive Teacher Rating Scale (ACTeRS)*. This is a norm-referenced, standardized behavior rating scale for diagnosing and monitoring the behavior of the student who manifests a deficit in attention in the classroom or is unusually active or restless. It includes twenty-four behavioral items rated on a five-point scale, which fall into four factors: Attention, Hyperactivity, Social Skills, and Oppositionality. This scale is also reported to be quite sensitive to medication influences, and might be used to monitor your child's behavior during medication trials.

The *Child Behavior Checklist—Teacher Report Form (CBC-TRF)* by Achenbach is a parallel form to the Parent version described earlier. It contains much of the same information as the Parent form. Different scales have been developed to reflect the child's work habits, level of academic performance, degree of teacher familiarity with the child, and happiness of the child.

The *School Situations Questionnaire—Revised (SSQ-R) is* the equivalent version to the Home Situations Questionnaire. The teacher responds to eight school situations, indicating whether or not a student has problems paying attention or concentrating. If "yes," the teacher indicates the severity. The useful scores are the number of problem settings and the average severity.

A final rating scale that can be completed by the classroom teacher is the *Academic Performance Rating Scale (APRS)*. This scale assesses a child's productivity and accuracy in completing schoolwork. While this information can be inferred from report cards, this form also contains questions that deal with attention and organization skills. This form can shed more light on the child's attention deficits, as well as provide more clues about how the child approaches his work. This will be useful in implementing practical suggestions during the intervention phase.

Clinicians need to remember that teachers are busy people and have twenty to forty other children to manage. Most of the forms mentioned here take only a few minutes to complete. I usually have parents deliver the forms to their child's teacher with instructions and a return envelope with my address. That way the teacher is able to send the forms directly to me. Sometimes teachers will be a bit more candid in their comments if they know the parents are not receiving the forms.

Clinical Assessment of the ADHD Child

To the utter bewilderment of parents, highly active, destructive, and inattentive children have come to my office and acted like angels. Even if they have just been picked up at school for fighting in the lunchroom and setting off the fire alarm, they are able to smile and make pleasant conversation.

If I didn't know better, I might look at such a child, have him play a few minutes of video games on my computer, and conclude he was a pretty normal kid. On the other hand, I might look at Mom and see her eyes bugging out and veins popping from her neck. My conclusion could be the child doesn't need medication, but Mom does.

The error here is to jump to a conclusion from nonrepresentative data. An accurate diagnosis of ADHD must be made from a variety of sources, in different situations, and across several samples of time. That is why we need to collect the many different observations from alternate sources in order to get a clear picture of how the child really acts.

Clinical measures of attention disorder

Structured psychometric testing has the potential to provide the clinician with standardized, norm-referenced data about the child. Both quantitative and qualitative data can result from testing that is well-designed and well-administered. However, in spite of the extensive research on ADHD, there is still no single test or battery of tests that have been shown to be *the* test for diagnosis of attention disorders. The most common psychometric tests used for the attention deficit child include tasks that measure *reflection, vigilance, impulsivity, short-term memory,* and *sustained attention.* None of these tests are pure measures of attentional ability, and questions are frequently raised about reliability and validity. However, with caution and understanding, the competent evaluator can utilize some of these tests to obtain *quantitative* objective data regarding the child's attention-related skills. Also, important *qualitative* observations can be made about the process the child goes through while responding to the test items.

Several clinic-based tests of sustained attention and impulsivity have recently been standardized for use in evaluating symptoms of ADHD. Some of the most widely studied laboratory measures of vigilance or attention span with the ADHD population are the *Continuous Performance Tests (CPT)*. Several such tests are available. They include the Conners' *Continuous Performance*

Test (CPT), the *Test of Variables of Attention (TOVA)*, and the *Gordon Diagnostic System (GDS)*.

The Gordon Diagnostic System is a portable, solid-state, childproof computerized device that administers a nine-minute vigilance task, where the child must press a button each time a specified, randomly presented numerical sequence occurs. This system is able to discriminate ADHD from normal children, and is sensitive to stimulant medications.[4]

Any of the continuous performance tests are expensive, and probably only clinicians who do a lot of ADHD evaluations will be able to justify their purchase. Like rating scales, a continuous performance test provides one source of information to be integrated with the balance of data gathered by the evaluator.

Other tests are used to measure a child's impulsivity and ability to attend. The *Stroop Word-Color Association Test, Kagan Matching Familiar Figures Test,* and the *Hand Movements Test* are some examples. Different clinicians may choose to use various tests, depending on their experience and preferences.

The *Wechsler Intelligence Test for Children—Third Edition (WISC-III) is* the most common individually administered test for determining a child's general level of academic potential or IQ. The test is divided into two sections called Verbal and Performance. Within each section there are five or six subtests which measure different aspects of intelligence and problem-solving. Three subtests from the WISC have been factor-analyzed into a category called "Freedom from Distractibility." The subtests used are Arithmetic, Coding, and Digit Span. Data is conflicting on whether these subtests can discriminate ADHD children from normal children. Since the WISC-III is often used in determining at least general intelligence, the data from these subtests will frequently be available. Your evaluator may or may not highlight these scores as part of the diagnosis.

With older students and adolescents, several self-report forms or structured interviews may be used. These can include the *Conners-Wells' Adolescent Self-Report Scales*, the *Achenbach Youth Report Form,* and the *Brown ADD Scales*.

Direct observation

Systematic formal behavioral observations in natural settings can be another useful component in the diagnosis and assessment of ADHD children. Direct observations are time consuming and expensive, and they can also be difficult to standardize. However, when combined with parent, child, and teacher interviews and rating scales, observational data can add greater validity, integrity, and rigor to the clinical process.[5]

On occasion, I will observe the child in the classroom. I may count the number of talk-outs and out-of-seats compared to on-task behavior. Later I will ask the teacher if that period was a representative sample of the child's behavior. If so, I can compare this with my other classroom experiences. This process does give a better sense of depth to the assessment, and also sets the stage for implementing classroom interventions that are relevant and appropriate. Because I have been there and talked to the teacher directly, I have a better appreciation of what kinds of recommendations to make. The only problem is the increase in cost that this procedure adds to the total evaluation.

The clinician may give other tests to round out the assessment. The *Piers-Harris Self-Concept Scale* is a brief self-report measure to evaluate self-concept in children and adolescents. Subtitled "The Way I Feel about Myself," this true-false questionnaire is designed to evaluate a child's conscious feelings about himself. This test might be given if a clearer impression of self-esteem were needed. If depression is suspected, a test such as the *Children's Depression Inventory* may also be administered.

Many other measures may be used to get at the emotional features of a child. I will often give the *Bender Gestalt, Draw-A-Person*, or *Draw-A-Family*, along with several types of sentence completion forms, and portions of the *Education Apperception Test, Thematic Apperception Test*, or *Projective Story-Telling Test*. These latter tests show a series of pictures of various types to which the child responds by telling a story about what is happening in that picture. The results give the clinician an idea of the emotional themes a child uses to describe various life situations.

For additional cognitive and achievement assessment, the clinician may give tests such as the *Wide-Range Achievement Test 3, Peabody Individual Achievement Test,* and all or part of the *Woodcock-Johnson Psychoeducational Assessment Battery—Revised.* The revised Woodcock-Johnson test is quite comprehensive. Cognitive skills similar to WISC-III results can be obtained, along with reading, math, spelling, and writing achievement levels. This allows the clinician to obtain a clearer definition if learning disabilities are suspected. It also allows us to compare actual achievement levels to the child's potential ability.

Medical Evaluation

It is essential that children being considered for a diagnosis of ADHD have a complete pediatric physical examination. To be useful, however, the exam must be thorough enough to help achieve a diagnosis or identify other accompanying conditions. Your physician's role includes directing the search for a remediable medical cause of ADHD, as well as participating in the multidisciplinary diagnostic evaluation. If and when medication is indicated, your physician will supervise the medication intervention program. To these ends the following *components of a medical evaluation* should be included, as outlined by Goldstein and Goldstein.[6]

One of the goals of the physician is to determine if there are any medically remediable causes of the child's symptoms that could look like ADHD. Such things as hyperthyroidism, infection with pinworms, or iron deficiency need to be explored and eliminated from consideration. The major purpose is to provide a differential diagnosis of ADHD from other medical conditions and to treat those problems appropriately.

The physician will also need to decide if there is a need for more complete medical diagnostic testing. The purpose is to determine whether some type of medical illness is present which might duplicate some of the ADHD symptoms. The test may be as simple as a blood screening or as involved as an MRI. At this time, there are no lab tests or measures that can confirm an ADHD diagnosis, so neurological tests such as an EEG, CAT scan, and PET scan are not normally needed, unless the child's neurological history is significant.

The doctor will conduct an appropriate physical and brief neurological examination. The research is confusing in regard to the usefulness of soft signs and minor physical anomalies in the diagnosis of ADHD. Revisions in the examination for neurological abnormalities, now called "subtle signs," have been made and offer better discrimination potential.[7]

Goldstein and Goldstein recommend assessment of eye movements, finger sequencing, tandem gait, and choreiform movements (a type of finger movement). Storm has recommended the pediatrician conduct a neurodevelopmental exam which includes: minor neuorologic indicators, fine-motor function, language screening, large-muscle skills, temporal/sequential organization, and visual processing.[8]

Your child's hearing, vision, and blood pressure will also be screened, along with height, weight, and head circumference measurements. These measurements will be compared to normative tables of similar-age children, and are usually normal for most ADHD children. The purpose of the physical exam is to eliminate the unusual case of vision, hearing, or central processing problems that can look a lot like ADHD symptoms.

The final aspect of the medical evaluation is to determine if there are any contraindications to medication intervention, and to serve as a comparison at future reevaluations. Gathering information on risks of possible medication intervention is part of the physician's initial evaluation. The actual decision to prescribe medication is made only after a diagnosis of ADHD. The intent here is for the physician to look for medical features that would preclude the use of certain medications, should any type of medication trial be considered.

How Is the ADHD Diagnosis Made?

All of the tests have been given, the forms are scored, and now it is time to make sense of everything. How will your clinician go about evaluating the data? The following format has been found useful in analyzing the various sources of information. This approach describes the types of multimodal data necessary to make a diagnosis of ADHD and provides a guide for the integration of the assessment data. In making the diagnosis of ADHD, the following criteria, as articulated by researchers such as Barkley, as well as Goldstein and Goldstein, should be considered: [9]

DSM-IV diagnostic criteria

This is the most frequently used and best-researched definition available at the present time. Therefore, the child should meet these criteria. The DSM-IV definition specifies the child should demonstrate at least six out of nine of the inattentive and/or six out of nine of the hyperactive-impulsive criteria. These symptoms must be present to some degree before age seven, they must be present in two or more settings, and there must be clear evidence of clinically significant impairment in the student's social, academic, or occupational (if an adult) functioning.

Significant developmental history

From the parent interview and childhood history, the clinician should look for evidence of similar problems with inattention, distractibility, and impulsivity with either of the parents or with immediate relatives. Other notable features are irritability or unwillingness to be cuddled as an infant, eating or sleeping problems, allergies, or frequent ear infections.

Parents will also often describe a child who was constantly into things, excessively curious, unable to play with toys for any length of time, had frequent accidents and injuries, and experienced difficulty with both large and fine motor coordination.

These children seem bright, but their parents say they are forgetful, lose things, are messy, disorganized, and sometimes appear to be in a fog or constantly daydreaming. There are reports of excessive temper outbursts followed by immediate remorse and repentance, only for it to happen again and again. These children don't seem to learn from their mistakes, discipline seems ineffective, and some parents report their child even wears out his shoes more rapidly than other children.

Elevated rating scales

The child must score at or beyond 1.5 to 2 standard deviations difference in comparison to the same chronological age and sex on at least one questionnaire sensitive to attention problems. This means your child should score at the 93rd percentile or higher on any measure of ADHD symptoms. The scales used in this category will often include the Conners' Revised Parent and Teacher Rating Scales, the Achenbach Child Behavior Checklist, the ACTeRS, or other similar rating scale. This criterion must be met by two independent raters, usually the child's parent and teacher(s).

Objective measures

There is no single test that measures ADHD. However, there are a number of objective, norm-referenced measures which range from computer-based tests to paper-and-pencil tasks. The ADHD child should demonstrate difficulty with attentional skills such as reflection, vigilance, persistence, and poor visual concentration. The tests I draw from include the Gordon Diagnostic System, Matching Familiar Figures Test, the Hand Movements Test, various subtests from the Woodcock-Johnson Tests of Cognitive Abilities, the Freedom from Distractibility score on the WISC-III, and the Stroop Word-Color Association Test.

I would expect the majority of the tests given would show borderline to abnormal results in an ADHD child.

Situational problems

The inclusion of situational data allows the evaluator to assess the impact of the child's attentional problems on daily living. Children with attention disorder will often have problems across numerous situations. There is usually a consensus between parents and teachers concerning the severity and frequency of these problems. If there is not agreement between the home and school reports, the clinician needs to carefully consider why there is a disparity. The difference could result from rater disagreement or measurement errors, as well as the fact the child has more problems in one situation than the other. The more pervasive the behavior, the greater the need for comprehensive intervention.

The standard for this criterion is that there are problems in at least half of the situations screened on the Revised Home Situations and School Situations Questionnaires developed by Barkley and DuPaul.

Differential diagnosis

The clinician must gather sufficient historical, behavioral, and assessment data to rule out or minimize the contribution of the following conditions to an attention disorder: medical problems, learning deficits, language disorders, auditory processing disabilities, specific intellectual deficits, and psychological problems of childhood.

Clinical interviews, projective testing, IQ and achievement tests, and standardized tests such as the *Personality Inventory for Children* can be used to rule out other pervasive developmental problems or establish the coexistence of other features, such as oppositional disorder, conduct problems, depression, anxiety, posttraumatic stress disorder, inadequate parenting, abuse, or learning disabilities.

In 25 to 35 percent of the cases, ADHD children also have learning disabilities. With this in mind, the clinician must carefully evaluate the learning characteristics of the student in order to make the most appropriate recommendations for educational intervention. Language difficulties, auditory, visual, or motor processing dysfunction, short- or long-term memory problems, and various learning style features are examples of the kinds of considerations to be used in the differential diagnosis.

ADHD, primarily inattentive versus primarily impulsive-hyperactive

It is important to remember the above criteria are probably more true of the attention disordered child with hyperactivity. The child who experiences attention difficulties, but without hyperactivity, may not show up with as many behavioral problems in school or at home. The ADD child without hyperactivity will have difficulties during individual seat work and in small group activities. Otherwise, he may not experience any problems. Overactive and aggressive behavior is easy to see because it disrupts others. The nonhyperactive child may go unnoticed because he or she doesn't make waves and cause trouble.

Research paints two dramatically different pictures of attention disordered children. Children who are primarily impulsive-hyperactive exhibit aggressive conduct problems, bizarre behavior, appear guiltless or unpopular, and perform poorly at school. They show less self-control, greater impulsivity, and markedly worse internalizing and externalizing. This child is more noisy, disruptive, messy, irresponsible, and immature. Impulsive children have a higher risk for serious aggressive or oppositional behavior and antisocial conduct. These children will also have a higher number of relatives with ADHD, aggressiveness, and substance abuse.

The impulsive-hyperactive children tend to have lower scores on the arithmetic subtest of the WISC-III and will show more commission errors on the Vigilance test of the Gordon Diagnostic System.

In contrast, those attention deficit children who are primarily inattentive tend to be anxious, shy, socially withdrawn, moderately unpopular, poor in sports, and have low school performance. The inattentive student often is seen staring into space or daydreaming, is often forgetful in daily activities, appears to be low in energy, and is sluggish and drowsy.

This student often seems lost in thought, apathetic, and lethargic. He or she is less aggressive, impulsive, and overactive, both at home and school, and has fewer problems in peer relationships.

On tests, the inattentive student has fewer off-task behaviors during the Vigilance test of the GDS, and tends to perform worse on the Coding subtest on the WISC-III. Also, this student has greater problems on any measure of consistent retrieval of verbal information from memory.

The inattentive child is also found to have a higher number of relatives with anxiety disorder and learning problems.

Both categories of ADHD can experience depression and low self-esteem.

If the above criteria are met, the conclusion can be made that your child has ADHD. The diagnosis may also include other coexisting conditions, and will need to describe whether hyperactivity is present.

The diagnosis should not stop with merely placing a label on the condition. The crucial part of the process is determining the specific treatment plan appropriate for your child.

How an Assessment Becomes a Treatment Plan

At the conclusion of the assessment procedures, you will not leave the doctor's office with a tidy plan drawn out in ten easy-to-follow steps, but you will have some definite direction to follow. The nature of ADHD requires a continuing effort to manage and deal with its ongoing challenges. The following steps summarize how the diagnostic information described in this chapter is translated into a tentative treatment plan.

1. The major concerns or problem areas for the child are identified and described. This information is gathered through all of the assessment procedures described earlier.

2. The identified problems are clustered or grouped into categories for ease of description. Categories can include: academic, social, emotional, spiritual, and physical. These broad categories can then be broken down into specific areas. For example, academic can be divided into intelligence and achievement. In turn, these can be divided into their specific components. Achievement, for example, can include reading, math, language, and writing skills. All of the various components of intelligence would also be examined, with any deficiencies or learning disabilities identified for remediation and compensation.

3. The counselor will end up with a broad picture of your child, covering the entire spectrum from academic to medical needs. The diagnosis takes place when these various descriptions of behavior and symptoms are compared to the criteria and guidelines established for all of the disorders of childhood. If your child meets the combined criteria for ADHD as described in chapter 1, then the diagnosis of ADHD would apply, along with any other handicapping conditions.

4. The next step is to prioritize the various problem areas into some type of treatment plan. The list allows you and the clinician to decide which interventions need to be started immediately and which ones can be undertaken later.

5. The clinician will also need to identify the unique aspects of your child's life—what features of your culture, family, marriage, financial condition, community resources, stressors, medical conditions, and so on, impact your child. The relevance and practicality of each intervention idea must be evaluated in terms of the context in which you and your child live.

6. Next, a list of the various treatment options is prepared. Intervention ideas are set forth to address the specific needs of your child and family. What kinds of adjustments would help in the classroom? What can parents do at home to help teach self-control and organization? Would medication be appropriate? Dietary changes? Marriage or family counseling? The list goes on until all of the needs are covered.

7. The treatment ideas are then evaluated. What are the pros and cons for your child of each of the proposed forms of intervention? Are the resources present to actually carry out the suggested treatment plan? Are there risks that need to be weighed against possible gains? These kinds of questions are considered as thoroughly as possible before the various parts of the treatment are implemented.

8. The treatment components are identified and the necessary resources gathered to begin working the plan. As the specific ideas are tried, there is always ongoing evaluation. Is the plan working? What needs to be changed? How can it be done better?

As each part of the plan is implemented, there will be adjustments and changes to fit the conditions. What works for another child may not work for yours. Treatment consists of trying previously established ideas that have been found to help children with ADHD. However, if a given tactic doesn't work, it must be adjusted in some way so that it benefits your child. This ongoing evaluation fits the basic principle in working with ADHD problems, "If at first you don't succeed, try, try again."

References

1. D.P. Cantwell, "Attention Deficit Disorder: A Review of the Past 10 Years," *Journal of the American Academy of Child & Adolescent Psychiatry*, 35(8) 1996, 978–87.

2. M. Gordon, *ADHD/Hyperactivity: A Consumer's Guide* (Dewitt, New York: GSI Publications, 1991), 42–46.

3. S. Moses, "Letter on ADD Kids Gets Mixed Reactions," *The APA Monitor* 22.12 (1991):36–37.

4. M. Gordon, "Microprocessor-Based Assessment of Attention Deficit Disorders," *Psychopharmacology Bulletin*, 22 (1986):288–90.

5. R.A. Barkley, *Attention-Deficit Hyperactivity Disorder. A Handbook for Diagnosis and Treatment* (New York: Guilford Press, 1990), 334–53.

6. S. Goldstein & M. Goldstein, *Managing Attention Disorders in Children* (New York: John Wiley & Sons, 1990), 52–71.

7. M.B. Denckla, "Revised Neurological Examination for Subtle Signs," *Psychopharmacology Bulletin* 21 (1985):773–89; M.B. Denckla, et al., "Motor Proficiency in Dyslexic Children with and without Attentional Disorders," *Archives of Neurology*, 3 (1985):231–33.

8. G. Storm, "ADHD and the Developmental Pediatrician," *Medications for Attention Disorders and Related Medical Problems*, ed. E.D., Copeland (Atlanta: SPI Press, 1991), 69–79.

9. R.A. Barkley, *Attention-Deficit Hyperactivity Disorder. A Handbook for Diagnosis and Treatment*, 169–205; S. Goldstein & M. Goldstein, *Managing Attention Disorders in Children* (New York: John Wiley & Sons, 1990), 152–71; S. Goldstein & M. Goldstein, "The Multi-Disciplinary Evaluation and Treatment of Children with Attention Deficit Disorders," 16th ed. (Salt Lake City: Neurology, Learning and Behavior Center, 1991), 51–60.

CHAPTER FOUR

WHAT HAPPENS TO US?
Family Reactions to a
Diagnosis of ADHD

A diagnosis of ADHD often brings a mixture of relief and anxiety to parents. There is relief brought about by finally having a medically accepted name to call the phenomenon. Parents often express relief when they are told their parenting skills did not cause the ADHD. I have had parents break out in tears when I affirmed that their actions did not cause their child to act the way he or she does. Parenting, like schooling, does not bring about the presence of ADHD, but the environment can certainly intensify or calm the symptoms.

When a family receives the diagnosis of ADHD, the process of grief is activated. Many of the same feelings and reactions brought about by a significant loss, such as death, become a part of the family's emotional processing. The well-known reactions of denial, guilt, anger, depression, and acceptance begin their cycle. Anguish, fear, helplessness, hopelessness, and shame are some of the related feelings that are likely to emerge at this time. I would emphasize that these phases are cyclic, and not fixed or sequential. These reactions will ebb and flow, disappear and reappear like winter fog along a riverbank. My descriptions are intended to help you process these reactions, not to suggest a rigid progression of events.

• *Denial* is often the first reaction to the discovery of ADHD. This can be true for one or both of the parents in the months or years prior to ever seeking professional help. "Oh, he's just being a boy," or "If you would just be more firm and consistent with her, everything would be OK," are a couple of examples of expressions of denial prior to a formal diagnosis. "There's nothing wrong with my child," or "It can't be true—the doctor is wrong," and "She just needs more time to mature, and more understanding teachers" are examples of denial following a formal diagnosis.

• *Anxiety*, along with many other emotions, usually accompanies the formal diagnosis. Most of the feelings are generated around the questions of: "What do we do?" "How is ADHD treated?" "What caused the ADHD?" "What happens next?" It is important for you to acknowledge your feelings of anxiety and then work with your team of professionals to outline a positive course of action. Having a sense of direction and a plan intended to help your child can be helpful at this stage.

• *Flight* can be another expression of denial. Here the denying parents of a problematic child may go from one doctor to another looking for one who will tell them what they want to hear— "There's really nothing wrong with your child that time and love won't cure." Parents of an attention deficit child need to understand that love is crucial, but without understanding, structure, and appropriate intervention, an ADHD child will not get better.

• *Cover-up* is another form of denial. One parent, often the mother, wants to "protect" the other parent by not sharing the results of the diagnosis or minimizing the problems the child is having. The cover-up may continue by the one parent hiding the fact the child is in a special program or receiving outside help for the ADHD. This results in two major problems. The uninformed parent continues with unrealistic expectations and tends to make inappropriate demands on the child, resulting in further tension and conflict. The child perceives the reason for the cover-up as lack of acceptance and believes the family has to pretend that s/he is more different than s/he really is. This leads to anger, depression, and struggles with self-esteem.[1]

• *Anger* often follows the denial phase. This anger may be directed inward, against yourself, often in the form of guilt, or it may be directed outward, blaming the other parent or some outside source. "We never had anything like this on my side of the family." "That pediatrician should have paid closer attention to those ear infections." "These psychologists are for the birds!" "The kindergarten teacher should have seen the problem and told us to get help three years ago." All of these expressions are signs of anger displaced toward others. Similar to the guilt reaction, blaming an outside source places responsibility somewhere else, and protects you, the parent, from feeling helpless. One major problem coming from this reaction is the effect on the child. If the ADHD child hears the parent making constant disparaging and critical remarks about the major sources of help in his or her world, the child's faith and respect are undermined for the very people the family must turn to for help and hope.[2]

Sometimes the feelings which tend to emerge during the anger phase of grief may focus on God because He let you down. "Why does my child have to struggle with these problems? Why hasn't God answered my prayers?"

I cannot deny the pain, and I cannot explain why such things happen. I just know God can work and be glorified even in the middle of our problems. He understands our anger. The process of raising an ADHD child to health and maturity is a tedious journey, not an overnight trip. The process of identifying your fear and anger will take a while. As the journey proceeds, you will find anger and doubt turning to hope.

The change from doubt to hope happens, in part, because of *where* you place your faith. That's why a portion of faith the size of a mustard seed is sufficient. If you look to yourself for all of the answers in handling a difficult child, you will be disappointed, frustrated, and continually angry. That is the wrong place to put your belief. By placing it in God, you are assured of help and healing (Psalm 37:5; James 1:5).

God accepts you in the process of dealing with your anger and learning to believe. A father once asked Jesus if He could heal his son who had an evil spirit. Jesus replied, "Everything is possible for him who believes." Immediately the boy's father exclaimed, "I do believe; help me overcome my unbelief!" Then Jesus proceeded to cast out the evil spirit and the boy was made whole (see Mark 9:14-27). The process of grief will include times of anger and doubt. The exciting thing is that God will accept you even in your angry and doubting state.

• *Isolation* can be a significant feeling in the initial stages of identification and treatment of your child's ADHD. You may say to yourself: "Why doesn't anyone care?" "Nobody seems to understand." "Why can't they make more accommodations and allowances?" These are some of the expressions of isolation. You feel alone, helpless, and powerless to make sufficient improvements in the daily functioning of your child.[3]

• *Guilt* is another common reaction. "Why me?" "It's all my fault." "God is punishing me because . . . " or, "If only I hadn't let him bump his head, had played with her more, had been more strict, or had followed the doctor's advice." These are all manifestations of a judgment of guilt by the parent, followed by feelings of sorrow and remorse. Dr. Larry Silver describes identification of guilt as an attempt to establish control over a situation that a parent perceives as hopeless and out of control. If a parent can lay the blame or attribute the cause to himself or herself, that person then "conquers" the situation by explaining it, however erroneously. The "logic" used is that if this happened for a reason, on account of something I did, and if I do not practice that transgression again, then nothing like it will happen again.[4]

Guilt may also be used as a stimulus for penitent behavior, with the petitioner hoping resolution takes place once the penance has been paid. If you are struggling with guilt, it might be wise to talk with your pastor or counselor and sort out the difference between true and false guilt. Then you can go on to understand and experience the place of God's forgiveness and loving acceptance. A spiritual approach to feelings of guilt can be a major source of comfort.

• *Fear* is another possible reaction to a diagnosis of ADHD in your child. It can be expressed by thoughts such as: "Maybe it's worse than they say." "Is it a progressive disease?" "Will she ever be able to finish school, hold a job, or live a normal life?" As a parent, you will have many legitimate questions when a diagnosis is given. Any competent professional you work with should provide as much information and reassurance as possible. In my own practice, I try to be factual and honest with the family. I don't want to give false hope or foster unrealistic expectations. However, family members need reasons to hope and to believe things can improve for their child. I will often tell stories of other ADHD children I have known and how they have been helped. There are increasing numbers of materials such as books, tapes, and videos that can be used by the family which illustrate the growth and improvement of other ADHD children, and I will often point out these resources to the parents.

Many of the materials are listed in the resource section of this book.

• *Overprotection* is one outgrowth of fear that can emerge as the parent is trying to cope with the demands and stress of dealing with an ADHD child. Children definitely need the protection of parents. It is part of your responsibility to keep your child safe and to expose him or her only to those challenges that are developmentally appropriate. The goal is to protect the child when needed, and yet to encourage learning and exploration even if frustration is involved. Only through taking on new, untried challenges will a child become a confident learner. An overprotective parent covers a child's weaknesses, but this also smothers the child's strengths. Overprotectiveness keeps a child immature and delays growth. It also makes a child feel inadequate. If a child looks around and sees other siblings doing chores, taking on a paper route, and trying out for the ball team, but never gets the same opportunities, he or she will conclude, "I can't do anything."[5]

Parents need to identify tasks that are appropriate for the ADHD child, as well as learn to "engineer" the environment so as to maximize success. Taking on a daily paper route, for example, may not work. However, a once-per-week paper delivery might be possible. Your counselor should be able to help you with this and similar issues.

• *Envy* may also frequent the experience of the parents of a high-maintenance child. "Why do other parents have it so easy?" "Everything good happens to them and everything bad happens to us." "It's not fair. We work so hard and get so few results." These statements come from thoughts of envy or even jealousy of other families who don't appear to have the same struggles as ADHD parents. I might tell parents with whom I work, "These comparisons are normal. However, we don't want to dwell on the differences between your child and other children. Let's focus on what is good about your child."

It's entirely possible, of course, that many of those "well-adjusted" families have their own problems and frustrations. The parents of an ADHD child should not assume that everything is always rosy with the family across the street. As their counselor, I try to point out this reality to the ADHD family.

Also, I highlight the many unique qualities and creative potential found in many ADHD children. Many characteristics of ADHD children are quite appropriate and desirable. As was mentioned earlier, their spontaneity, zest, tirelessness, enthusiasm, intensity, curiosity, stimulating brashness, and life-of-the-party energy have their useful moments. These children have rich imaginations and can quickly generate new and different ideas. They can pick up on emotional nuances that other people miss. They can combine ideas in creative ways through art and writing that no one else has tried. The need is to bring the ADHD child's problem behaviors under control. Then the useful abilities can be harnessed for good.

I encourage you to remain optimistic and hopeful. The future will hold times of discouragement. Even so, you, your attention deficit child, and your family can experience joy and success.

• *Bargaining* is another well known part of the grief process. For the ADHD family it may take the form of: "Maybe he'll be OK if we move." "I'm sure she'll be fine next year." "Maybe if we get a computer, everything will be easier." "Maybe if I quit work and stay home, he will do better." The important distinction between bargaining and appropriate action has to do with evidence and function. Simply moving from one neighborhood to another will not affect the presence of ADHD. If moving, however, allows the child to be placed in a more progressive and appropriate school, this plan is being based on evidence and a rationale that has *functional* potential. The move has the potential to improve the child's educational success, based on professional opinion and a careful analysis of the child's needs. The move is not dictated or solely motivated by some general impression that the grass will be greener someplace else.

Here again, your counselor can help you sort through your motivations and reasons for proposing changes. If there is evidence that a change in plans has credibility for the benefit of your child and family, it can be implemented. If not, the relationship of bargaining to the grief process should be explored.

The bargaining phase can be a time when you may be tempted to invest in quick cures and unproven treatment programs. You want to believe with all your heart that your son or daughter can be "normal" and not have to struggle with the problems of inattention and distractibility.

During this phase, some parents look to spiritual or quasi-medical promises for elimination of the problem. I wish they worked. I readily acknowledge God's power; I know that He can heal anything, including ADHD. However, I worry about the feelings of a child who did nothing to deserve the problems of ADHD in the first place. Now he might have to endure unfruitful spiritual interventions which come up empty. The tendency will be for that child to internalize the blame, and conclude it is his fault that he wasn't cured.

I think it is more realistic to acknowledge the presently incurable nature of ADHD and focus on the methods of intervention that have been shown to be helpful. Included in those interventions are spiritual resources, including prayer. However, I ask you to be discerning and cautious about creating false hope.

Another aspect of the *deal-making* part of grieving occurs when you promise God you will make changes in your life *if* God will heal your child. If God convicts you to make necessary additions or deletions to your life, by all means be obedient to that call. I just don't believe a child's health should be made a bargaining chip in that process. God isn't in the business of authoring illness to bring us to repentance. Periods of hardship, including illness of a family member, can result in life-changing commitments, but those are by-products of God's grace. It was not that God caused the original problem. It is that He is great enough to work His ways, in spite of the problem.

• *Mourning* is a time of grieving specific losses. These losses can be primary, such as the death of a loved one. Or they may be secondary, such as the realization that a child may not be able to reach certain goals the parent had established. "I guess he won't be a doctor." "She'll not be able to go to the same college I did." "I was a good student, I guess my child will never be on the honor roll." These are examples of mourning the fact that certain accomplishments may be unreasonable for a particular child.

Take the time to examine whether your expectations are, in fact, accurate. We never want to put a ceiling on any child. At the same time, over the course of the years, the evidence can certainly point in a given direction. Try to be objective as you sort through the months and years of evidence regarding your child's abilities and interests. Try to focus on what the child can do, rather than on what he or she can't do. There may need to be a shift in goals and expectations from what you had initially visualized for your child. However, the key here is "shift," not "lower." Seek to identify the strengths of your child and find ways to cultivate those strengths.

• *Depression* is certainly understandable as a response to loss. "I've failed my child." "I'm a lousy parent." "No wonder she is having so many problems, look at her parent(s)." "I had the same problems as a kid. I never got any better and neither will my child." "I can't do this. I'm not cut out to be a parent." These expressions of hopelessness and depression are frequent companions of many parents of ADHD children.

Many parents are burned out and need some time of physical, spiritual, and emotional restoration. Depression can be a very normal reaction to extended stress. Like a warning light on the dashboard of your car, depression can be a signal that something is out of balance and needs attention. Don't ignore the signal.

Many different alternatives are available to you. A medical evaluation may be needed. Respite care may need to be arranged. Periodic case reviews may be scheduled for your child to make sure everything is being done to maximize the management plan at home, in school, and with peers. Talk to your counselor, pastor, or physician about your negative feelings and thoughts. Medication, emotional support, reassurance, and attention to negative thinking, false assumptions, and incorrect perceptions are some of the therapeutic interventions that may help you deal with your depression.

• *Acceptance and hope* are eventual goals for the grief process. If the process goes the way it should, acceptance and hope become more a part of your family's day-to-day experience. There will still be those days when hope subsides and you will consider moving to Tasmania. Remember, you have the same choices as your child in regard to the presence of attention disorder. An ADHD child can pity herself and be miserable and dependent the rest of her life. Or she can do the best with what she has and work hard in the process.[6]

"OK, my child has ADHD. What are we going to do to help?" "My child has some weaknesses and some strengths. How can we build on those strengths?" "It will take the help of a team of professionals, a loving and supportive family, and our faith in God, but we'll make it." These are the comments of parents who have accepted the reality of the diagnosis, know there is work to be done, and have committed to being an advocate for their special-needs child.

Like any other context for grief, a person may get stuck on any of these phases or emotions. Chronic denial, anger, or guilt are the most common. The normal reaction of denial, for example, after learning of a child's ADHD, is to be expected. However, if that reaction, as evidenced by continual flight or blame, goes on for months, rather than days, the progress and health of both you and your child will be compromised.

Grief work is difficult. My experience suggests two years is a common time line for moving from initial denial to acceptance, in persons dealing with the death of a loved one. Dealing with a diagnosis of ADHD may take that same kind of patient, but persistent, effort. Remember, this process does not end at the end of some arbitrary interval, such as two years. Managing life with an ADHD child (often with the frustrations of also being an ADHD parent) is a continual challenge. Yet, experience and faith allows us to be confident in the outcome.

Reactions of Other Children in the Family

When one member of a family hurts, everyone feels the pain in some fashion. This certainly includes the siblings of the ADHD child. A variety of reactions, such as anxiety, anger, guilt, acting out, and covering up success, are possible reactions to living with an ADHD brother or sister.[7]

• *Anxiety and worry* may occur for some siblings. Lack of information about the nature of ADHD can feed these feelings. In families where there is little discussion or disclosure about the problem, siblings can wonder if ADHD is contagious or terminal. They may ask their parents, "What is wrong with my brother?" The unwise parent may respond with minimization or avoidance, which serves to feed the anxiety of the child asking the question. The sibling may wonder if there will be enough money to pay for all of the doctors and medicine, as well as other family needs. A sensitive or benevolent brother or sister may worry that his or her ADHD sibling will never find success in school or life after living with so much stress, conflict and failure.

• *Anger* can come from many sources in an ADHD family. The sibling may get angry when told there isn't enough money to buy a new bike because of doctor or tutoring expenses necessitated by the special-needs sister or brother. Where double standards are present regarding chores and other responsibilities, anger and resentment can also occur. "Why do I have to make my bed every day and Jesse doesn't?" "Why do I get punished for the same thing that you seem to ignore with Julie?"

A sibling may become angry over living with the moody, easily frustrated, accident-prone, forgetful, perpetual-motion machine, also identified as her brother or sister. Personal possessions may not be safe because of raids on her room, to say nothing of her reputation among friends. "Your brother is crazy." "How's the nutcase at your house?" "You're not weird like your sister, are you?" These kinds of statements are hard for a special-needs sibling to handle. The sibling is caught between defending the family member, risking alienating friends, or demeaning his sister to save face with peers. Frustration and anger are likely under all of these conditions.

• If the sibling begins to degrade his ADHD brother or sister with friends, *guilt and remorse* can occur. If siblings hear their parents say, "He really can't help it" or "It's not her fault," confusion can emerge as the siblings try to reconcile their resentment with the fact that much of the behavior is outside of the control of their sister or brother. Perhaps there have been thoughts like, "I wish I lived in another family" or "I wish my sister had never been born." Guilt and feelings of sorrow or shame will often be forthcoming.

• *Acting out* can become a by-product of any of the previous feelings. Siblings might develop night terrors from worry, or aggressive attacks from anger. Resentful brothers or sisters may provoke misbehavior in their ADHD sibling as a means of getting even. They may set up the other child as a scapegoat in order to get away with their own misconduct. Sometimes siblings may set up their ADHD family member to look bad so that they can look better.

Another version of acting out can be motivated by a desire for attention. Siblings may conclude that "the only way to get anything in this family is to have problems." So they act out to claim some of the center stage that had been occupied by their ADHD brother or sister.

• *Holding back* or *covering up success* is sometimes found in younger siblings of ADHD children. This will be true when the younger child has special talents in academics, music, art, or athletics. A few such precocious youngsters may see that they are in danger of passing up their older sibling and begin to hold back, believing it's not acceptable to perform at a higher level. This stifles their progress and can lead to additional resentment and rancor.

Many of these problems can be moderated with education and open communication. When I complete an evaluation with a positive diagnosis for ADHD, I try to get the entire family together to provide an overview of the process. I have several videos that can be used to explain the nature, causes, and treatment procedures for ADHD. This allows siblings to have most of their questions answered. There are programs and books directed to children who have siblings with special needs, and I will often direct the family to these resources.

One such resource is a program called Sibshop. Activities take place about once a month where children who have siblings with special needs such as autism, Down's syndrome, leukemia, severe learning problems, and ADHD can be together. They do fun things, such as bowling, cooking, and learning how to paint with a toothbrush in their mouths. Most importantly, they hear how other children get along with their sibling who has serious medical or learning problems. They are able to support each other and learn to see the good in having a brother or sister with special needs. Sibshop is active in a majority of states throughout the U.S.[8]

Reactions of Extended Family and Friends

Grandparents, aunts and uncles, as well as friends of the family can go through the same process as parents when a diagnosis of ADHD is given. There can be the initial denial and disbelief. "Those doctors don't know anything. All they do is take your money and come up with fancy terms that have no meaning." "He'll grow out of it." "She's no problem at my house. We play games or bake cookies for hours at a time."

• *Denial* can be accompanied by blame and shame. "You just need to be more strict with that child." "If only you would. . . ." "Why do you indulge her so much?" "A good old-fashioned spanking is all he needs." The themes of more love or more discipline are preached, along with the message that poor parenting is the basis of the problem. The end product is guilt, along with no improvement in the quality of life for the ADHD family.

• *Alternative explanations and solutions* are frequent contributions from well-intentioned friends and family members. Suggestions of dietary changes, vitamins, special herbs, lighting conditions, or exercise programs are made. While there could be value in some of these nontraditional interventions, the family is tempted to disregard the advice of the professionals and pursue unproved techniques. Usually disappointment will follow.

• *Noncooperation* is a frequent characteristic of unaccepting extended family members or friends. A reward system, for example, may be established for compliant behavior. The intention is that the ADHD child is to earn a point each time he cooperates or complies with a directive from his parent. The counselor has emphasized that structure is important and that the more pervasive the management scheme, the more quickly the child will improve. However, after explaining the system in detail and leaving

Grandma to baby-sit, the parents come home to find the place in shambles, and Grandma completely oblivious to the point system. She doesn't believe Johnny has a problem; therefore, the point system is a waste of time. I have had some parents who reached a point where they had to tell the grandparents they would have no contact with the children unless they agreed to educate themselves about ADHD and follow the system outlined by the professionals.

Many families can, in fact, be bonded together by love and strengthened by the trials of raising an ADHD child. This can result in a unified family-support group that provides a crucial foundation for the growth and happiness of a special-needs child. However, it does take intelligent cooperation.

Summary

The diagnosis of a special need, such as ADHD, can be a traumatic experience for all members of a family. The common reactions of grief certainly apply. Denial, guilt, anger, depression, and bargaining are usually present, serving as stepping-stones to eventual acceptance of the diagnosis and family lifestyle it requires.

As parents, you will need ongoing encouragement to follow through on professional and support-group advice. There may be times when you will need specific help in areas of stress management, conflict resolution, anger management, communication skills, time management and organizational skills, respite care, as well as how to maintain and enhance your marriage relationship. Don't be afraid to ask for and search out these kinds of resources.

The general principle in the treatment of ADHD is *consistent structure* along with *consistent effort*. There are no short and sweet methods for dealing with these children and adolescents. All along the way, it takes persistent efforts to provide and maintain structured learning experiences. It isn't easy. The challenge never goes away. However, there are rewards, and ADHD children do grow up to be well-educated and productive adults.

References

1. L.B. Silver, *Dr. Larry Silver's Advice to Parents on Attention-Deficit Hyperactivity Disorder* (Washington, D.C.: American Psychiatric Press, 1993), 93–94.

2. Ibid., 95.

3. S.L. Smith, *No Easy Answers: The Learning Disabled Child* (New

York: Bantam Books, Inc., 1979), 158.

4. Silver, *Dr. Larry Silver's Advice to Parents on Attention-Deficit Hyperactivity Disorder*, 94–96.

5. Ibid., 96.

6. Smith, *No Easy Answers: The Learning Disabled Child*, 159.

7. Silver, *Dr. Larry Silver's Advice to Parents on Attention-Deficit Hyperactivity Disorder*, 98–102.

8. D. Meyer, P.F. Vadasy, & D.J. Meyer, *Living with a Brother or Sister with Special Needs: A Book for Sibs*, 2nd ed. (Seattle: University of Washington Press, 1996); D.J. Meyer & P.F. Vadasy, *Sibshops: Workshop for Siblings of Children with Special Needs* (New York: Paul H. Brookes, 1994); S.D. Klein & M.J. Schleifer, *It Isn't Fair!: Siblings of Children with Disabilities* (New York: Bergin & Garvey, 1993).

PART TWO

Treatment of ADHD

" 'I will restore you to health and heal your wounds,'
declares the Lord."

Jeremiah 30:17

CHAPTER FIVE

HOW CAN PARENTS HELP?
Parental Intervention
with the ADHD Child

Julie and Jeff sat in their car for a few minutes after leaving Dr. Howard's office. The report on Julie's lap indicated very clearly that Danny had ADHD. The doctor had done a comprehensive evaluation and was very compassionate as she described her conclusions.

As the rain beat down on the roof of their car, Julie thought, *This isn't true . . . it is not happening to my child . . . my child can't possibly have ADHD . . . you must be wrong.*

Jeff gripped the steering wheel until his knuckles were white. His thoughts turned more to anger: *Why didn't Danny's teacher say something last year? What's wrong with these doctors that they don't have some way to cure this thing once and for all? What kind of loving God would allow this to happen to an innocent child? Danny doesn't deserve this.*

"What's going to happen to Danny?" Julie said to no one in particular. "Is he going to be frustrated his whole life? What are we going to do?"

"Do you suppose it's my fault?" Jeff asked. "Dr. Howard said this is probably inherited. I guess it means Danny got this from me. How was I to know? Maybe we shouldn't have had any kids."

"No, honey, it's not your fault. It's not anybody's fault, I guess," Julie responded. "We're both feeling pretty helpless right now. But, as Dr. Howard said, at least now we know what's wrong. We realized Danny wasn't like the other kids. Now we know why."

"Yes, I suppose you're right," Jeff said. "It helps to know what the problem is. Now we can begin to help work on the solutions. It's just so frustrating to make sense out of all this."

This dialogue represents the questions and feelings of most parents when they learn their child has ADHD. There is a sense of relief about knowing the exact nature of the problem. Some of the guilt is removed because the parents have learned they didn't cause the problem through faulty discipline. But there is anger and sadness in hearing that ADHD does not have a cure at the present time, and that the condition is something their child will have to deal with the rest of his life.

Parents need a chance to grieve. If you learn your child has attention deficit, don't be in too big a rush to run out and make all sorts of changes. Take your time. Shed some tears and vent your anger. Punch a few pillows or chop up a cord of wood. Let God know how you feel. Talk to some trusted friends or family members about the situation. Don't try to keep up a false front of confidence and faith when you don't feel strong.

There is "a time to weep and a time to laugh, a time to mourn and a time to dance" (Ecclesiastes 3:4). And yes, there is every reason to have hope. The rest of this book is about how to bring that hope to fruition. But before you can reorient your thinking and behavior to the specifics of dealing with an ADHD child, you need a time to mourn. Allow yourself that expression.

• *Feelings of the ADHD child.* Most children will be confused when they learn about the ADHD diagnosis. They might think there is something terribly wrong with their bodies or brain, and even wonder if they are going to die. Some may use this diagnosis as an excuse, saying, "I can't help myself. I have ADHD."

Remember, children go through the same grief process as their parents. They will need time to adjust to the diagnosis and its implications. Your child needs acceptance, love, and understanding. Much as an abused child is told time and time again, so your child needs to hear, *"It's not your fault."*

Most children will be relieved, because now people will realize why they have struggled so much. Adults will now have a greater appreciation for why they have so much trouble paying attention and following the rules. They probably really *want to* behave, but have had a terrible time doing so.

In the resource section, I have listed a number of books or videos you can use to explain ADHD to your child. Check out one or two of these and use them with your child, as well as other members of your family.

• *How to explain ADHD to your child.* One of your most difficult tasks is to explain ADHD to your child. You don't want to say the wrong thing so that he feels inferior or defective. You also are reluctant to say too little and have him remain uncertain and confused. Some children could take parts of an explanation and use them as an excuse to misbehave. Because of these fears, many parents try to avoid the issue, but there will eventually be a day of reckoning. When you do approach the subject, it should be done in ways that are honest and helpful. Ideas drawn from the materials mentioned above can help you compose your explanation. In addition, I want to give you a few pointers.

You do need to explain ADHD to your child. He needs to know that you realize he has a difficult time sitting still, stifling interruptions, and keeping his mind on a job. Without some type of explanation, your child will conclude he is dumb or inferior. He needs to know his academic problems are not his fault. Tell him you understand he is doing the very best he can, but that he has a very real problem which makes it hard for him to concentrate and get his work done. Part of treatment begins with an understanding of the nature of ADHD. Just as I began this book with an explanation and definition, so your child needs the same information at a level he can understand.

You can use the checklists on pages 108 and 109 to help your child identify behaviors that characterize ADHD. The lists itemize some of the things that kids have said about themselves. Read them and have your child make a check mark in the box next to each comment that is just like him or her.

The answers to the checklists can be used to help your child acknowledge that his problems are much like those of many other kids who have attention deficit. You can then go on to give the rest of the explanation.

That explanation needs to be simple and phrased in word pictures your child can relate to. Tell him that every person is unique and that we all have specific strengths and weaknesses. Some people have certain parts of their brain arranged in such a way that

Home Situations

❏ I have trouble paying attention unless something is very interesting.
❏ I often forget to do things my parents ask me to do.
❏ I seem to get into more trouble than other kids.
❏ I keep getting into trouble for doing the same things over and over.
❏ I have lost lots of my things, like coats, gloves, or school materials.
❏ I get bored easily.
❏ Mealtimes can be real hard because I always do things wrong.
❏ I can get angry quickly.
❏ My parents get after me because my room is so messy.

School Situations

❏ I have trouble listening in class.
❏ My mind often wanders off when I should be paying attention.
❏ I often have trouble sitting still.
❏ I have trouble getting my written work done in the time allowed.
❏ My teacher often has to tell me to be quiet or to keep my hands to myself.
❏ I have trouble getting my assignments done, or I forget to turn them in.
❏ I make lots of careless mistakes in my schoolwork.
❏ I don't like to read.
❏ Sometimes I can get so interested in something that I tune out everything else around me.
❏ I have trouble with my handwriting.

Social Situations

- ❑ I don't have very many friends.
- ❑ I often play with younger kids.
- ❑ I seem to do things without thinking.
- ❑ I have had lots of spills and accidents.
- ❑ It is real hard to play quietly by myself.
- ❑ I like to do things that adults say are dangerous.
- ❑ It is hard for me to wait or take turns.
- ❑ Other people complain because I interrupt too much.
- ❑ I seem to have trouble following the rules in games, at school, and around home.
- ❑ Sometimes I can be too bossy.
- ❑ I tend to be shy and quiet, especially around other kids.

---

they can't see very well. These people wear glasses to allow them to view their world more clearly. Other kids have teeth that need straightening. They wear braces and retainers to correct their teeth so they can eat correctly, play the horn, or whistle.

You might tell a primary-age child something like this: "Danny, your mother and I want you to know what Dr. Howard told us about why it is so hard for you to listen to your teacher and get your schoolwork done. Everybody has little highways in their body, and they have things that work like tiny little cars to carry messages to their brain. If your teacher is telling you how to do a problem, these little "car-like" things called axons have to travel fast to get all the messages to your brain. Danny, your body doesn't have enough of these little cars or cells. So when the teacher talks to you, all of her ideas don't get to the right place in your brain. In fact, sometimes these little cars run out of gas and never get to the brain at all. However, maybe another message *does* get to the brain, like a noise in the room or a bird outside the window. Because these messages don't require you to concentrate so much, it's easier for them to get to the brain. They don't need as many cars. Then what happens is that you pay attention to the broken pencil or bird outside, and miss what the teacher is saying. This isn't your fault. It's just the way your body works."

It's important to let your child know he is not the only one in the world with this problem. There are probably lots of kids in his school who also have attention deficit. If someone else in his extended family has the same problem, share this fact also. There are many parents, even teachers, who have attention problems. Above all, convey your total love and acceptance for your child just the way he is.

Your explanation should be a beginning point for responsibility and problem-solving about how to deal with ADHD. Your comments need to serve as a departure point for discussing how the entire family is going to work together to manage the effects of attention deficit. You want to give a basic definition about the nature of ADHD, and help motivate your child to persevere. Managing the symptoms of ADHD is not easy, but there are many resources to assist you. Let your child know that you, his teacher, counselor, and his doctor are going to help.

You can ask your child to describe his problems to you. Various word pictures might emerge: "I have a tiger in my tank." "My engine runs too fast, and I can't make it stop when I want." Or "I'm like the Little Engine That Could, except my engine runs too fast and sometimes jumps off the track." A child who has seen the film *Bambi* would recognize the little rabbit that was rather impulsive and seldom waited long enough to identify the source of a sound.

For the inattentive child, the word picture might be, "My TV screen sometimes gets fuzzy or tries to show too many channels at once," or "It's like I'm listening to a CD and it loses track of what song it was playing."

Each of these descriptions could be turned into a discussion about how to regain control by: "Grabbing hold of the tiger's tail," "Turning off the switch," "Putting on the brakes," or "Changing to a better channel." The discussion could then proceed to the specifics of how each of the self-control actions would be accomplished.

Any topic, cartoon character, or metaphor that focuses on channeling energy can be used as a working explanation. It all depends on the child's age and interests and what you can use to hold his attention.[1]

Guidelines for Parenting

I would like to give you some general parenting guidelines that can be critical in raising an attention deficit child. Many of these principles could also be applied to parenting any child, including most types of special-needs children. I have adapted these instructions for parents to the unique features of ADHD children. Read them over, discuss them with your spouse or other caretakers, and find ways to implement them or refine your existing approaches to parenting.

Don't ignore this section. These ideas are based on extensive research and experience and have been found to be extremely important to the process of loving your child into his full potential.

☞ Treat your child as a capable human being. Compliment his or her strengths. Support efforts your child makes to explore the world through any reasonable means. Allow your child to take healthy risks, and to try new situations. Don't foster dependence by being overprotective. You're not going to let a nine-year-old hitchhike to Disneyland, but you will consider an overnighter at a friend's house or a scouting campout at the state park.

☞ Focus on what your child *can* do, not on what s/he can't do. Give attention to your child's special qualities and strengths. Find ways to maximize those strengths, both to help compensate for weaker areas, as well as to enjoy an activity for its own sake. Your child may have difficulty concentrating while reading to himself, but does much better when listening to someone read aloud. Rather than force silent reading, which leads to frustration, let your child learn new information by reading to him, listening to a book on tape, or watching a videotape. If your child has a creative side, look for methods to nourish that creativity. In short, celebrate the uniqueness of your child in any way possible.

☞ Take special opportunity to let your child know you enjoy spending time with him or her. Say it with words, "You know, Shelly, I really look forward to these times when we share a cup of cocoa and just talk." Write notes and put them in the lunch bag, leave cards on the dresser, and add comments when providing feedback for homework. Of course, this means both Mom and Dad make time in their schedules to spend one-on-one time with each of their children.

☞ Remember the big picture. Schoolwork is important, but a child's love for God is more basic and has eternal implications. Be thankful for all the things that are going well in other parts of your child's life. Don't just dwell on your child's problems with attention or self-control.

☞ Share with your child some of your own struggles as a student. Talk about how you felt, how your parents handled things, and how you coped with frustration. The point is to communicate empathy and understanding toward your child's difficulties and to encourage hope for the future.

☞ Teach and model that mistakes don't equal failure. An ADHD child may tend to see his or her mistakes as huge failures. Parents can model, through good-humored acceptance of their own mistakes, that errors can be useful and can lead to new solutions. Mistakes are not the end of the world. When your child sees you taking this approach to your mistakes and the mistakes of others, s/he can learn to view his or her mistakes in the same light.

☞ Reward the process, not just the product. It is important to acknowledge the effort toward a goal as well as the achievement of the goal. Model this behavior in yourself. For example, let your child know you enjoy the preparations for a birthday party as well as the actual party. Take as many opportunities to highlight and celebrate honest efforts as you do for productive results.

☞ Communicate the concept that this is a family effort. Yes, your child has to take responsibility for doing her chores, completing homework, and putting out her best effort. However, your child is not in this alone. The resources of the entire family will be brought to bear to deal with the challenges of ADHD. No stone will be left unturned to find ways to help. Everyone will pull together to make school as successful as possible. Generally speaking, don't keep secrets about how things are going for your child. Pray together, work on projects as a family, and take suggestions from other family members on how to approach a problem. Make everything a team effort. Emphasize family traditions, stories, and legacies to help keep the problem of attention deficit in perspective. In the larger scheme of things, family, faith, and loving relationships are truly what is important. Try to live out that concept.

☞ Love your child unconditionally. No matter what happens, no matter how bad things get, communicate love with no strings attached. Sometimes that rotten, crummy attitude will show up. Expect it, both in your child and yourself. As a parent, you are entitled to some "no good, very bad days." When these inevitable things occur, you will need to draw on God's strength and that of your family and friends. However, whatever happens, keep the love messages going strong. Show your child you love him or her by your actions. Give your child a big hug when s/he gets home from school or you get home from work. Ask your child about how the day went. And take the time to really listen or to draw out more of a description when the first response is "I don't know," or "Oh, fine." Show an interest in the papers and projects your child brings home from school. Look for what has been done correctly more than the errors.

☞ Do not compare your child with any of his brothers and sisters or classmates. Accept your ADHD child as s/he is. Telling a child his sister was reading two years above grade level at his age will only reinforce his low opinion of himself. Comparisons can only tear his heart out. Believe in your child and have faith that s/he will get better. Continue to give support and encouragement. Let your child know you understand s/he is doing the best job possible at the moment. You will be the best cheerleader your child will ever see, and you won't be comparing your child to any other team.

☞ Be realistic in your expectations. Don't ever put a ceiling on what your child can do or be. At the same time, be realistic about the moment. Your child's reading or math skills may improve dramatically over the next several years. Anticipate that that can happen. Today, on this particular assignment, be realistic about how much the child can do, given recent experiences. Be ready to help your child stretch to new horizons, and yet don't push him or her so hard s/he gives up in the process.

☞ Your child needs encouragement to take responsibility for his or her actions. ADHD should not be allowed as an excuse for not trying, for misbehavior, or for wrongdoing. Attention problems can give rise to frustrations and mistakes. Help your child learn to differentiate "can't" from "won't." Difficulty in maintaining concentration in a noisy classroom is not something an ADHD student can easily control. Refusing to take his medication, choosing to sit beside a very distractible classmate, or throwing away his teacher's note to his parents, are examples of "I won't do it." These situations may be dealt with as acts of disobedience, because the element of choice is involved.

☞ Encourage problem-solving at every opportunity. Children with attention and learning challenges will have to learn to deal with frustration and disappointments. Parents will need to foster problem-solving at an early age. I have taught families to use the SODA approach for problem-solving.

S stands for stop and examine the problem. What is going wrong? What needs to change or be handled differently?

O is for options. Brainstorm possible options or solutions to the problem. Be creative, allow crazy ideas onto the floor. Help each other tap the right side of your brains to find ways to solve the problem.

D stands for decide. The next step is to choose which of the options is the best solution for this problem. Look at the pros and cons, apply principles of fairness and consistency, and decide what to do.

A is the action step of SODA. The final step is to act on the solution. Implement the idea. Set a plan into motion and then evaluate how the solution works. If everyone isn't satisfied, have another SODA and try again.

☞ Be aware that struggling with your child over homework can create an adversarial relationship. This conflict just sends another failure message to the child. Some parents make very poor tutors. Their own egos get so involved they can't remain objective while working with a struggling child. Try not to lose your temper or ridicule your child about his schoolwork. If this is true for you, back off. Let somebody else take over the homework monitoring role. The relationship is more important than the math papers.

☞ Understand the difference between unwilling and unable. You wouldn't punish a four-year-old child because she can't read the newspaper. In the same way, the child's tendency to become overaroused and easily frustrated, as well as impulsive and restless, is often unintentional. By successfully distinguishing between when your child is unable to behave from when s/he is unwilling to respond appropriately will reduce some of the stress. This will help stop the development of a more intense oppositional behavior pattern. Your goal is to model, teach, and reinforce appropriate compliant behavior, as well as ignore, extinguish, and/or punish noncompliance or unwilling behavior. At the same time, you will need to teach your child how to adapt and compensate for behaviors which he is unable to do because of the restrictions imposed by his ADHD. Here is an example.

Most elementary-age ADHD children cannot be expected to remember multiple directions or commands. If you tell your seven-year-old child to take out the garbage, feed the dog, and get the mail, you may find garbage in the dog's food bowl, and the dog in the mailbox. It's simply too much information to process. The result is not unwillingness, it is inability. This was not an act of willful disobedience. Education is more appropriate. Initially, you need to give one direction at a time. After a while (ranging from six months to twenty-one years!), teach your child to make lists, or use memory devices. An example of the latter would be to give the child the previous three directions, along with the mnemonic cue of "GDM." This stands for "garbage," "dog," and "mail." These prompts would then be used by the child to sequence the list of chores. I can't promise even this suggestion will work all the time, but it can help.

Let me quickly add that the question of, "Can he help it?" is a tough one. There is no easy way to sort out inability. There are going to be many occasions where you probably won't know for sure. You just need to do your best to assess the situation and determine your own course of action. Prayer for God's direction needs to be a daily requirement. Also pay attention to the angry, defiant, vengeful attitude, as opposed to the accidental, momentary flare-up or reaction.

Suppose you walk into the family room and find your child sitting precariously on the back of the couch. With concern in your voice, you say, "Sally, don't sit on the back of the couch." You fully expect she will get the picture and resume a normal sitting position. However, since Sally is an ADHD child, many expectations are questionable. You turn around and Sally is now teetering on the arm of the couch, ready to fall onto the nearby lamp table, which is next to the china cabinet containing your prized French figurines. As your blood pressure shoots through the ceiling, you shout at your daughter, "I told you to sit down. Now do it!"

"But, Mom," your daughter retorts, "you said I couldn't sit on the back of the couch. You didn't say anything about sitting on the arm of the couch."

Your patience is exhausted, the beans are boiling over on the kitchen stove, and you say to Sally through clenched teeth, "I want you to sit on the couch with your bottom on the cushion, and your feet on the floor. Is that clear?"

At this point, if Sally does not sit properly on the couch, as instructed, you have an "unwilling" or compliance problem, not an "unable" or ADHD problem. Now I realize this particular episode may not take two hours of prayerful discernment to figure out. Other situations can be far more difficult to determine how to handle. Most parents report, over time, they are able to decipher from body language, tone of voice, context, and history, just what behaviors are "can't" and which ones are "won't."

If your child's behavior is aggressive and harmful, I would recommend some type of instructional consequence or punishment. The child's reality includes living in a society that censures most forms of violence. Our Christian values certainly emphasize peaceful problem-solving. ADHD should never be an excuse for tolerating hitting, harsh language, or defiance.

☞ Keep to a regular routine. Children with ADHD need a predictable schedule. Try to keep daily events such as bedtime, meals, and homework on a definite schedule. Limit the amount of TV. Don't fall into the trap of using TV as a babysitter. If you restrict TV, be prepared to take the time to expose and encourage your child to follow other pursuits. Be firm about limits and consistent about enforcing them.

☞ Take care of yourself. Parents need to prevent burn-out. Most ADHD children are high-maintenance kids. The constant advocacy, attention to details, and remediation efforts require large amounts of energy. The concentration and patience needed for a child with attention disorders can wear down the best parent. There will be days when you are at your wit's end and will seriously consider running away. You've had a very bad day, and you feel like giving up and trading in the family minivan for a one-way ticket to Australia.

The important thing is that even if you have these feelings and thoughts, you won't act on them. You will find a way to process your feelings, and then remember that your loss of control will not help matters. When your child can't control himself, he needs your stability. He will be comforted by your sense of control, but feel frightened and confused when he sees you lose it. This is where God's strength and comfort, along with the support of friends and family, is crucial to your survival. This is also where a general game plan or strategy for behavior management is necessary. The ideas given so far, and the suggestions that follow, will all help establish the structure you and your child need to deal with his impulsive world.

Parents need time for each other and for friends. Single parents have a double load, so the need is even greater for them. Find time to foster some of your own talents and interests. Cultivate your faith in God as a source of comfort for those tough times. Participate in a network, either of other ADHD parents, or family, friends, and/or church community. You can't manage the entire process by yourself. A support system takes time to build, so start right away.

☞ Maintain your sense of humor. Laughter is good for the soul. Home needs to be safe and supportive. A large part of what makes it safe is humor and mirth. Not the sarcastic, stinging humor that puts family members down—we are looking for the playful, sometimes self-effacing humor that rolls with the punches that life throws at you. Cultivate the kind of humor that sees the silliness in life and the comic relief in accidents. Share the Sunday comics and magazine cartoons and relate how seeing the funny things in life helps us cope with the sad and traumatic things.[2]

Strategies for Encouraging Compliance

The previous parenting guidelines focused on the emotional aspect of development. In this section, we will look at ten procedures I have found necessary to be successful in the training and shaping of appropriate behavior in an attention deficit child. Because of their tendency to live in the moment and their apparent reduced ability to extrapolate a current lesson into the future, these children need a great deal of what we might call environmental engineering. Some children seem to learn from their day-to-day experiences through natural events. Parents don't have to give as much thought to occurrences such as going to the store, birthday parties, or having company over for dinner. With many ADHD children, each of these situations needs preplanning. This aspect of environmental engineering involves setting specific expectations and some type of consequences, depending on whether the child is successful or not. Let's examine these building blocks for successful parenting of challenging children.

Choose your battles

Where do parents begin? Many of the parents of ADHD children I see are so frustrated with their child they can't find a place to begin. Everything seems so overwhelming and negative. Much of what they can describe are negative characteristics and concerns: "My child never listens," "She always forgets," "He is chronically in trouble on the playground," or "I can't seem to get her to do anything I ask."

In this context, I advise the parents to choose their battles. Establish priorities. Determine the most important objective. Decide what really has to change right away. We can't change things overnight. This is a long-term project that requires perseverance and patience, so we have to identify those behaviors in the ADHD child that require immediate attention.

Behavior that endangers the child or others must take on a priority. This would be followed by behavior that is most disruptive to the family, would result in academic improvement, or improve a child's social standing. Each family will set its own priorities. Some things will have to be overlooked for a time in order to get other, more urgent, behaviors established.

As parents, talk with each other about the behavioral priorities for your child. Make sure that you agree about your goals. Then be ready to focus on those areas of highest concern and not make an issue of the less important areas.

Give immediate consequences

A consequence is something you do or provide following a child's response. An example would be giving your child a dollar for cleaning up her room. Another type of consequence would be taking away your son's video game privileges because he went to a friend's house without asking permission. Both of these situations involve a consequence. One consequence was positive, the other was a negative.

One of the most basic understandings in human behavior is the Law of Effect. This "law," simply put, says if you reward certain behavior, it is more likely to continue to occur and to occur more often. Conversely, if you punish a behavior, it is not as likely to occur or will happen less often. There are two ways to reward behavior and two ways to punish behavior. The two methods of rewarding behavior are to provide a positive consequence following a response (called positive reinforcement), or to reduce or take away an aversive or punishing event (called negative reinforcement). Removing restrictions, or telling a child she is no longer grounded because she has been displaying more cooperative behavior, would be an example of negative reinforcement.

There are also two methods to punish behavior. One is the administration of an unpleasant event, such as a spanking or making your child write 100 sentences. The effect of punishment is also seen by taking away a positive circumstance, such as eliminating phone privileges or making a child stay in his room.

At one time or another, a parent is probably going to use all four types of consequences. In the discussions to follow, I'll give several examples.

ADHD children need immediate consequences. That means parents need to be alert to apply either a reward or punishment as close in time as possible to the targeted behavior. The consequence should also be clear and specific. A general comment, such as "Good job," is not as likely to have strong reinforcement power to your attention deficit child. "Good job. Now give yourself two points on your Good Behavior Chart," is more likely to have the desired effect.

Give frequent consequences

Besides rewarding them right away, ADHD children require that parents apply consequences more frequently. These children need tangible and regularly applied consequences to help overcome their relative difficulty in learning from daily experiences. Because the executive functions of their brains are somehow impacted, these young people require ongoing feedback about their behavior.

Each child is different. Some will need more structured feedback than others. One child may require a fairly comprehensive point or token system that identifies and rewards many aspects of his behavior all day long. Another child may only need points added up and recorded at the end of the day, and only for a few high-priority behaviors. You will need to find what works for your son or daughter.

Some parents resist using a token or point system with their children, saying that it seems like bribery and teaches a materialistic approach to life. First, a true definition of bribery is to give something of value to someone for behavior that is illegal or immoral. The behavior we are targeting with our ADHD children is far from being illegal. We are trying to teach acceptable, ethical, moral, and desirable behavior. So using consequences certainly does not qualify as bribery.

It is true that we don't want our children to get the idea that they should only do something if they are going to get paid for doing it. This is where value education comes into place. As a concerned parent, you want to first model altruistic and benevolent behavior. Your children need to see you giving your time, talents, and resources to worthy causes. They need to hear Mom and Dad talking and teaching about the importance of recognizing, understanding, attaching meaning to, and internalizing virtues or values such as honesty, courage, peaceableness, self-reliance, responsibility, self-discipline and ambition, relationship commitments, loyalty, perseverance and dependability, respect, love and compassion, unselfishness and sensitivity, kindness and friendliness, justice and mercy, and faith. We'll talk more about this aspect of teaching in the final chapter on spiritual issues in parenting.

One final response to the parent who is reluctant to use a point system. May I ask, "Why do you work?" Most likely your answer will include something about making money. Most of us work to earn a living. It is necessary to functioning in our society. My point is, for almost everything we do there is a consequence. Either directly or indirectly, there is some kind of payoff for all that we do. Even for those who are Christian, there are benefits: eternal life, a God who answers prayer, peace of mind, and a purpose for living. However we view it, there is some kind of positive consequence even for our spiritual decisions.

If consequences are an inevitable and pervasive part of everyday life, why shouldn't we use a systematic approach to consequences that has been shown to be necessary, functional, and beneficial to all children? All children require a balanced and healthy diet. Some children are anemic and need extra iron, and we don't hesitate to provide it. I believe we take the same approach to an ADHD child who needs extra structure in order to learn and behave most effectively. Using immediate, frequent, and meaningful consequences are a part of that necessary structure.

Give meaningful consequences

For a reward or a punishment to be effective, it must mean something to the child. I recall a situation where I had recommended a point system be established to help a young girl complete her homework. It worked fine for a few weeks, and then her performance began to deteriorate. Upon investigation, I discovered her parents had neglected to provide any kind of exchange program for the points their daughter was earning. She got points for turning in her work to the teacher, but when she brought the points home, they were ignored. The parents had promised to set up a menu of activities their daughter could earn, but they never got around to doing so. As a result, her performance declined. This was a case of parental error, and not a problem with the basic idea.

Likewise, if you told your child he wouldn't be able to eat any spinach for two weeks if he didn't get busy and clean up his room, I seriously doubt if your proposal would have the desired effect (unless of course, your child is named Popeye).

ADHD children seem to require meaningful consequences to motivate them to change their behavior in the desired direction. Verbal comments and parental praise just aren't sufficient for most of these children. You will need to look to more meaningful consequences such as privileges, special snacks, toys, or access to desirable activities such as video games, TV, or the telephone.

One twelve-year-old boy I worked with took about two years to earn a motorcycle. He lives in an area where he has easy access to unlimited riding space, and his parents were willing to help him with the total cost of a used bike. Usually this would be too long of a delay for an ADHD child. However, because of his high level of motivation, it proved to be quite successful for this young man. To sustain interest, his parents would occasionally take him to a motorcycle shop. Together they would look at ads in the newspaper, and the family would talk about the day when Jeff would get his bike. Just recently, Jeff came beaming into my office and announced he had just purchased his motorcycle. He hardly touched the floor as he excitedly told me all about the new bike sitting in his driveway. And, of equal importance, was the fact his behavior at home and school had gone from highly disruptive to pretty much normal preteen activities. A meaningful consequence system was partly responsible for his improvement.

The use of natural or logical consequences is another way to make them meaningful. Many times the normal course of events will provide consequences to behavior. If a child goes outside on a cold day without a coat, he may catch a cold. That is a natural consequence. Your child calls from school and says she lost her lunch money for the umpteenth time. The temptation may be for you to rush to school with more money or a sandwich. Natural consequences should apply here (your daughter isn't going to starve by missing one meal). Unless there are medical reasons to do otherwise, let her learn from this event by telling her you are sorry, but you will have a light snack ready when she gets home from school. Until then, she must do without.

When my two boys were young, we had a schedule of chores that rotated from week to week. Sometimes there would be an argument between them about whose turn it was to feed the dog. I instituted a logical consequence. If the dog did not get fed by the evening meal, then the boy whose turn it was would not eat, either. We had no more problems with that issue. The boys made very sure that Chex got her meal, even if they weren't sure whose turn it was.

Be more positive than negative

Avoid the criticism trap. It is common for families with challenging children to become focused on punishment as the exclusive form of management. One of the first things I will do is try to get the parents to implement some type of positive reward system. The concern may be for fighting with his sister. We will redefine the goal to increasing cooperative exchanges between the two siblings. Instead of sending Sam to his room every time there is a fight, we institute a token system where both children earn rewards for getting along with each other.

Research has suggested there needs to be a ratio of about eight positive exchanges to every single negative exchange in healthy families. Worded another way, there need to be eight warm fuzzies to every cold prickly. In many families I encounter, the ratio is reversed. The emphasis is on the negative almost to the exclusion of any positive interaction between parent and child. Make sure you are endeavoring to highlight the positive approach as much as possible.

Very often I end up suggesting a system of consequences that involves both rewards and punishments. So I am not saying we must eliminate punishments of any kind—far from it. The real world includes negative consequences and our children need to be prepared to deal with that reality. My plea here is to get away from a highly negative focus often found in ADHD families.

Be specific in your expectations

To be effective in improving a child's behavior, a parent must establish specific, observable, and measurable targets. It is too vague to say, "I want my child to behave himself." Rather, you need to specify exactly what it is you wish your child to do. "I want her to comply when I ask her to do her chores," is an example of a more specific target.

Don't describe attitudes, feelings, or personality features such as "more pleasant," "less negative," "more energetic," "or be happier." These features can't be managed effectively, as stated, because they are too vague. They are too open to differing opinion by various caretakers as to whether a child is or is not displaying that characteristic.

Therefore, when you are establishing target behaviors in your child, make sure you have a clear, specific, and observable behavior in mind. One way to ensure a specific description is to ask yourself if the behavior in question contains some type of movement, so that you can count it. Brushing your teeth, completing chores, taking turns, doing what your parents request, all contain some type of action or movement.

Another part of this requirement for expectations is to clearly define the time limits for satisfactory completion of the task or behavior you expect. "Clean your room today" may work for some children, but probably not for the ADHD child. More appropriate would be to say, "Your room needs to be clean by ten. Look at your list to remind yourself what to do. After it's done, you may go to your friend's house." You have provided a time limit, a written list of what is to be accomplished in "cleaning your room," and a statement of the consequence for satisfactory completion of the task.

Be consistent in carrying out your plan

This can be a difficult goal to accomplish, but it is very important. Consistency has three applications. The first involves the consistent application of a management plan over time. As the parent, you are responsible for any management program and its maintenance over the weeks ahead. It is not your child's job to remind you of your responsibilities to award points or provide the rewards. Don't give up too soon. It may take weeks before some of the stubborn habits of your ADHD child begin to change for the better. If you have made a rule, which, if broken, is to be followed by a certain consequence, make sure you follow through.

Another aspect of consistency is to respond with the same management scheme regardless of the setting. At home, in the grocery store, while at church, riding in the car, or while eating dinner at Grandma's house, make sure you follow the plan. If your child sees that he can get by with noncompliant behavior when you are shopping, you'd better believe he will try it. I know it can be quite demanding. There are times you will be too tired to move. Yet, the more consistent you can be, the better the results.

The third aspect of consistency is from caretaker to caretaker. Usually this means both parents need to be following the same program. It does very little good if your child sees that when Mom leaves and goes to the store, Dad does not follow the plan. Discuss your expectations and how you intend to apply the consequence system. If there are disagreements, iron them out upfront. You are only making things worse for your child if there are unresolved disagreements about the management plan.

Experience tells me that for about one-half of the ADHD children I see, one of their parents is likely to also have ADHD. This inevitably leads to problems with consistency and follow-through. If this could be a problem in your family, I strongly suggest you confirm the possibility of parental attention disorder, and if true, start your own intervention program. Both the effectiveness of efforts on behalf of your son or daughter, as well as your own quality of life, can be improved.

Think ahead
Think about the troublesome times for you and your child. While at the grocery store, whenever other children come to visit, or when only one parent is present? Most parents, because of repeated difficulties, can predict when their child is likely to be disruptive. Is this true for you and your child?

I recommend you take some time and write down the most difficult situations. When and where do they occur? Your next step should be to devise a plan to deal with your child's behavior using some of the ideas from this chapter.

Once you have devised a problem-situation plan, review that plan with your child whenever you approach that situation.

Identify the specific behaviors you expect from your child, followed by the consequences the child will earn if he follows, or doesn't follow, the rules. Have your child repeat the rules and the consequences out loud while making sure you have good eye contact. Finally, make sure you follow through with the consequences, consistent with your statement of the rules to your child. Then as you enter and progress though the problematic situation, give your child frequent feedback about his or her compliance or noncompliance, along with the appropriate rewards.

Use multisensory instructions

Remember when you are giving instructions, making requests, or explaining concepts, most ADHD children respond best to multisensory input. I am talking about the combined use of touch, sight, and sound. Whenever possible, combine the tactile, visual, and auditory modes of learning.

This means, if you want to have maximum impact, lay your hand on some part of your child's body, perhaps his arm or shoulder, as you speak. Look your child in the eyes and use clear voice inflections. Sometimes you may need to add visual references, graphic illustrations, pictures, or gestures to the entire mix in the hopes of getting through to your child.

Keep it simple

Whatever you come up with as a management plan, make sure you can implement it. Keep it simple. It is far better to have a simple point system marked on the calendar which gets used, than a complicated system which gets dropped because nobody can keep it straight. Be easy on yourself. Take on only what you know you can handle. If a particular system of consequences seems a bit out of your reach, go with something you know you can manage.

This same concept can be applied to the entire intervention program. ADHD children often have numerous medical, emotional, social, academic, and spiritual needs. Pace yourself, as well as the rest of your family. Take on only those activities and programs that can realistically be accomplished with the resources available. Don't stretch yourself so thin that you risk burning out somewhere down the line.

Illustration of Management Techniques

Within the principles outlined above, there are a number of specific management techniques which can be illustrated. I'll summarize several of them and give illustrations of each. The purpose of the techniques is to help you react to what your child does in a way that will encourage the repetition of desirable behaviors and discourage unacceptable behaviors.

Pinpoint, record, change, and try, try again

The steps described below have been used by many parents to get started on a behavior-change program for their child. These steps can be used for almost any type of concern you may have for your child. Here is how you proceed:

1. You *pinpoint* the behavior(s) you are concerned about. Think about both *uppers* and *downers*. *Uppers* are acceptable or desirable behaviors, such as following directions, which you would like to see occur more often. You want their frequency to go up. *Downers* are undesirable behaviors, such as fighting, which you wish to occur less often. You want their frequency to go down.

2. You then *record* the frequency at which these behaviors occur so you know later if things are getting any better. Any simple chart will do the job. Tally marks on the calendar, beans in a jar, or create a simple bar graph. Both the A.D.D. WareHouse and Childswork/Childsplay mail-order companies listed in the resource section, as well as your local school supply stores, have charts for this purpose. You usually want to keep track of the count over a constant time period. For example, the number of times a child follows or does not follow directions should be recorded over an entire day, or from the time he gets home from school to bedtime. This record should be kept for the same times from day to day, so the count is comparable.

3. Next you *change* the way in which you are dealing with the behavior, usually using some type of positive or negative consequences. This is the actual intervention tactic. You might set up a daily reward if your child has more compliance instances than noncompliance. Every time you give a request, such as "Brush your teeth," or "Feed the dog," a bean goes into the smiley-face jar if he complies. If he does not do what you ask in a reasonable fashion, a bean goes into a frowny-face or Mr. Yuck jar. At the end of the day, he earns a reward if there are more beans in the smiley jar. I'll give a number of other ideas in the next section.

4. Then you *evaluate* the results of your intervention. The charting system should show whether there is an increase in positive behaviors and a decrease in negative behaviors. Your general impression will usually reflect how things are going.

However, sometimes behavior changes slowly and you need a daily record to monitor those gradual improvements. I have often worked with parents who bring in the chart, not having paid much attention to it, and then tell me, "Things aren't working. The intervention just isn't doing the job." I say, "OK, let's look at the chart and see what has been happening." Sometimes I will see that the desirable behavior has improved only modestly over the past two weeks. However, the inappropriate behaviors have dropped by half. The parents haven't been looking at things closely enough. They can't see the forest for the trees. When I point out the gradual improvement, they are more encouraged. This allows them to continue the effort; without the charts, they might prematurely stop a workable idea.

5. The final step is to *try, try again*. If your first form of change didn't work, you redesign the effort and try something else until it works. If you run out of ideas, your psychologist or other mental health professional can be of help. The ADHD support groups may suggest creative alternatives that have been used by other parents.

• *Examples of the five steps.* To illustrate this process, let me describe an idea I have used for years. The *pinpointed* (step 1) behavior may be leaving personal articles or dirty dishes all over the house. The goal is to get your child (or family) to pick up after themselves. If someone takes a bowl and a glass into the family room to watch TV, you expect the items to be placed in the sink or dishwasher after usage. The same is true for coats, shoes, and toys. When the person is through using the item, it is supposed to be placed in the appropriate storage area—closet, toy box, or storeroom.

For a few days you *count* (step 2) the number of items left lying around the house. This record of items per day left unattended becomes your baseline of comparison.

Next you implement the *change* (step 3) tactic. Through discussion with the child or family members, you suggest the *Sunday Box Strategy*. This is how it works. Whenever an object used by a family member is not returned to its proper storage area, it is placed in the Sunday Box. And the rule is this—any item placed in the box cannot be used until the following Sunday. If the remote control for the TV is left in the laundry room instead of on the TV, it goes into the box and you do without it until Sunday. The same is true for coats, shoes, toys, and maybe even books. You have to use discretion and common sense in regard to schoolbooks and homework. Also, if Dad leaves his billfold or checkbook out on the coffee table overnight, you will have to weigh the value of enforcement versus a ticket for driving without a driver's license.

Each Sunday the box is emptied and a *count* (step 4) is made of all the items, either for the entire family or for each individual. This weekly total serves as the measure of change. The number of items should go down. If it does and then stays down for a few weeks, you can dispense with the box. If people fall into relapse, you can always use it again as needed.

If these ideas don't bring about a desired change, you should look for a way to customize or adjust the initial strategy (step 5). You *try again*. Perhaps you can add a reward, such as a trip to the hamburger stand, if the total one week is lower than the previous week. You keep at it. Try, try again, until the goal is achieved.

Time-out Strategy

This is a method of removing a child from a problem situation and giving him time to cool off and think about what he has done. Time-out is an appropriate tool for children between eighteen months and ten years of age. It is most useful for the younger child, and can be instrumental in controlling behaviors such as tantrums, biting, hitting, and throwing things.

Both parents need to agree on the specific behaviors that will result in a time-out. The offenses should be clearly evident, and significant violations of the house rules.

Dullness is the key in selecting the appropriate place for the time-out chair. The child's room is sometimes used for time-out, but a separate quiet spot in a hallway or corner is better. That way his room doesn't become associated with punishment. Besides, there are too many interesting things to do in most children's rooms. A bathroom has the same drawbacks.

The chair should be located where the child cannot see the TV or be within reach of toys. The place should not be dark, frightening, or dangerous. Do not use closets, basements, or attics. This could inadvertently teach your child to be fearful of small or dark places. The location should be boring. You will also need some type of timer for enforcement.

Before using this technique, explain the entire process to your child. Describe the specific behaviors that will result in a time-out. Emphasize that time-out will be used every time the child engages in a certain misbehavior. Remember to continue the positive incentive programs to teach appropriate behavior that can replace the misbehavior. Thus, your child can earn stars for playing nicely with his sister, or he can earn time-out for hitting or teasing her. Never use time-out by itself. It should always be coupled with techniques that focus on increasing appropriate behavior.

Explain that the time-out begins when he is sitting quietly on the chair. His bottom must be in contact with the chair at all times. If the child remains on the chair until the timer rings, he can get up and resume activities. If he gets up before the timer rings, you will reset the timer, and the interval starts all over again. The child is not allowed to go to the bathroom, get a drink, or eat while in time-out.

A guideline is one minute of time-out per year of age, up to five minutes. A two-year-old would have two minutes of time-out, a three-year-old, three minutes, and so on. The purpose of time-out is to remove the child from the situation and assure him that you are in control. Five minutes will usually serve that purpose. Longer intervals defeat your purpose. After ten minutes or so, an ADHD child may lose track of why he earned a time-out in the first place. Remember though, time-out is to be a continuously quiet time.

If your child refuses to comply with the time-out, use a firm, clear voice, and guide him to the chair. If you have to carry him, be firm but not aggressive. Try not to get into physical battles or chase after your child. Retain control and impose additional consequences. Do not use threats. Phrases such as, "Wait till your father gets home," mean nothing to an ADHD child. If your child argues or objects too strenuously, calmly state an additional consequence. Don't use additional time-out beyond a total of ten minutes. You might state that he will see no TV for the rest of the day, or have to go to bed half an hour early.

Warnings have no place in a time-out program. They just teach a child that he has at least one free transgression. Also, don't accept excuses or let the child talk you out of the consequence. Impose the time-out even if your child says, "But, Mom, I forgot." Give him five minutes to remember what type of behavior is acceptable. Don't let him throw you off course by saying, "Fine, put me in time-out! I don't care!" This is a form of manipulation. Impose the time-out as planned, and evaluate the effect after a week or two.

Some children may get upset enough to make a mess or create damage while in time-out. If this happens, administer a logical consequence. If he draws on the walls, following time-out he has to clean up the mess. If he breaks the chair, let him know he will have to pay for it out of his allowance, or through extra chores. (The grounding program with various cards could be used here. See the next section.)

When the child's time-out is over, his slate is wiped clean. Don't give a lecture or nag about what happened. You can give a brief reminder about why he went to time-out, along with a simple suggestion for future acceptable behavior. Do not apologize for putting your child into time-out. After all, it was his choice to misbehave. Also, do not require your child to apologize or express regret in order to be able to leave the time-out spot. If he does so spontaneously, be sure to give positive attention. However, do not make it a requirement.

Within a few minutes, look for an occasion to praise the child for behaving appropriately. If your child went into time-out because of disobedient behavior, such as refusal to pick up his toys or turn off the TV, it is very important to repeat your original command the moment time-out ends. If he refuses to obey, immediately send him back to time-out. If he obeys your request, give him verbal praise. This sequence may need repeating several times (up to ten or fifteen minutes maximum), until the child learns you are serious and consistent about this program. Remember, immediate consequences, whether positive or negative, are important for the child with attention deficit.

If your child misbehaves away from home, calmly point out the misbehavior and inform him there will be a time-out when you get home. Make sure you follow through with the time-out later. Some parents make up "time-out tickets" on small pieces of paper and hand them to the child when he acts out away from home.

Another option is to give time-out on the spot. Find a secluded spot where your child must stay for five minutes. This can be a corner of your friend's house or the backseat of your car. When at the park or some other outdoor setting, you could identify ahead of time a particular tree or bench as the time-out place. This reminds your child the rules still apply, and gives you a definite routine to follow.[3]

Grounding and Community Service Strategy

This method of discipline teaches the child the consequences of improper conduct, while at the same time giving him a chance to earn back privileges through appropriate and responsible behavior. Sometimes we tell a child he is grounded for three days or two weeks. That may seem to work, but the only thing that can end the grounding is that the time runs out.

The form of grounding I am suggesting is a combination of restrictions and community service or chores. It works best in this form with children who are at least eight years old. With adjustments, it can certainly be used with adolescents.

As in time-out, the parents must agree about the rules and infractions. Then they need to sit down with the child and prepare a list of ten jobs that he is capable of doing, but which are not part of his regular assignments. Each job should be roughly comparable in time and effort. Examples might be cleaning the bathroom, raking the front yard, sweeping and cleaning the family room, and so forth.

Each chore or item of community service is recorded on an index card with a detailed description of all parts of the task. Nothing should be omitted from the listing, so that there is no chance of an argument later about the task criteria. You then explain to the child he will be assigned a certain number of job cards when he breaks an important rule. If he lies about having homework to do, for example, the parent will assign a certain number of job cards from the file box, and the child will be grounded until those chores have been completed.

While grounded, the child must attend school, perform required tasks, and follow house rules. This usually means he must stay in his room unless he is working, eating, or attending school. No entertainment of any type is permitted. Also, there will be no contact with friends outside of school and no phone calls. This grounding lasts until every last detail on the job cards is completed. Parents will check to make sure all parts of all chores have been adequately done. If the chores are done correctly, praise your child and end the grounding. If a job requires more work, let your child know exactly what has to be done to end the grounding.

One value of this approach is that your child is actually determining how long he is being grounded. It can take fifteen minutes or two days. The second advantage is that the sequence ends after a positive completion of a task. You are able to end this chain of events by complimenting your child for the chores completed.

The ideas discussed in this chapter should help you get some sense of direction in the management of your ADHD child. Remember it takes patience and consistency to bear fruit in terms of permanent changes in behavior. Additional ideas can be found in the various materials listed in the resource section in part 3.

References

1. S.W. Garber, M.D. Garber, & R.F. Spizman, *If Your Child Is Hyperactive, Inattentive, Impulsive, Distractible . . . Helping the ADD Hyperactive Child* (New York: Villard Books, 1990), 52–63.

2. Grant L. Martin, *Help! My Child Isn't Learning* (Colorado Springs: Focus on the Family, 1995), 96–100. Used by permission.

3. Further discussion of time-out can be found in the following references: Russell A. Barkley, *Taking Charge of ADHD* (New York: Guilford Press, 1995); Grad L. Flick, *Power Parenting for Children with ADD/ADHD* (West Nyack, N.Y.: The Center for Applied Research in Education, 1996); R.A. Moss, *Why Johnny Can't Concentrate: Coping with Attention Deficit Problems* (New York: Bantam Books, 1990).

CHAPTER SIX

HOW CAN MY CHILD CHANGE?
Self-esteem, Self-control,
and Social Issues
for the ADHD Child

If you could give only one gift to your child, what would it be? Good health? Wealth? Perhaps it would be peace of mind or academic success. The Christian parent may quickly think about the gift of God's love in the person of Jesus Christ. A child's eternal destiny is of paramount importance, and a personal faith in Jesus Christ is an absolute necessity. After the spiritual dimension, most parents would want to give their child a good self-concept or proper self-esteem, for without this, he will never find happiness and contentment. There must be a basic foundation of having a realistic appraisal of oneself, accompanied by good feelings about who one is. This is self-esteem.

No one is born with self-esteem. It is learned day by day. Your child's sense of worth began the moment you first held him in your arms. That physical closeness provided your child with a sense of security. At ten minutes of age, the infant did not say to himself, "All right! This big person thinks I am special. I can tell by that smile on her face." But over time, as you cuddled him, fed him, responded to his cries, and cheered his first steps, he began to get the message. As each new skill was added to his repertoire, another dimension was added to his thoughts about himself.

Most children naturally grow up feeling good about themselves. However, ADHD children have fewer successes, hear more no's, and face more rejection. As a result, their self-esteem is lower, and this carries into adulthood. Many of the specific sources of trouble and conflict will pass away as they leave their youth. How often does an adult have to sit still in a classroom with his hand raised, waiting for the teacher to ask a question? An adult can make excuses for some of his inattention or forgetfulness. But the residue of negative experiences, parental criticism, peer rejections, and failures of childhood remain. These feelings and thoughts continue to influence behavior long after the lunch box is stored away and the report cards are put in the attic.

Self-esteem, or the way a person sees himself, is an accumulation of many experiences. He may consider himself to be a good soccer player, a loyal friend, a poor speller, a mediocre reader, a great whistler, and a lousy brother. These all add up to some type of summary evaluation of who he is and how others see him.

The image one has of self is important because it gives a sense of fulfillment for the life that one lives. Self-esteem is essential to personal achievement, accomplishment, or value. A person with good self-esteem will be able to take risks. Some of those risks will result in more successes. These achievements, in turn, give the confidence to take more risks, to try more things, and can yield more positive feedback. However, for ADHD children, this cycle can work in reverse. They don't succeed, they develop less confidence, their judgment about themselves is low, and so they are less willing to try new things.

As you are learning about the nature of ADHD, the needs of your child should be coming more clearly into focus. It is my hope that you can be more systematic in helping your child accumulate more positive experiences on which to build a realistic positive opinion of himself. This section is intended to aid you in cultivating this important area in your child's life.

Notice my initial definition—a realistic appraisal of self accompanied by good feelings about who one is. Self-esteem is a cumulative opinion or judgment based on the feedback one receives throughout his lifetime. This total impression comes from many different experiences. To help you make sense of such a large concept, I am going to break self-esteem into four major categories—*security, belonging, competency,* and *purpose.* We'll discuss what each one means, along with ideas for enhancing the child's experiences within that area.

Sense of Security

Every child needs structure and limits set on behavior. The new infant needs to be wrapped in a blanket and held close to ensure bonding and health. As a child grows older, he desires more freedom. Yet, it must always be in the context of limits.

Imagine a single-lane highway bridging a river gorge. The narrow roadbed is suspended a thousand feet above the raging current and dangerous boulders below. There are even a few ferocious crocodiles and thousands of flesh-eating piranha just waiting for some type of food to fall from the bridge above.

You have to drive across this bridge. Unfortunately, it was constructed by the same people who built some of our downtown Seattle freeways. They were left unfinished—giant roadways in the sky with no access and abrupt endings; ribbons of concrete atop giant pillars, but going absolutely nowhere. Your bridge had the same contractor. There are no guardrails on this bridge—just a flat, one-lane surface with no warning markers. How would you approach the task of negotiating your way across this macabre bridge? My guess is that you would do it with extreme trepidation and considerable anxiety. Because there are no protective boundaries to the bridge, it is hard to tell where the relative safety of the road ends and the downward journey into the jaws of the crocodiles begins.

This bridge is a metaphor for the life of any child. But let's complicate the picture a bit. Suppose you have to drive across this bridge in a high-powered sports car. Even more problematic, the car's accelerator has a mind of its own. Sometimes the engine roars to life and wants to go a hundred miles an hour. Also, the brakes are very unreliable and may or may not work properly. Such an unpredictable car would be a challenge in itself, without having to negotiate this bridge of horrors. Such is the experience of your ADHD child.

Self-esteem can be aided by establishing guidelines and limits

Your child's sense of security is enhanced by knowing exactly what is expected of him and by experiencing consistent consequences for keeping or breaking those limits. All of the ideas presented in chapter 4 will contribute to this aspect of self-esteem.

Parents should strive for reasonable consistency in enforcing rules, and avoid unexpected enforcement. ADHD children don't handle change very well, and they will be more erratic when faced with new requirements without prior notice.

Consistent enforcement of positive and negative consequences is more important than severity

Regular use of five minutes of time-out, for example, will be more effective than intermittent corporal punishment.

The use of positive reinforcement is very important in building a child's self-image. Punishment is necessary, and you need to learn how to use it effectively. A key concept here is to make sure there are more positive, reinforcing events than negative ones. Remember the earlier recommendation to try to give eight positive exchanges, or warm fuzzies, to every single negative event, or cold prickly. These do not have to be material rewards—quite the contrary. Hugs, compliments, mutual activities, shared jokes, laughter, common interests, and private moments together are examples of positive exchanges.

A relationship with your child can be seen as a *savings account* at the bank. You have to make deposits in that account for it to have any value. At some point, it is inevitable you will have to make withdrawals too. However, if you withdraw without making deposits, the account will eventually be depleted. Your relationship with that account comes to an end.

The same is true with your child. You made many early deposits when your child was an infant. But as he grew older, it became necessary to discipline and make some withdrawals from that account. You need to make sure you keep ahead of the balance sheet. The eight-to-one positive ratio will help you do that.

Trust is another aspect of your child's sense of security

An ADHD child needs to know the significant adults around him can be depended upon to do what they say. It is important to keep your promises. Don't make idle statements about possibly going to the zoo unless you intend to do so. Keep this kind of verbal brainstorming to yourself. Once your child hears about it, in his mind it is already happening.

On the other side of the coin, don't make threats about restrictions, grounding, time-outs, or other forms of punishment. If these are needed, impose them immediately. Don't just get emotional and rant and rave. (Do that in the privacy of your bedroom, support group, or in the soundproof laundry room.)

Imagine a traffic cop whose job it is to make frustrated and irritable drivers obey the speed limit. The problem is that this particular policeman only has his whistle. So he valiantly stands on the sidewalk, looking sternly at each passing speeder and blowing his whistle as loudly as possible. While this may startle the drivers upon first seeing the man in blue with the red face and puffy cheeks, the long-term effect is quite predictable. With no ability to enforce or apply consequences, the policeman is powerless to slow people down. The same is true of the parent who makes threats and seldom follows through. This does nothing to build your child's sense of security.

Sense of Belonging

The next important component of self-esteem is the child's awareness of belonging and of being a meaningful member of a family. Your child needs to know he is a part of a unit of humans who care for one another, have a common heritage, and aspire to common goals. Individual meaning and value are gained because of this perception of participation and identity.

This could be called a sense of family or community. The child needs to know his home is a place where he can be safe, no matter what happens in the outside world.

Plan family activities that build this feeling of belonging and that strengthen an awareness of fun, unity, and unique identity. Appreciation of your family name and your unique heritage is important. Contact with extended family helps tremendously, assuming that the relationships are positive. Hearing stories about grandparents, family histories, and traditions all give a child an appreciation for what has gone before, and how he is a part of the ongoing family line. Continue important traditions that reflect your family culture and religious beliefs. Also, find ways to include your child in the planning and expression of these traditions. *Building memories* around the family unit is important.

Individual activities such as creating a family crest, making a picture collage, or designing a family banner can be used to identify and express the various elements of your family identity. Participation in the design and decoration of the family home and individual rooms can also help. Encourage the expression of the inclusive "we" in discussions relating to family activities, needs, and interests, instead of the exclusive "I."

Avoid highly competitive games with your ADHD child. Often he can't be successful, so don't expose him to additional frustration and failure with intense games of Scrabble or Monopoly. Your child probably wouldn't have the patience to sit through such a game, anyway. Also, be careful about academic, artistic, musical, or athletic comparisons. Differences in abilities are inevitable. Just do the best you can to highlight successes. Encourage cooperation and mutual problem-solving, rather than wins and losses. Ridicule and teasing should be minimized. Playful joking is fine, but do all you can to keep mean and cruel statements to a minimum.

Responsibilities are an important part of belonging to a family unit. Teach respect for property and personal space. If each child has a room, bed, closet, or toy box, s/he should be able to exercise control over who has access to that space. See that each child respects the rights of others, as well as receives reciprocal respect from other family members. Shared chores and mutual responsibility for the physical condition of the house and related property should be encouraged. Children usually can't be responsible for major chores or house repair, but activities should be identified that fit the skills of each child, including your ADHD child. He needs to be part of a team effort and to have that effort recognized and praised.

As your child grows older, outside groups will take on increased importance. Sports teams, music groups, clubs, classes, and friendship groups will be additional places where your child can have a sense of belonging. We know, of course, that many ADHD children have trouble fitting into these groups, due to their impetuous and awkward style. This only serves to highlight the importance of making the family unit a comfortable, warm environment in which to belong.

There is one additional crucial element to our sense of belonging. It is found in our identity as children of God. We will discuss this later.

Sense of Competency

Nothing helps build a child's confidence faster than large doses of success. Your child gains a sense of competency as those closest to him are able to affirm his uniqueness. Abilities, interests, personality traits, and learning styles all go together to make each person a special creation. Our culture tends to emphasize intelligence, physical beauty, and material possessions. If your child has these attributes, your task may be easier. However, the ADHD child needs a balance of feedback that recognizes his hidden, as well as conspicuous, strengths.

The many ideas for skill-building and compliance-training which are discussed in this and other chapters all contribute to your child's assessment of competence. All of this fits together to build up self-esteem. It is very easy for an ADHD child to fall into the habit of "nothing ventured, nothing lost." If he believes most of his choices or actions will result in failure, he won't try. Your goal is to help him improve his skills so that he will more often be successful. In addition, you want to discover ways to help him compensate for weak areas by using his strengths.

I had an ADHD client who, when he first came to see me, was struggling with his homework and had no friends at school. He was very bright, but tended to talk a mile a minute. Usually he failed to give his classmates a chance to get a word in edgewise. He had many skills to draw on, but as I was doing some assessment in the early stages I found out he had an incredible visual memory. Besides the formal test results, I found confirmation of this strength while playing the card game called "Concentration." The game is played by randomly laying rows of cards face-down on the table. You take turns examining each card, one at a time, and then try to remember where each half of the pair is located. If you turn up a particular card, you can keep it if you can also turn up its complementary card. You have to turn up both matching cards in the same turn. Your turn is over if you guess at the wrong card.

Playing against this fourth-grade boy, I lost 25 to 2. I couldn't believe how he could remember the location of each card once he had examined it. I mentioned this to his mom and she confirmed his fantastic skill in this area. We then tried to draw on his visual memory skills as we looked for ways to control his excessive talking. He used pictures we created in counseling sessions to help remind himself to slow down, look at the bored expressions of his peers, and tell himself to "stop." This is an example of *using a strength to compensate for a weakness*. It is a vital tool for building competency.

One of the most important ways a parent can encourage a child's striving toward competency is through *unconditional love*. I have mentioned several times how an ADHD child usually has a history of criticism, failure, and rejection. Your child needs large doses of love and affirmation with no strings attached.

The self-rating scale on page 141 allows you to evaluate how you are doing in regard to the sacrificial love described in 1 Corinthians 13. Don't be too hard on yourself—nobody but Jesus could score a perfect ten on everything. Use this as a way to examine yourself and establish some goals for improvement in your family, and particularly for your ADHD child.

Sense of Purpose

A sense of purpose gives *direction* for our lives. Direction is crucial, for if we don't know where we are going, we will get lost. Knowing our purpose under God gives us a compass bearing. The spiritual instructions you give to your child should respond to the question, "Why am I here?" A child doesn't need a detailed course in theology, but he does need continual exposure to those values and concepts that give meaning and purpose to life. These concepts are taught over many years. There will be formal times of instruction, such as during family devotions. There will be informal instruction when your child asks a specific question such as, "Dad, why are we Christians?"

The Bible tells us that God has given humankind the task of subduing and ruling over the earth as His representatives (Psalm 8:6). We are here to be of service to God. We are called to worship and honor our Creator (1 Chronicles 16:29; Psalm 95:6). We are asked to be wise and good stewards over creation (Luke 19:13ff; Romans 14:12).

As children of God, our purpose includes enjoying fellowship with our Father (Psalms 34:18; 145:18; Acts 17:27). Our calling is to be God's representatives on earth. As stewards of all that He created, we have the major purpose of *bearing fruit* (John 15:16). As we use our abilities and gifts in service to others, the fruit of love, joy, peace, patience, kindness, goodness, faithfulness, gentleness, and self-control will be nourished and multiplied in us (Galatians 5:22-23).

To bear fruit, then, becomes our response to the nagging question, "Why do we exist?" We can know that God placed us here. Living a life of faith can give us a solid sense of purpose. As we focus on the maturation process, knowing our labors are to result in love, joy, and peace, we will be better able to keep on course and fulfill our destiny.

There are many ways to apply these concepts to your child. First, you need to know and claim them for your own life. Once

HOW DO I OFFER THE GIFT OF LOVE?

Love is patient, love is kind. It does not envy, it does not boast, it is not proud. It is not rude, it is not self-seeking, it is not easily angered, it keeps no record of wrongs. Love does not delight in evil but rejoices with the truth. It always protects, always trusts, always hopes, always perseveres. (1 Corinthians 13: 4-7).

Considering the scriptural definitions of *agape* love, rank yourself on a scale of 1-10 (1=very weak, 10=very strong). Circle one number for each description.

LOVE IS PATIENT: I am slow to get angry with the ones I love. I do not yell or lose my temper. I can hang in there no matter what happens.	1 2 3 4 5 6 7 8 9 10
LOVE IS KIND: I am thoughtful and considerate, generous in my praise, unsparing with my time, always looking for ways to uplift others.	1 2 3 4 5 6 7 8 9 10
LOVE DOESN'T ENVY: I am not jealous or threatened by the successes of others. I don't pout or pick flaws. I'm happy when others succeed.	1 2 3 4 5 6 7 8 9 10
LOVE DOESN'T BOAST: I don't hog the conversation, bragging about myself, or exaggerating the facts to leave a better impression.	1 2 3 4 5 6 7 8 9 10
LOVE ISN'T CONCEITED: I don't harbor an inflated view of my importance. I don't have to be coaxed to do my part. I don't twist the conversation to draw attention to myself.	1 2 3 4 5 6 7 8 9 10
LOVE ISN'T RUDE: I'm not cruel, nasty, crude, cutting, sarcastic, or cocky, but am polite, courteous, gracious, and complimentary.	1 2 3 4 5 6 7 8 9 10
LOVE ISN'T SELFISH: I'm not self-centered, making others fit into my mold, or setting expectations on others for my own interests. I'm not possessive of others, nor do I insist on my own way.	1 2 3 4 5 6 7 8 9 10
LOVE ISN'T EASILY ANGERED: I'm not touchy, cranky, defensive, brittle, or supersensitive. I'm not easily hurt by little things.	1 2 3 4 5 6 7 8 9 10
LOVE KEEPS NO RECORD OF WRONGS: I'm able to forgive. I don't have to seek revenge, retaliate, or defend myself when hurt.	1 2 3 4 5 6 7 8 9 10
LOVE DOESN'T GLOAT OVER THE SINS OF OTHERS: I don't rejoice when others make mistakes or are proven wrong. I don't take pleasure in reminding others of their faults or by saying "I told you so."	1 2 3 4 5 6 7 8 9 10
LOVE REJOICES IN TRUTH: I'm glad when right and justice prevail, no matter who gets the credit. I'm strong in my own convictions while still leaving room for my own error. I'm happy when others succeed.	1 2 3 4 5 6 7 8 9 10

that is in process, the fruit will begin to show and touch the life of your child. Your goal is to teach and model a life of faith and reliance on God. As your child sees that faith result in patience, even in times of crisis and stress, he is learning valuable lessons about drawing on God's resources. I will say more about this in chapter 8.

The other key component of teaching our children a sense of purpose is our identity as children of God. We need to do everything we can to expose our children to the biblical evidence of our individual worth. We were fearfully and wonderfully made (Psalm 139:13-16). We are products of God's workmanship (Ephesians 2:10). We are created in the image of God and His likeness resides within us (Genesis 1:27). He doesn't look at us, see our imperfections, and say, "I've made a mistake here. I'd better try again."

God values us enough that He seeks our worship (John 4:23). Christ, His Son, accepts us as we are, with no strings attached (John 6:37). We are precious in God's eyes (Isaiah 43:4). We are important enough to God that He allowed the death of His Son for our redemption (1 Peter 1:18-19). Further, we have been adopted by God and made His sons and daughters (Romans 8:14-17). We are children of the King (1 John 3:1).

These promises and descriptions define who we are in a spiritual sense. They are the facts of our existence. While we may not always feel like they are true, these are the basic cornerstones on which we can claim to have a solid identity or self-esteem. Belonging, security, and success are human requirements. However, the basis of our ability to look past the problems of an ADHD child rests in our rights as children of God.

How to Deal with Certain Difficult Situations

As I have worked with many ADHD children and their families, several situations seem to come up again and again. How to deal with morning and bedtime routines are two of the most frequently asked questions. Social groupings, such as birthday parties and sports participation, are also discussed.

In the following sections, I will discuss some possible solutions. No single technique will work with all ADHD children. Hopefully, enough alternatives are included to provide you with a workable strategy.

Morning routine
Many parents report to me that mornings, particularly on school

days, are the very worst time for their attention deficit child. Even with sufficient hours of sleep, some kids will be hard to get up, and once they do get out of bed, they act as if they have glue in their arteries. They're slow as can be, often getting distracted by nonessential tasks, acting as if they have all day to get dressed, eat breakfast, and catch the school bus.

Other ADHD children wake up much too early, and in the process disturb everyone else in the household. While this type of child seems to have lots of energy, he has trouble channeling that energy and getting through the morning routine without a great deal of hassles and reminders by his parent.

Then there are those children who wake up moody, angry, sullen, and oppositional, regardless of how they went to bed the night before. These kids seem to get up on the wrong side of the bed no matter how cheerful their parents try to be in the wake-up process.

Of course, you can have any combination of these morning personalities. The question is how to deal with them and get the day started with a minimum of stress and conflict. Here are some suggestions derived from parents who have been there.

• Make up a schedule for the morning routine for your child to follow. Get the child's input on how he would like to organize his morning from the moment he gets out of bed to the time he leaves for school. Post specific times by which each of the activities should be completed. For example, out of bed—7:00; bathroom routine finished—7:15; fully dressed—7:30; morning chores completed—7:45; breakfast eaten—8:00. If everything is completed on time, the child gets some type of reward, such as watching TV before he has to leave for school.

• Variations on this program would include giving points or tokens for each task or section of the morning that is completed satisfactorily. The points can be blended into the total management program used for other behavioral concerns. Or you can just make the morning routine the focus of the project. The morning routine points are charted and the points accumulated toward some type of weekly prize.

• You might also make a tape recording that matches the morning routine. Various verbal reminders or prompts could be spaced throughout the tape identifying what the child should be doing and approximately how much time he has left to meet his deadline. Music could fill in between the periodic voice prompts. Some parents have had their child make his own tape so that he is hearing his own voice giving the prompts on the tape.

• Another option some parents have used for children who are on medication is to wake their child up approximately thirty minutes early, administer the medication, and then let their child stay in bed. Then at the regular wake-up time, the normal morning routine is initiated. For some children, this makes all the difference in the world. For others, some type of rewards or prompt system is needed, along with the medication. If medication has the effect of reducing appetite, then this strategy may not work, as the child is not hungry for breakfast.

• A partial solution for some families with problems getting chores done in the morning is to try to get them done the night before, or delay them until after school.

• Another approach is to make a race out of the routine. This can be done between siblings or with a parent. The goal is to be the first one done with either the entire morning routine, or each of the individual components of the routine. Be careful with this option. Some hyperactive children may get too fired up over this early morning race and it can cause more problems than it solves. It may work better with the more distractible or lethargic type of child.

• Be ready to use natural or logical consequences. If your child takes too long to get ready and misses the bus, make her walk to school, if that is feasible. Even if the walk is a long one, it may be possible to arrange it so the child is safe, but still has to experience the natural consequence. Have friends or neighbors watch over your child as she makes her way to school. Maybe you could follow along in the car or on your bike, but the child still has to walk the entire distance. For most kids, if they realize their parents are really serious about the follow-through, they will make sure this consequence doesn't happen again. You will need to make a judgment about whether this type of arrangement would work in your situation.

• Another option is that if your child is late and misses the bus, he has to pay you for the time spent driving him to school. Payment could be made in terms of loss of allowance, points off of the reward system, or by completing extra chores.

• Putting the morning routine and your expectations, along with consequences, into a contract format may also help. Write out the details of the agreement, spelling out exactly what the child is to do, along with the specified rewards and punishments. Then have all concerned parties sign the document.

• You might also use the grounding and chores system

described in chapter 5, and a consequence for failure to keep to the schedule or for the occurrence of unacceptable behaviors such as fighting, name-calling, or refusal to comply.

• If your child is one of those early risers who really doesn't need a lot of sleep, he shouldn't be penalized for having a "morning personality." Just make the rule that as long as he stays in his room, or engages in some type of quiet activity that doesn't disturb others, he may do so. Set an alarm clock for the time the morning routine should start. When the alarm goes off, the child is expected to follow the routine. Prior to the alarm, he can read, study, play quietly, or otherwise occupy himself. This ability to not disturb others may take some training, so you might need to set up a point scheme to provide some type of reward for quiet, nonintrusive activity in the morning.

• You may want to experiment with following the same morning routine every day of the week. Many ADHD children have difficulty adapting to any type of change. If the weekend routine is markedly different from the weekday schedule, there may be more problems adjusting back and forth. The same consideration may also be appropriate for vacation times. See what works best for your family.

Bedtime routine

Another problem time for many families is at the end of the day. Disengaging from playtime activities, taking a bath, getting ready for bed, and settling into bed, are difficult transitions for many. Even after getting into bed, many ADHD children and teens have trouble turning off their thoughts and getting to sleep. Here are some strategies that might work for you and your child.

• Some of the same ideas discussed in the previous section on morning routine would be equally applicable to the nighttime routine. Adapt and apply any of those procedures you think would work.

• Always start with a set routine. This may be hard for some families who tend to live life on a more spontaneous note. This is a totally acceptable and desirable lifestyle for many. However, if you are having trouble getting your child down for the evening, you may need to be more systematic for this part of your life.

Make sure there is a fixed time for starting the process. Those times may vary, depending on the ages of your children. Let's say your seven-year-old needs to be in bed by 8 o'clock. Give your child an advanced warning, usually fifteen to thirty minutes. Tell him he has fifteen minutes to finish up his construction project and then begin getting ready for bed. It may help to set a timer at that point for fifteen minutes. When the timer goes off, make sure a parent is ready to help with the process. If Dad is preoccupied with the newspaper and ignores the timer, his child will soon learn the timer has no real meaning.

Preparation for bedtime needs to be a calming process if at all possible. Allow sufficient time for you and your child to get through the entire process without being rushed, yet still getting into bed at the appropriate time.

Most kids, ADHD or not, like a routine. They like to be read to, listen to a tape, have a back rub, or just talk about "things." Try to keep to that routine. Sure, there are days when you are too tired, stressed out, or preoccupied with other matters. On those days, the temptation is to speed up the bedtime routine in order to get it over with as soon as possible. That's certainly understandable. Don't let that become the standard procedure, however.

Make the bath, tucking in, reading, storytelling, cuddling, back rubbing, and prayers a happy, fun, and relaxing time. Many parents report it is at these times, while settling down for the night, that most of the meaningful discussions with their children have taken place.

Use this time to affirm and state your love for your child. Listen to his concerns. Do some problem-solving. Don't put off your child's questions or concerns for another day. He will go to sleep much better if there has been some attempt at answering or resolving his concerns. Developing this type of relationship and history with your child also lessens his tendency to be oppositional or angry at nighttime. He will learn that good things tend to happen around the bedtime routine. It's not something to be avoided, but a special time of the day to be appreciated and valued. Yet it takes initiative and cooperation from both parents to build up this type of atmosphere. For a single parent, the challenge is even greater because there is no one else with whom to share the responsibilities. Do the best you can.

• In spite of everything you do, some children still have a hard time falling asleep. Medication, while usually beneficial throughout the day, can contribute to problems with sleep. If the problem seems medication related, talk to your physician. If serious enough, there may be some alternative medications without the same side effects.

Another possibility is to take another medication, just to help your child sleep. Antihistamines such as Benadryl have been suggested by physicians for some difficult situations.

Certainly, you want to take precautions such as avoiding caffeinated beverages or foods prior to bedtime. Also, watch for any negative reactions any other foods might have on the sleeping patterns of your child, and avoid those foods also. Some parents report remedies such as drinking warm milk or certain herbal teas can be helpful in getting their child to sleep.

Another consideration is to avoid highly stimulating activities prior to bedtime. If your son has just spent an hour engaged in a nerve-racking video game, he may have much more trouble calming down. Some parents, especially fathers, like to wrestle or "horse around" with their children. As fun as this may be, it may not be the best type of activity just before bedtime. Save it for another part of the day.

I have also used relaxation techniques to help some children and teenagers get to sleep. The steps in teaching a child how to relax are presented below.

As we well know, an ADHD child does not handle the unexpected very well. Transitions pose an ongoing obstacle because the child tends to become overexcited. If he is tired, the results are even more problematic. He is more susceptible to overarousal and less able to be attentive.

Calmness training or relaxation offers a partial solution to these problems. This technique provides a skill that can be taken anywhere. It can help your child fall asleep, reduce his fear of new situations, keep him calm during an argument, and even help him be in a better state of mind before taking a test.

Relaxation is not a form of self-hypnosis. It is simply a method of progressively flexing and relaxing each muscle group in the body until the person is more calm and relaxed. Basically, it consists of measured breathing and muscle relaxation. It is a biological process. It is not supernatural in any way unless one contaminates it with various mystical beliefs and practices. All we are going to do is to increase the blood flow to the muscles and the brain and help the child to think about positive, calming ideas.

Remember, this is a skill that takes repeated practice. Your child may not immediately recognize the value of this training. Some rewards may be necessary to get him to cooperate and continue.

Have your child sit in a comfortable chair or sofa. His feet should be on the floor and the back of his head should be able to rest on the top of the chair. His arms should rest easily by his sides, the palms of his hands lying on the seat. Sit opposite the child so he can see and mirror your activity. When he is in position, ask him to freeze for a short time. Praise this effort and offer the prospect of more rewards if necessary.

Begin by making a big wide yawn with your mouth wide open, your eyes squeezed tightly shut, and your nose wrinkled. Hold this position for a few seconds, inhale deeply through your mouth, and then suddenly exhale and sigh, almost closing your mouth so it remains only slightly open and relaxed. Do this a few times and ask your child to repeat the yawning routine. Praise his cooperation, administer points as needed, and remember to practice at various times, such as sitting at the dinner table or while riding in the car.

The next step is to teach diaphragm breathing. Here you place one hand, palm down, over your belly button. Take big, slow breaths that fill the abdomen with air. As you slowly breathe in to the count of five, your abdomen should rise as it inflates with air. As you exhale, your stomach should sink.

You want to produce full, easy breaths at the rate of about five seconds in and five seconds out. Your goal is four to six inhale-exhale cycles a minute.

Have your child copy your actions and give him constructive feedback and praise. Combine the big yawn with the breathing. Practice this routine for several minutes. Use a timer to indicate when your child has reached his goal.

Another feature to relaxation is to think about words such as "calm," "relaxed," "still," and "peaceful." The child could also think about a favorite place, such as the beach or a mountain lake. Help him recall what it feels like to be floating on a raft or lying on the warm sand. I have asked older children to think about favorite Bible verses or the words to a hymn or Scripture song.

The next step in the sequence is to continue the relaxed deep breathing and, at the same time, to systematically tense and relax your body, starting with your arms and hands. Clench your fists, flex your arms, and then relax them completely. Do this for each side of the body, and repeat it three times. Have your child copy your actions, and help him focus on the difference between the tense and relaxed state. After the hands and arms, you can move to the legs and feet. Tense each by tightening the muscles on the back of your calf and your foot by pulling your toes back toward your body. If you are susceptible to any kind of muscle spasms or back problems, be sure to check these activities with your doctor.

Lead your child through this entire sequence several times. You might even make a tape with instructions paced for each activity. Background music can fill in the practice times. The advantage of the tape is that the child can use it to practice when you aren't around. This also helps him accept responsibility for his learning. You can promote this kind of initiative through verbal praise and handing out bonus points.

Continued daily practice is essential to make this skill a useful part of your child's life. The more you practice, the more automatic it will become. Encourage your child to try relaxation several times a day. You might want to make a chart that monitors the number of daily or weekly practice sessions. Bonus points can be given for beating last week's practice total. Always make sure the practice is of sufficient quality and duration to be of value.

Try out ways to apply the relaxation techniques while sitting in the car or in other public places. Make a game of seeing if you and your child can practice without others knowing. Yawning and deep breathing will be easy to do. Tensing and relaxing the various muscle groups may not be possible to conceal, unless you have refined the techniques so that a more simple form of tension is sufficient. An example is to tense up the stomach muscles and then relax them. This can be done without obvious external body movement. Remember, you are going to gain from this technique also. Each of you can realize benefits as relaxation is applied to school, home, and social situations.[1]

Sometimes I have made up a tape for the child to listen to while preparing for sleep. The tape can include music, comforting phrases, Scripture verses, as well as prompts on getting more relaxed. It can be quite effective, with sufficient practice, and is a definite alternative to using medication to assist a child in getting to sleep.

Sports involvement

There are many things to consider surrounding the question of involving an ADHD child in some type of sports activity. For those who are naturally gifted with athletic ability, participation in team sports can be a very positive experience. It certainly can contribute enormous amounts to their self-esteem.

For other ADHD children, team sports can be problematic. Parents have told me of their anguish in watching their son or daughter play baseball. Especially at the younger ages, baseball can be very difficult for the child who has problems with attention and concentration. A baseball game can move relatively slowly, involving mostly the pitcher and catcher. The players in the out-field can easily become preoccupied with chasing butterflies or digging in the dirt. When the occasional fly ball does come their direction, it can be difficult for all concerned to see Sally dancing in the grass, staring at the flagpole, completely oblivious to the baseball flying toward her.

This phenomenon isn't limited to baseball, of course. I recall watching one of my grandson's soccer games when he was about four years old. I had made an official diagnosis of ADHD, inatten-tive type, while watching one of his teammates fill the goal. This young lad, with his back turned to the playing field, was busily dig-ging in the dirt and inspecting the back of the net. Suddenly, out in front of the goal, one of the opposing players broke loose and was dribbling the ball toward the goal. The parents on our team started yelling for the goalie to turn around and stop the ball. All the goalie heard was his name and all of this attention suddenly directed toward him. He thought it was great! He smiled, jumped up and down, and waved back to all these vocal supporters, keeping his back to the oncoming player the whole time. He didn't know what the commotion was all about until the opposing player kicked the ball into our goal, hitting our goalie squarely in the back.

This type of situation is pretty normal for a four-year-old. So my "diagnosis" may have been a bit premature. Soccer is actually quite a good sport for many young people, including those with ADHD. Problems with concentration can show up, even on the soccer field, but it tends to be less pronounced than baseball.

If your child does not have above-average athletic ability, but wants to participate in a sport, encourage him or her. However, be prepared to spend extra time coaching and practicing skills. Your child will need all the head start he can get, so that his problems with attention or impulsivity won't set him up for failure.

As ADHD kids grow older, some of them seem to prefer indi-vidual sports such as track and field, swimming, cross-country, golf, or the martial arts. Some parents have reported that activities such as tae kwon do seemed to be helpful in improving the con-centration and self-control of their ADHD children. I believe it would be important to choose a martial arts instructor very care-fully. You want to make sure the methods, goals, and instructional content is consistent with your values. The same could probably be said about any coach or instructor.

Parties

Parties, family gatherings, holidays, and other group activities can be particularly difficult for many ADHD children. I recall a mother telling me about one of the worst experiences of her life surrounding her daughter's ninth birthday party. This took place before a diagnosis of ADHD was made. Mom thought it would be nice to expose her daughter and friends to some culture. So they made arrangements to take Dad, Mom, Alicia, and six or seven of her friends to the ballet. Everybody dressed up in their finest clothes and off they went. Well, almost. Alicia was slow getting ready, some of her friends were late getting to the house, so they were straggling in after the performance had started. Dad, who hated ballet and was also ADHD, went immediately to sleep, the girls got bored and started talking loudly, Alicia became distraught with all of the activity, Mom ended up in tears, and the entire group left the theater at intermission. The party was to include a sleepover, but while the parents where scrambling to get the treats prepared, several of the girls got into a fight, and Dad ended up taking everybody home before the night was over. It was a complete fiasco.

The selection of who was invited to the party, the choice of activity, and the lack of preplanning for the activities at home, all spelled disaster. However, the story doesn't end here. During the ensuing year, Alicia was diagnosed with ADHD and learning disabilities. A treatment and intervention program was initiated, and the parents became better informed about how to organize problematic situations, such as a birthday party. The next year's birthday party was much better. The parents took care on who to invite so there was maximum compatibility. They kept the number of guests small. And they carefully orchestrated the activities for the evening. Every detail was planned out and every activity had the necessary materials readily available. Such a contrast to the year before! It all boiled down to careful planning and environmental engineering.

Space limits coverage of other common problem areas for attention deficit children and their families. I would recommend to you an excellent book, *The ADHD Parenting Handbook*, written by Colleen Alexander-Roberts. She has an entire chapter on "Problems That Drive You Wild." In that chapter, the author discusses topics such as: morning and evening routines, mealtime, chores, riding in the car, when company comes to visit, siblings, baby-sitters, taking your child to public places, when you are trying to talk on the phone, temper tantrums, nonstop talking, and traveling.[2]

Social Skills

The majority of ADHD children experience either social incompetence or aggression, or both. While medication has been shown to be effective in reducing aggressive behavior, a component of social-skills training is essential for the ADHD child having problems in these areas. Two of the major goals of social-skills training are that the ADHD child will become more knowledgeable about appropriate and inappropriate social behavior, and will learn the specific social skills targeted and identified during the assessment process.

There is quite a bit of overlap between social-skills training and self-control training. Most programs seem to focus on four major skill areas: social entry, conversational skills, conflict resolution and problem-solving, and anger management.[3]

As you observe and try to teach your child more appropriate social skills, Dr. Barkley suggests you pay particular attention to several key prosocial skills. The first is how your child initiates his interactions with another child or with a group. The second is how he starts and maintains a conversation with another child. This would include listening skills, asking relevant questions, taking turns in the conversation, and showing a genuine interest in the other person. The third characteristic is his ability to resolve conflicts. And the fourth major category is your child's ability to share things with other children.[4]

ADHD children can be one or two years behind in their social development. Most experts believe that this delay is related to the child's inability to pick up on the social cues and nonverbal messages that are present in all social contexts. Many of these children need help in one or more of the following five areas: listening, following instructions, sharing, working and playing cooperatively, and displaying social graces. Social graces would include greeting others, saying thank you, introducing others, giving and receiving compliments, offering to help, being sensitive to what others are feeling, and apologizing. Daily hygiene can also be a part of social graces.[5]

One author makes the following recommendations for parents in regard to improving their child's social skills. First, monitor and supervise what movies and TV shows your child watches.

Regulate his exposure to violence and other forms of inappropriate material in books, videos, electronic games, and computer programs.

Also, practice appropriate social behaviors of the type listed above. Be a good model for your child. Throughout the day, label and demonstrate each of these skills, such as sharing, or offering help. Point out when these behaviors are occurring in real life or on TV. Reinforce and praise your child when you see him or her demonstrate these skills. Be systematic in illustrating these social graces, but don't be overbearing, obnoxious, or embarrassing to your child in public.

A final point made by Dr. Flick is to carefully assess your child's social needs and work on those areas in which your child is lacking. Use any teaching strategy available, including multisensory methods, to illustrate, engage, and reinforce your child's use of these important social behaviors.[6]

In the resource section, I have listed a number of materials that have been designed to help ADHD children improve their social skills. If this is an area of concern for your child, consult some of these resources for specific help.

The major theme that emerges from the evaluation of both self-control and social-skill training efforts for ADHD children is the need for active and comprehensive parental involvement. Attempts to improve the self-control or social skills of an ADHD child will have little effect unless there is involvement from the natural change agents in the child's life. These include the people closest to the child—parents, close relatives, teachers, and classmates.

References

1. Adapted from S.W. Garber, M.D. Garber, & R.F. Spizman, *If Your Child Is Hyperactive, Inattentive, Impulsive, Distractible . . . Helping the ADD Hyperactive Child* (New York: Villard Books, 1990) 108–15.

2. Colleen Alexander-Roberts, *The ADHD Parenting Handbook* (Dallas: Taylor Publshing Co., 1994), 46–94.

3. Russell A. Barkley, *Attention-Deficit Hyperactivity Disorder, A Handbook for Diagnosis and Treatment* (New York: Guilford Press, 1990), 550–72.

4. Russell A. Barkley, *Taking Charge of ADHD* (New York: Guilford

Press, 1995), 182–83.

5. Grad L. Flick, *Power Parenting for Children with ADD/ADHD* (West Nyack, N.Y.: The Center for Applied Research in Education, 1996), 114–20.

6. Ibid., 120.

CHAPTER SEVEN

HOW CAN THE PHYSICIAN HELP?
Medical Treatment
for the ADHD Child

Jeff and Julie had just returned from the second planning session with Dr. Howard. As they had discussed several intervention strategies for their son, Danny, the doctor raised the question of medication as something Danny's parents should consider.

"I just don't know whether I want to give Danny medication," Jeff said.

"Yes, I agree," replied Julie, "but I think we should at least weigh the pros and cons. If it can help his brain to function better, maybe it's worth trying."

"But what if it stunts his growth, or causes him to be dependent on drugs when he's older?" asked Jeff. "I'd hate to give him something that seemed to help for now, but would cause more problems later on."

"I know what you mean, Jeff," answered Julie. "Let's look at this material Dr. Howard gave us and see if it answers any of our questions."

One of the most difficult decisions you will face as the parent of an ADHD child is whether to use medication. If your child has an infection, you may give an antibiotic for a few days, and the problem is resolved. In contrast, the drugs given to manage ADHD must be taken for months and sometimes years. You can't help but wonder how this long-term usage might affect your child. The following discussion will attempt to answer the most common concerns parents have about medication for attention deficit.

Psychostimulant Medication

Psychostimulant medication is the most common treatment for children with ADHD. More children receive medication to manage ADHD than for any other childhood disorder. More research has been conducted on the effects of stimulant medications on the functioning of children with ADHD than for any other treatment modality for any childhood disorder. This extensive research helps us be fairly definitive about the benefits and liabilities of medication.

There has definitely been an increase in the use of stimulant medications in recent years. A recent study utilized several data sources to derive a best estimate of the use of methylphenidate over the years 1990–1995. These researchers found that approximately 1.5 million children, ages five to eighteen years, were on this type of medication. The estimate is that there has been a 2.5-fold increase during these years in the usage of methylphenidate for children with attention disorder. Some media pronouncements in recent years have stated that there has been a sixfold increase in the use of stimulant medication. This comprehensive study strongly refutes this high figure.

The increase in medication is thought to be a result of children being on medication for longer periods, an increase in the number of girls diagnosed and treated, and the increased inclusion of more children who have mainly the inattentive form of ADHD. Increased public acceptance of medication as a viable form of treatment for this disorder may also contribute to these trends.

It should also be remembered that during the 1980s, a major media propaganda campaign was carried out by a certain religious group against the use of stimulant medication. The campaign, while inaccurate, did appear to cause a dramatic decline in prescribing this type of medication in the years preceding 1990. Part of the increase noted in the early 1990s, then, may just be a return to the pre-1987 prescription levels.

While the increased use of stimulant medication is obvious,

the study found than only 50 to 60 percent of children who could be diagnosed as ADHD are actually being medicated. This finding does support the position that we are not overmedicating children who have ADHD. The general consensus is that the incidence rate for ADHD in the U.S. is 5 percent. Yet, only 2.8 percent of the children, five to eighteen years of age, are being given stimulant medication.[1]

In general, we can say that medication intervention is a significant help to ADHD children. Stimulant medication has been shown to be effective in improving behavior, academic work, and social adjustment in from 70 to 95 percent of children with ADHD.[2] How your child will respond depends on many factors, so each situation has to be carefully evaluated as to the best type of medication and dosage. There are certainly situations where medications are improperly administered. If medication is to be considered, it must follow strict controls, appropriate dosages, and careful monitoring.

The most important concept to emerge from the vast amounts of research about ADHD is that no treatment approach is successful alone. Neither medical, behavioral, psychological, nor educational intervention is adequate by itself. We must be conscious of treating the *whole* child or adolescent. Successful intervention makes a difference both in the short-term and in the long-term. We want to make changes which will help bring about the necessary confidence, competence, organization, discipline, and character in your child. We also want changes that will last a lifetime. The teacher may complain that your child won't sit still in the classroom. You may be unhappy that he can't remember directions. We must deal with those immediate concerns, as well as look to his future needs. Giving the child 10 milligrams of Ritalin may help him sit in his seat and remember directions. However, it will not necessarily help him make friends.

Research has shown that multidisciplinary approaches to the treatment of ADHD work better, in the long-term, than medication alone.[3] Possibly one of the greatest benefits of stimulant therapy is that it maximizes the effects of concurrently applied treatments. What we often see is that the total treatment is far more effective than any of the components taken alone. Medication will not make your child act perfectly, nor will it make him smarter. However, what it can do is to reduce many of his attention difficulties so that he can tackle his problems more successfully.

The history of stimulant drug use dates back to the discovery by Bradley in 1937 of the therapeutic effects of Benzedrine on behaviorally disturbed children. In 1948, Dexedrine was introduced with the advantage of having equal efficacy at half the dose. Ritalin was released in 1954 with the hope it would have fewer side effects and less abuse potential. Today Ritalin is used in over 90 percent of cases where some type of stimulant medication is prescribed.

It is thought that stimulant drugs act by affecting the catecholamine neurotransmitters (especially dopamine) in the brain. Some believe that ADHD develops from a dopamine deficiency, which can be corrected by stimulant drug treatment. At one time it was felt stimulant drugs created a paradoxical reaction in ADHD youngsters. The paradox was the calming response to taking a stimulant drug. This is no longer believed to be the case. We now have a better, although incomplete, understanding of how the calming reaction is produced in the brain.

Many parents feel guilty about having their child take medication because they mistakenly think they are tranquilizing him. This is simply not true. The medication helps stimulate the parts of the brain needed to concentrate and attend. The decrease in external movement does not mean he has been tranquilized. It means he is able to focus more effectively. When your child is watching TV or playing a video game, he may seem oblivious to the outside world. However, that doesn't mean he is tranquilized by the TV. Rather, his attention is temporarily focused so that he seems mesmerized, in contrast to his more usual distractible and inattentive condition.

Attention deficit results from the malfunction of the attention system. This system allows the brain to discriminate between situations where focused, deliberate behavior is appropriate and situations where quick, impulsive actions are needed. ADHD children are not able to control their attentional skills. They may be intently concentrating when they should be aware of their surroundings. On the other hand, they may be too easily distracted and ready to run off when they should be focused. Medication works to enhance the functioning of the attentional system, so that children can choose when to be sensitive to outside distractions and when to focus their attention. The attention center is stimulated by these medications with the result that the child has better control. In other words, with medication, the child is better able to put on the brakes.[4]

The decision to proceed with medication intervention must be based on the comparison of the risks, benefits, and alternative treatments available. We will look at these considerations one at a time.

Short-Term Side Effects

After reviewing 110 studies, including more than 4,200 hyperactive children, one researcher concluded that the primary side effects noted for stimulants were insomnia, anorexia or loss of appetite, weight loss, and irritability. These and other side effects were reported to be transitory and usually disappeared with a reduction in drug dosage.[5]

Most of these side effects appear at the beginning of treatment. For example, your child may say to you, "My stomach doesn't feel good." Usually this feeling is not nausea, although young children may locate the sick feeling in their stomach. These complaints normally last for about a week and may not be affected by whether the child takes the medication before or after meals.

Appetite suppression is common. Your child may be less hungry for a time. This may be less noticeable if the drugs are taken after meals, since the effects wear off before the next meal. Adjusting the dosage will often alleviate this symptom over a week or two. Since the effects of Ritalin last for only three to four hours, the dosage around mealtimes can usually be adjusted to avoid any serious problems with appetite. Make sure your child eats a good breakfast and dinner, and supplement with nutritious after-school and bedtime snacks. This helps avoid any temporary weight loss.

Other mild, but less common, side effects can include sadness, depression, fearfulness, social withdrawal, sleepiness, headaches, nail biting, and stomach upset. These symptoms will usually resolve spontaneously with a decrease in dosage. For example, if a child gets a headache right after taking the medicine, he may be taking too high a dose. Late-in-the-day headaches can also occur. These should be monitored closely. If they persist or are severe, the doctor will need to adjust the dosage. Some of these symptoms can be considered acceptable side effects in light of clinical improvement. The parents and physician will need to make the decision regarding the advantages of decreased distractibility versus side effects such as nail biting. These side effects are mild, but they can occur in some children treated with stimulant medication.

Toxic psychosis and seizures have occurred in a very few cases. The symptoms resolved when the medication was discontinued. Children with a family history of epilepsy may be at greater risk, and the physician should consider this when evaluating the possibility of stimulant medication treatment.

Another possible side effect is nervous tics produced by stimulant medications. A number of irreversible instances of Tourette's syndrome has also been reported as a result of stimulant treatment. Tourette's syndrome is a neurological condition composed of multiple, persistent motor tics and uncontrolled language. The combination of motor and vocal tics is considered an important diagnostic sign, although they need not occurr at the same point in time. It is essential that a child who shows signs of tics be carefully evaluated by an expert before ever taking any medication.

Perhaps fewer than 1 percent of ADHD children treated with stimulants will develop a tic disorder. Also, in 13 percent of the cases, stimulants may exacerbate preexisting tics. Therefore, it is prudent to screen children with ADHD for a personal or family history of tics or Tourette's syndrome prior to initiating stimulant therapy.

Another side effect that has been reported is a "behavioral rebound" phenomenon. Typically, this is described as a deterioration in behavior that occurs in the late afternoon and evening following daytime administrations of medication. What parents report is that the child becomes very moody and irritable for the first hour or two after the medication has worn off. Research has suggested that this usually happens only for the first two or three weeks that the child is on the medication. If the problem continues or is severe, adjustments in the medication dosage and scheduling should resolve the problem.

The general consensus is that stimulant medication is relatively safe, but side effects do occur. In the vast majority of cases, either the side effects cease after one or two weeks of continued treatment, or adjustment in the dosage alleviates the problem. You can protect your child by making sure both you and your doctor are closely monitoring side effects, as well as effectiveness. Most of the serious side effects show up right away. They will also disappear quickly if the drug is withdrawn. Then a trial of a different stimulant medication can be initiated.

Long-Term Side Effects

There are no reported cases of addiction or serious drug dependence with these medications. Studies have examined the question of whether children on these drugs are more likely to abuse other substances as teenagers, compared to children not taking stimulant medications. The results suggest there is no increase in the likelihood of drug abuse. In fact, some youngsters adopt a stand of staunch opposition to any drugs. More research is needed on this topic since all of the issues are not yet clear. But the risk of future drug abuse appears to be quite low.[6]

Since ADHD is a long-term condition, medical treatment may be required for a prolonged period. This also raises the question of whether the child will become tolerant of the medication. The answer appears to be no. Over time, the child's dosages may need to be increased. However, this probably relates more to his increase in body weight than to his becoming tolerant of a certain dose, although it is possible for a few children to become tolerant of Ritalin. You and your doctor should continue to monitor its effectiveness very closely.

Another possible long-term side effect is the suppression of height and weight gain. Presently, it is believed that suppression in growth is a relatively transient side effect in the first year or so of treatment, and has no significant effect on eventual adult height and weight. Furthermore, there is evidence to suggest that if medication is discontinued at various points in the year, a growth rebound will occur. Most physicians will suggest a "drug holiday," especially for all or part of the summer, to provide a catch-up period. One flaw in this idea is that children often have growth spurts in the summer, regardless of whether they are on medication or not. If you take your child off of the medication and he grows an inch or two, you might assume that this drug holiday caused the growth spurt. Yet it might have happened anyway, because this is the time when most surges in height and weight take place.

Meanwhile, the summer may have been anything but a vacation. If there was a resumption of the overactivity, impulsiveness, and distractibility, you need to evaluate the relative value of stopping the medication. Ultimately, these children will reach their projected adult height. Still, it is wise for the physician to monitor growth in children receiving stimulant medications.[7]

About the time they hit adolescence, a number of children who had cooperated previously become resistant to taking their medication. Parents begin to find pills fertilizing the ferns in the family room. If they are unaware of the noncompliance, parents might assume the medication is losing its effectiveness. In reality, the child has outgrown his willingness to take the medication.

Teens don't want to be different. Taking medication separates them from the crowd. Even time-released pills taken in the privacy of their own room may not overcome the resistance. Open discussion, careful supervision, and understanding of your child's feelings can help him work through this opposition.

Contraindications: Reasons for Avoiding or Stopping Medication

With what we now know about stimulant medication, *contraindications* include: known hypersensitivity or allergic reaction to the drug; seizure history; glaucoma; hypertension; history of tics; hyperthyroidism; and pregnancy. One of the main objectives of the physical exam is to determine whether your child fits any of the predisposing categories. Liver disease, certain forms of heart disease, and high blood pressure are the clearest contraindications to stimulant therapy. Children with seizure disorders should probably not take stimulants, since the drug can lower the seizure threshold and increase the likelihood of seizures.

Doctors are also reluctant to use stimulants in children with a family history of tics, because stimulants can increase the possibility of tics developing. Stimulants can also aggravate anxiety. If a child who has ADHD is also quite anxious, an alternative to stimulant medication may be appropriate.

Most physicians will be reluctant to prescribe medication for a preschool child. Only if there are extreme symptoms, and if the child is a danger to himself, would stimulant medication be appropriated. The use of behavioral management techniques is a preferred method of treatment.

Benefits of Medication

Between 70 and 90 percent of children appear to exhibit a positive response to stimulant medication. There seem to be three general categories of response to medication.

For about one-third of the children, medication brings about a dramatic improvement. This would be the *miraculous* category. The effect is both immediate and obvious. Often within the first hour after treatment, a perceptible change in handwriting, talking, motility, attending, organization, and perception may be observed. Classroom teachers may notice improvement in deportment and academic productivity after a single dose. Off-task activity levels seem to decrease and the child becomes more compliant and less aggressive. Parents will report a marked reduction in troublesome sibling interactions, inappropriate activity, and noncompliance. Even peers can identify the calmer, more organizing, cooperative behavior of stimulant-treated children.[8]

Another third of those who receive medication fall into the *moderate* category of responsiveness. While parents and teachers notice improvement in the child's attention and self-control, the effects are not astonishing. The child is definitely easier to teach because he's not quite so fidgety and distractible, but he still requires a ton of extra attention. There are significant improvements, but not wholesale changes.

The final third of children fall into the *minor* response category. Some children either don't respond, or react poorly to medication. Despite all efforts to find the right medication at the right dose, a positive reaction is not obtained. In other cases, there is some positive effect on attention and self-control, but the side effects make the improvements not worth it. It has been estimated that 1 to 3 percent of children with ADHD cannot tolerate any dose of stimulant medication.[9]

In summary, the primary benefits are the improvement of the core problems of ADHD—hyperactivity, impulsivity, and inattentiveness. Attention span seems to improve and there is a reduction of disruptive, inappropriate, and impulsive behavior. Compliance with the commands of authority figures is increased, and children's peer relations may also improve, primarily through reduction in aggression. In addition, if the dosage is carefully monitored and adjusted, the medication has been found to enhance academic performance.

Medication does little to rectify any cognitive functioning or learning disabilities. If a child has visual or auditory processing deficits, medication will probably not change this learning problem. What it may do is help him pay attention better, so that remedial instruction will have more of a chance to impact the learning disability.

Although these medications are certainly helpful in the day-to-day management of ADHD, they have not been demonstrated to lead to enduring positive changes after their cessation. Research has been very clear that stimulant medications are not a panacea for ADHD, and should not be the sole treatment employed in most cases. The numerous skill deficits which these children have will still need attention and remediation.

It would be a mistake to assume that because a child responds to medication, he must be ADHD. Likewise, it is an error to say a child is not ADHD if he fails to respond to medication. This says nothing about his condition. It certainly does not indicate that his problems are any less real than those who do respond. The key is a thorough evaluation that identifies all of the child's needs, followed by a detailed treatment plan. Medication may be one component of that plan.

When to use medication

One of the most difficult decisions for both the parent and clinician is deciding when to use medication. The fact that your child has been diagnosed as ADHD does not imply an automatic recommendation for drug treatment. You want to make your decision based on accurate information about the nature and use of various medications and upon a clear understanding of your child's specific needs and family situation. It is important to be an informed consumer in this process. Don't be rushed into a decision. Yet, on the other hand, if there is the prospect of significant help being available to your child, don't procrastinate too long and allow your child continued unnecessary frustration and failure.

Guidelines for recommending medication

Doctors Barkley, DuPaul, and Costello have identified the following guidelines regarding the decision to initiate a medication trial. I believe this is an excellent set of instructions, and would advise you to consider them carefully and discuss them with your physician before you start medication.

❑ Has the child had adequate physical and psychological evaluations? Medications should never be prescribed if the child has not been recently examined in a thorough manner.

❑ How old is the child? Pharmacotherapy is often less effective or leads to more severe side effects among children below the age of four, and is therefore not usually recommended in such cases. In extreme situations, I have suggested a medication trial, but this is an exception.

❑ Have other therapies been used? Usually, we want to try some type of behavioral management before medication is initiated. On the other hand, if your child has been experiencing a great deal of failure and his behavior is deteriorating, it may be wise to bring about some improvement as soon as possible.

Further, if your family cannot participate in child management training, medication may be the most practical initial treatment.

❏ How severe is the child's current misbehavior? In some cases, the child's behavior is so unmanageable or distressing to the family that medication may prove the fastest and most effective manner of dealing with the crisis. Once medication has been initiated, we can then proceed to implement other forms of intervention.

❏ Can you as a family afford the medication and associated costs? Long-term compliance is very important. You need to be willing and able to stick with the treatment program as long as your clinician recommends it. This means the $60 to $120 per month for medication, plus office visits.

❏ Do you feel able to supervise and monitor the use of the medications and guard against their abuse? If your own life is too disorganized and stressful, you may not be able to see that your child maintains the proper medication schedule.

❏ What is your attitude toward medication? Some parents are simply antidrug and should not be coerced into agreeing to this treatment. If you really don't want your child on medication, your underlying attitude will probably sabotage its efficacy.

❏ Is there a delinquent sibling or drug-abusing parent in the household? If so, psychostimulant medication should not be prescribed, or security measures should be implemented, since there is a high risk of its illicit use or sale.

❏ Does your child have any history of tics, psychosis, or thought disorder? If so, the stimulants are contraindicated, as they may exacerbate such difficulties.

❏ Is your child highly anxious, fearful, or likely to complain of psychosomatic disturbances? Such a child is less likely to respond positively to stimulant medications, and may exhibit a better response to antidepressant medications.

❑ Does your physician have the time to monitor medication effects properly? In addition to an initial assessment of drug efficacy and establishment of the optimal dosage, periodic reassessment of drug response and effects on height and weight should be conducted throughout the year.

❑ How does your child feel about medication and its alternatives? With older children and adolescents, it is important that the use of medication be discussed with them and its rationale fully explained. In cases where children are antidrug or oppositional, they may sabotage efforts to use it. Sometimes the "wearing glasses for a visual handicap" metaphor can help explain medication without a stigma.[10]

❑ If your teenager is considering service in the military, he should know that a diagnosis of ADHD and current or recent medication usage may be a basis to disqualify a person for entrance into the military. Some of the guidelines are not very clear, and may be subject to change. There may also be some variation among the various branches of the service. Check with the local recruiting office if this is an issue for your adolescent.

Prescribing procedures

Following is a description of the common medications used in the treatment of ADHD. This overview is provided for your education only. Be sure to discuss the specifics of medication with your physician.

Ritalin (methylphenidate) is available in 5, 10, and 20 mg tablets. This is a short-acting tablet which most commonly lasts four hours. Ritalin-SR is a sustained-release product with effects lasting six to eight hours. Some physicians report unsatisfactory reliability with the sustained-release form of Ritalin, with the child getting only about 8 mg of actual medication benefit. It may be necessary to administer a 5 to 10 mg standard tablet in the morning, along with the 20SR.

The usual dosage is .3 milligrams per kilogram (about 2.2 pounds) of body weight, up to 1 milligram per kilogram in a 24-hour period. The usual starting dosage of the standard Ritalin for children under eight is a single 5 mg tablet in the morning, and for children over eight, a single 10 mg tablet in the morning. Each week the daily dosage can be increased by 5 mg and 10 mg a day, respectively. Usually tablets are taken at breakfast and lunch. Occasionally, an after-school dose is necessary. The total maximum daily dosage usually does not exceed 60 mg, although under some situations, 80 mg per day dosages are prescribed.

The amphetamines are quite similar in their pharmacologic makeup. **Dexedrine** (dextroamphetamine) comes in 5 mg tablets, in a liquid elixir preparation with 5 mg per teaspoon, and in slow-release Spansules of 5, 10, and 15 mg. The dosage is approximately half that of Ritalin. The slow-release or Spansule version of Dexedrine may work better for some children than the Ritalin SR. Since methylphenidate is not approved by the FDA for use in children under the age of six, dextroamphetamine may be preferable for children ages three to five.[11]

Generic formulations of methylphenidate and dextroamphetamine are also available. They will typically cost less than the brand name, and are sometimes required for insurance reimbursement. Because there is greater latitude in the manufacturing process for generic versions, the actual pills may contain more or less of the active ingredient than the same formulation of the brand name. This might result in a more varied and unreliable response pattern by the child. All of this depends on how your child reacts to the medication. In many cases, there may be no difference in how your child responds to the generic versus brand-name form of the medication. Talk to your physician and get his or her opinion. It may be wise to start with the brand-name formulation, and once you have a clear idea of how your child responds, then try the generic for a few weeks and see if you can tell any difference in the day-to-day behavior of your child.

Some doctors will also advise that patients do not take stimulant medication with aspirin, or acidic foods such as citrus fruit or orange juice, because they can prevent absorption of the medication.

Another concern may be the yellow dye contained in the 5 mg tablets of Ritalin. A few children have become more active and agitated when they took this version of the medication. It is possible to have an allergic reaction to the yellow dye contained only in the 5 mg Ritalin tablets. If your child has an adverse reaction to the 5 mg tablet, you might ask about trying the 10 or 20 mg tablets of Ritalin, which do not contain yellow dye.[12]

Adderall is a newer stimulant which combines amphetamine and dextroamphetamine. It is available in 10 and 20 mg tablets. For children, the usual starting dosage is 5 mg once or twice daily, increasing by 5 mg weekly, until optimal response is obtained. Total dosages of 40 mg per day, or more, are rare. Adderall does last longer that Ritalin or Dexedrine, perhaps six to eight hours. This may allow the child to avoid the noontime dosage necessary for the other stimulants.

Cylert (pemoline) is taken once a day, giving it an advantage over the shorter-acting preparations. It has a gradual onset of action. Significant clinical benefits may not be evident until the third or fourth week of treatment, and they may take as long as six weeks. The drug is available in 18.75, 37.5, and 75 mg tablets; and in 37.5 mg chewable tablets. The recommended starting dose is 18.75 to 37.5 mg, and the dosage is increased in daily increments of 18.75 mg per week until the desired clinical effects are reached. The effective daily dose for most patients is in the range between 56.25 and 75 mg. The maximum daily dose is 112.5 mg. Because of its association with life-threatening hepatic failure, Cylert should not ordinarily be considered as first-line drug therapy for ADHD. If used, initial and periodic liver-function tests are required.

Tricyclic antidepressants, including Tofranil (imipramine) and Norpramin (desipramine) have also been prescribed for the treatment of ADHD. Pamelor (nortriptyline) is another tricyclic that may be used. The bulk of the research suggests that overall, psychostimulants tend to be superior to the tricyclics in managing ADHD symptoms. However, there may be a subgroup of children, particularly those who show signs of anxiety, depression, sleep problems, or who have tics or psychoses, who may respond better to the tricyclics. These medications can also help those who are having trouble with anger, inability to sleep, or bed-wetting. Desipramine may have fewer side effects and thus be preferable. These medications can also be used in conjunction with stimulant medications.

The antidepressant medications are taken by mouth once or twice a day, but do not wash out of the body as quickly as the stimulants. This means it may take several weeks to build up a therapeutic level in the bloodstream. Side effects can include irregular heart rate, nervousness, sleep problems, upset stomach, dizziness, and dry mouth.

Another type of antidepressants is the SSRIs (selective serotonin reuptake inhibitors) such as **Prozac** (fluoxetine), **Paxil** (paroxetine), and **Zoloft** (sertraline). These medications increase the levels of the neurotransmitter serotonin by inhibiting the reuptake of serotonin, allowing it to remain active in the synapse for a longer period. These medications may be useful for children who have some mood disorder, including depression, anxiety, irritability, or who are highly aggressive. Improvement in attention span may result from this type of medication, but it is generally not as dramatic as the improvement seen with stimulants. Side effects can include nausea, mild weight loss, anxiety, headaches, sweating, or insomnia.

Clonidine (catapres) and **Tenex** (guanfacine) are antihypertensive medications that can also be used to treat ADHD symptoms. Clonidine is available in transdermal skin patches which allow the release of medicine evenly all day. Clonidine is less expensive than Tenex, but Tenex may cause less drowsiness during the day.

These medications have also been used for other disorders such as migraine headaches, schizophrenia, manic-depression, obsessive-compulsive disorder, panic disorder, and anorexia nervosa. Dr. Robert Hunt at Vanderbilt University has found this type of medication also helps control oppositional behavior, anger, aggression, cruelty, destructiveness, explosiveness, and frustration. Since these medications are also used for treatment of Tourette's syndrome, they may prove useful in ADHD children who have tics or who have developed tics on methylphenidate. The primary side effect is tiredness, along with decreased blood pressure, dizziness, and dry mouth.[13]

Some of the newer antidepressants such as **Wellbutrin** (bupropion), **Ludiomil** (maprotiline), **BuSpar** (buspirone) and **Effexor** (venlafaxine) have also been prescribed for treating ADHD. Your physician will advise you on whether any of these would be appropriate for your child.

No matter which medication is employed, some common principles should apply. I have summarized the major ideas proposed by various authors in regard to the use of medication with ADHD children.

Prescription principles

1. The dose should be the lowest possible and be given only as many times per day as necessary to achieve adequate management of the child's behavior.

2. Medication can be discontinued on holidays or summer vacations. The question is whether the deterioration of behavior without medication is so severe as to make the drug holiday not

worth the effort.

3. Titration (dosage) should be based on objective assessment of the child's resulting behavior and should start with the lowest possible increments.

4. Sufficient time (five to seven days for stimulants, up to three or four weeks for antidepressants) should be allowed for evaluation of the efficacy of each dosage.

5. Parents should never be given permission to adjust the dosage of medication without consulting the physician. This often leads to overmedication of a child, since the parents may increase the dosage every time the child misbehaves.

6. Never force medication on a child or family, particularly adolescents.

7. The physician should provide accurate information to the family about all aspects of the medication.

8. Obtain objective measures of medication effectiveness. The child or teenager self-report is often not an accurate source for determining the effectiveness of the medication. Many patients say they cannot tell the difference, even though teachers and parents see significant improvements in behavior.

9. Trial-and-error efforts will often be needed to fine-tune the proper medication and dosage for your child. It may take weeks or months to find the best dosing schedule. Also, be prepared that as your child grows older, the medication program will also probably need to change.

10. Timing is a very important consideration in the medication process. You need to learn how long it lasts, how long it takes to kick in, when it reaches its maximum effectiveness, and how your child's daily schedule matches up to the medication pattern. For example, if your child begins to have trouble the last period of the school day, it may be because the medication has worn off. Appropriate changes would then need to be made.

11. Medication must be taken regularly and consistently. To accurately measure its effectiveness, the medicine must be taken at about the same time, and under the same conditions, every day.[14]

Evaluation of Medical Intervention

Each child's response to medication is different. Therefore, it is important to collect objective data regarding changes in your child's behavior across several doses. The typical approach is to determine the child's optimal dose in the context of a double-blind, placebo-controlled assessment study that includes multiple measures of the child's behavior collected from the home, school, and clinic. Double-blind means neither the physician nor parent knows when your child is receiving the stimulant medication and when he is taking a neutral substance called a placebo. The use of a placebo reduces the effects of positive biases that can show up on rating scales when the rater knows the child is taking a medication. The problem with blinded drug/placebo trials is that they are time consuming, expensive, and often unnecessary for most children. Four types of situations have been identified which would suggest the need for the more rigorous double-blind trial.

One of these situations is when the parents disagree with each other about whether to consent to a medication trial. The second is if the school personnel are advocating drug therapy while the parents are strongly opposed (or vice versa). A third condition is if a child is so anxious about being medication free during an off-drug trial, the doctors are concerned that his anxiety will interfere with an accurate assessment. The final condition is if the patient, often a teenager, is very noncompliant with the medication because he is convinced that he has no problems and that the medication has no effect. The trial may help show that medication does help.[15]

This type of process usually takes three weeks. During one of those weeks the child is on a small dosage of Ritalin, such as 5 mg. A 10 mg dosage is often used during another week, and the placebo occupies the third week. The sequence is known only to the nurse, technician, or pharmacist who prepares or dispenses the prescriptions. Sometimes the physician will try a combination of medications, such as Ritalin and Dexedrine, during the study. This may extend the trial to four weeks.

It is also important during this time not to make any drastic changes in school or intervention techniques. To do so would contaminate the effects of the medication. Later on, several different treatment strategies will be used for your child. However, for the time the medication study is taking place, don't make other changes.

At the end of each week, both the parents and teacher complete a rating scale of some type. This is done to objectively measure the child's behavior during that particular week. The types of measures used to make the original diagnosis of ADHD now offer a comparison point for your child's performances on medication. The initial standardized score your child received allowed the clinician to compare him to other children. Now, the weekly scores provided by the parent and teacher allow him to be compared to himself. If there are any improvements in behavior that correspond to the introduction of the various medications, your doctor can assume the changes are primarily due to the medication. If one level of dosage was also accompanied by the most significant improvements in behavior, that level may become the initial therapeutic dosage. Periodic measurements are necessary to evaluate the continued efficacy of the treatment.

Whether or not your physician uses a double-blind study, some type of objective measures are needed. The *Conners' Teacher and Parent Rating Scales—Revised (CPRS-R/CTRS-R)*, the *ADD Comprehensive Teacher Rating Scale (ACTeRs)*, the *Revised Home Situations Questionnaire (HSQ)*, and the *Revised School Situations Questionnaire (SSQ)* are often used for this purpose. Their purpose is to make sure the medication is actually helping your child. If the data and your observations don't support any improvement, then the medication must be adjusted or dropped. Sometimes it takes a month or two to settle on a medication program that suits your child. Be patient. Don't drop the whole idea because there are no significant improvements in the first week. Also keep in mind the short-acting nature of Ritalin and Dexedrine. When you see your child in the evening, the effects may have worn off. The teacher may still see positive changes during the day. Make sure you look at all aspects of your child's day before you decide to stop the medication.

What to Tell Your Child

If medication is eventually prescribed, it is important to be honest with your child. Don't call it a vitamin or an allergy pill. Explain that the medication will make it easier to concentrate, complete his assignments, and get along with his friends. Your child needs to be told that medication will not solve all of his problems. It will not make him smarter—he is smart enough already. However, it will make it easier to pay attention to his teacher and schoolwork. A child can be told, "If you work very hard, you will probably finish your assignments and do better in school." The key idea is *hard work*.

Your child needs to be responsible for his own actions. Don't let him use forgotten or worn-off medication as an excuse for inappropriate actions or failure to complete homework. Also, refrain from making comments that link a child's undesirable behaviors to a need for medication. Avoid saying, "You're acting like you need another pill," or "You wouldn't have gotten in trouble today if you'd taken your medicine at lunch." The medication should not be seen as an all-controlling force outside the child. Medication can be beneficial, but the child must know that he is still in control of his actions. He alone is responsible for his academic and social accomplishments. On the other side of the coin, he is ultimately responsible for his mistakes.

The choice to use medication is important. The decision does not end when you start your child on a medication. Careful monitoring must be done to evaluate the effects and to determine the proper dosage. Side effects are possible, so careful observation of your child is necessary. Keep in contact with your physician.

Remember, medication is never the sole treatment program. What you do *after* the start of medication is where the major benefits accrue. The effects of medication alone are temporary. The effects of instruction and self-control will last a lifetime. Medication is one aspect of a balanced treatment.

Other Medical Interventions

Any concurrent illnesses or conditions, such as allergies, should be treated as effectively as possible. Research has not validated concerns about food additives, sugar, or diet. While this lack of evidence may be true for groups of children, there still may be a relationship with your particular child. I would encourage you to follow standard medical, nutritional, and psychological practice that has been demonstrated to be valid. If you wish to explore other forms of intervention, be cautious and be careful with your money. Examine the basis of the claims made for a particular treatment. Does it have only anecdotal support? Has it been submitted to scientific scrutiny? Has any professional organization taken a stand one way or the other on the particular idea you are considering?

Some health food devotees and nutritionists advocate massive ingestion of certain vitamins for a variety of problems. To the best of our knowledge, there is no evidence to support the efficacy of this for the treatment of ADHD. What studies do exist tend to support the idea that megavitamins are ineffective in reducing the symptoms of ADHD children. Of significant concern is the possibility of toxic blood levels from too high a level of vitamin intake. The supposed advantage of vitamin therapy over drug therapy, in being less toxic, thus becomes somewhat questionable. Too much of anything can be dangerous.[16]

Numerous studies have shown that caffeine, whether in coffee or in a tablet, has no measurable positive impact on the inattention of an ADHD youngster. About the only thing you can count on is that your child will have to go to the bathroom more often. This can add to his avoidance behavior, since he will now spend much of the morning running to the lavatory.

A book by Keith Conners, *Feeding the Brain: How Foods Affect Children,* presents a balanced and fair review of the effects of diet, vitamins, additives, and environmental toxins on children's behavior and functioning. It is a good resource if you wish to follow this topic in more detail. Another book, by John Taylor, *Helping Your Hyperactive Child,* presents a supportive view of the Feingold diet as one of several options for treating ADHD children. He reports no real data to substantiate his positive convictions about the Feingold program, but does provide guidelines for utilizing the program.[17]

Pay attention to your child's response to various environmental influences. You can develop a good sense of how different environmental factors influence your son or daughter. Remember to alter only one thing at a time. If you can see definite agents that cause your child's behavior to fluctuate, bring these to the attention of the appropriate professional. Don't give up. Some nontraditional approaches could have potential. However, don't commit yourself until there is evidence for trying a specific idea.

A scientific study should have most of the following characteristics or components:

• A placebo versus actual therapy trial where one group of children receives the actual treatment and another group receives treatment that appears to be similar, but omits the specific intervention being studied.

• A random assignment of subjects to each of the groups.

• Double-blind methods in which no member of the study knows who is actually being treated and who is not.

• A standard evaluation procedure where each child is followed for a specific length of time, with recognized measurement tools, so effects and side effects of treatment can be monitored.

• The use of appropriate statistical analysis, in which each study is analyzed with careful accounting methods to determine the actual success rate.

References

1. D. Safer, J. Zito, & E. Fine, "Increased Methylphenidate Usage for Attention Deficit Disorders in the 1990s," *Pediatrics*, December 6, Volume 98, 1996, 1084–88.

2. Russell A. Barkley, *Taking Charge of ADHD* (New York: Guilford Press, 1995), 249–69.

3. Dennis P. Cantwell, "Attention Deficit Disorder: A Review of the Past 10 Years," *Journal of the American Academy of Child & Adolescent Psychiatry*, Volume 35, Number 8 (August), 1996, 978–87.

4. S. Goldstein & M. Goldstein, *Managing Attention Disorders in Children* (New York: John Wiley & Sons, 1990), 221–66.

5. R.A. Barkley, "A Review of Stimulant Drug Research with Hyperactive Children," *Journal of Child Psychology and Psychiatry* 18 (1977):137–65; R.A. Barkley, "Predicting the Response of Hyperkinetic Children to Stimulant Drugs: A Review," *Journal of Abnormal Child Psychology,* 4 (1976):327–48.

6. K.D. Gadow, "Prevalence of Drug Treatment for Hyperactivity and Other Childhood Behavior Disorders," *Psychosocial Aspects of Drug Treatment for Hyperactivity,* eds. K.D. Gadow & J. Loney (Boulder, Colo.: Westview Press, 1981), 13–70.

7. R.A. Barkley, *Attention-Deficit Hyperactivity Disorder. A Handbook for Diagnosis and Treatment* (New York: Guilford Press, 1990), 573–612.

8. C.K. Conners and K.C. Wells, *Hyperkinetic Children: A Neuropsychological Approach* (Beverly Hills, Calif. Sage, 1986).

9. R.A. Barkley, *Attention-Deficit Hyperactivity Disorder. A Handbook for Diagnosis and Treatment,* 259; R.A. Barkley, "Tic Disorders and Tourette's Syndrome," *Behavioral Assessment of Childhood Disorders,* eds. E. Marsh and L. Terdal, 2nd ed. (New York: Guilford Press, 1988), 69–104; M. Gordon, *ADHD/Hyperactivity: A Consumer's Guide* (DeWitt, N.Y.: GSI Publications, 1991), 78–104.

10. R.A. Barkley, *Attention-Deficit Hyperactivity Disorder. A Handbook for Diagnosis and Treatment* (New York: Guilford Press, 1990), 259.

11. Michael Gordon and Irwin Martin, *The Diagnosis & Treatment of ADD/ADHD: A No-Nonsense Guide for Primary Care Physicians*

(DeWitt, N.Y.: GSI Publications, 1997), 4–57.

12. Chris A. Zeigler Dendy, *Teenagers with ADD: A Parent's Guide* (Rockville, Md.: Woodbine House, 1995), 85.

13. Robert Hunt, Lisa Capper & Patricia, O'Connell, "Clonidine in Child and Adolescent Psychiatry," *Journal of Child and Adolescent Psychopharmacology*, Volume 1, Number 1, 1990, 87–102.

14. R.A. Barkley, *Taking Charge of ADHD*, 261; *Attention Deficit Disorder Handbook*, 573–612; Goldstein and Goldstein, *Managing Attention Disorders in Children*, 221–66; Goldstein and Goldstein, *Hyperactivity: Why Won't My Child Pay Attention?* (New York: John Wiley and Sons, 1992), 169–90.

15. Michael Gordon and Martin Irwin, *The Diagnosis and Treatment of ADD/ADHD: A No-Nonsense Guide for Primary Care Physicians*, 4-19.

16. Michael Gordon, *ADHD/Hyperactivity: A Consumer's Guide*, (DeWitt, N.Y.: GSI Publications, 1991), 69–77.

17. C.K. Conners, *Feeding the Brain: How Foods Affect Children* (New York: Plenum Press, 1989); J.F. Taylor, *Helping Your Hyperactive Child* (Rocklin, Calif: Prima Publishing & Communications, 1990).

CHAPTER EIGHT

HOW CAN THE SCHOOL HELP?
Educational Issues in
ADHD Treatment

It's no wonder an ADHD child has problems with school. Nowhere else is he required to concentrate so long in the face of so many powerful distractions. Successful performance in school is dependent on an ability to persist and maintain concentration for long periods of time. All students must learn class routines, conform to teachers' rules, and inhibit their impulses to do otherwise. Furthermore, the student must control his body movement, maintain an appropriate level of arousal, and delay gratification until report cards are issued.

If you were to set out to design a situation that was most *contrary* to the needs and abilities of an ADHD student, you would probably come up with a typical classroom. We ask a child who has profound problems attending, organizing, and controlling his actions to spend hours per day attending, organizing, and controlling his actions. Would we ask a hearing-impaired child to listen to lectures all day, or a vision-impaired child to watch movies, and then hold them accountable for the content? I think not. But, in essence, this is what we ask of an ADHD child.

Our educational system is demanding more of these skills, and at an earlier age. As a result, the ADHD child will experience increased frustration and failure. Because of the child's problems, it is often the classroom teacher who raises questions that bring about referrals for an evaluation. While the teacher knows your child has a problem, confusion may arise over what *kind* of problem it is and what to *do* about it. Unless the teacher believes your child's diagnosis of ADHD is well-founded and real, it may be hard for you to convince him or her to make all the necessary modifications for your child.

Some teachers bristle at the idea of making adjustments. "Why should I give him more time to complete his assignment, or cut his assignment in half? He's smart enough to do the work if he'd only buckle down and do it. Your child has an attitude problem, not an attention problem." The prevailing opinion among unconvinced teachers is that ADHD children are just irresponsible, lazy, immature, or spoiled. One of your first jobs, as an advocate for your child, is to help school personnel appreciate the legitimacy of the ADHD diagnosis. They also must become familiar with the essential characteristics of the problem. This might require you to provide written materials, recommend workshops, identify videos, and organize training meetings to help bring the school personnel up-to-speed on the requirements of the ADHD student. The mental health professional who has worked with you so far should be a good resource for working with the school.

Appropriate Education for Teachers

I will highlight some general ideas for communicating the nature and needs of an ADHD student to his classroom teacher.

• The teacher must be *educated* about the cause and nature of attention disorders and understand the developmental perspective of the attention-related impairment. It is necessary for the teacher to make the same distinction as the parents do between noncompliance and incompetence. The differential effects of various consequences must be understood. An ADHD student may not respond to the same arrangement of rewards and punishments as do other students. How this impacts classroom management must be conveyed to the teacher in practical and nonthreatening ways.

• The next step in the process is to *pinpoint* the most problematic areas of concern. Because an ADHD child can have so many inappropriate classroom behaviors, it is necessary to identify and define those that need immediate attention. This is much like a triage decision in emergency medicine when many problems exist. Your child has numerous educational needs, but you can't work with all of those needs at once. Problems must be prioritized and specific intervention procedures developed for each area of concern. Usually, there will be two types of intervention. There are self-management procedures aimed at helping the child take control of his own behavior. There are also interventions which alter the school environment in order to help the child function more effectively. I will give examples of these interventions a little later in this chapter.

• Teachers can be educated about the *definition, cause,* and *developmental nature of attention disorders* through books, pamphlets, videos, workshops, and personal communication. Schools often provide such training resources. However, as an advocate for your child, you can become aware of some short texts and pamphlets written especially for teachers. I have identified some of these materials in the resource section of this book.

Obtaining Help from the School

• *Legislative mandate.* For a number of years, ADHD students could qualify for special-education services under Public Law 94-142 only if they had other problems such as learning disabilities or emotional disturbances. This has caused parent groups to become very active in encouraging Congress to allow ADHD to qualify for services.

In the fall of 1991, the U.S. Education Department sent a letter to state school superintendents advising them of their responsibility to service ADHD students. The letter outlined three ways students with ADHD could receive assistance through special-education programs.

The first method of eligibility has been available for some time. Students diagnosed with ADHD *in addition* to other disabilities, such as emotional disturbances or learning disabilities, may receive federally funded special education by virtue of those other diagnoses. This represents no change.

Children who have only ADHD, but whose alertness is chronically or acutely impaired by the disorder, may now receive services under the category of *"other health impaired."* Previous to this letter, there was confusion over whether this catchall category applied to ADHD children. As of this writing, it does apply.

The third way students may qualify is under Section 504 of the Rehabilitation Act of 1973. Schools do not receive any federal funding for students classified under Section 504. However, the law does obligate schools to modify classroom practices for any students whose physical or mental impairments substantially limit their learning ability. This section of the Education Department letter encourages interventions for the regular classroom. The examples of adaptations in regular education programs mentioned in the Department of Education letter include: providing a structured learning environment; repeating and simplifying instructions about in-class and homework assignments; supplementing verbal instructions with visual instructions; using behavioral management techniques; adjusting class schedules; modifying test delivery; using tape recorders, computer-aided instruction, and other audio-visual equipment; selecting modified textbooks or workbooks; and tailoring homework assignments.[1]

Examples of accommodations based on the government guidelines could include such things as:

- Taped textbooks so student can listen to content rather than read
- Allowing oral presentations instead of written for a student who has trouble expressing his thoughts in writing
- Extended time on tests
- Arrangement of room/space to minimize distraction, including test-taking in a quiet place
- Having a scribe write out answers to tests for student who has trouble writing, but can express ideas in verbal form
- Opportunity to take tests orally instead of in writing
- Using a reader during test-taking to assist student with reading problems
- Tutoring for specific needs by peer, aid, or teacher
- Large-print text and worksheets
- Using a computer to take notes and prepare assignments
- Computer-assisted instruction, multimedia presentation, and technological enhancements for various special needs
- Using a note-taker for students who can't listen and take their own notes
- Tape-recording of lectures and/or transcribing of tapes into notes for those with auditory or writing disabilities

There is still mixed opinion about providing services to

ADHD children. The guidelines are likely to change, so you are advised to keep abreast of the developments within your local school district. What this means, though, is that the chances are better now for you to get help for your child, even if he "only" has ADHD.

• *Obtaining educational services.* The specific process varies with each school district, but the following description should come pretty close to what can happen if you or the school should initiate the process. The first step is for a parent or teacher to make a referral. In my state it is called a "focus of concern." This means you fill out a form available from your child's school that identifies learning problems which impact your child's educational program. This referral is processed through the school principal and goes to the district pupil-services department. A child study team is formed to act on the referral. Usually this team consists of a school psychologist or counselor, nurse, and educational specialist, along with your child's teacher and principal. The school district is obligated to process your referral within forty-five to ninety days, obtain initial information about your child, and make a recommendation for services. During this time, various members of the team will review the child's school file, talk to the teacher, observe him in the classroom, obtain various rating scales, and possibly complete individual testing.

You will be notified of what is transpiring and probably will be given various forms to complete, including background information and descriptions of the current problem. A "focus of concern" child study is supposed to include the emotional, social, and physical dimensions of a child, as well as the educational. So you may be asked to have your child seen by your physician, who will then send a report back to the child study team. If the school district does not have a specialist available to evaluate a specific part of the referring question, they may refer to an appropriate professional such as a psychologist. Generally, when the school makes this type of referral, they are obligated to pay for it. Make sure that is clear in your case.

• *Development of an individual educational plan.* After the study team has gathered all of the data and observations about your child, you will be invited to a meeting to discuss the findings and recommendations and to agree upon some type of Individual Educational Plan (IEP). In the case of ADHD, you might agree to modifications in classroom management and assignment reductions. Medication may or may not be recommended. All of this would be discussed at that meeting. In complicated cases, several such meetings would be held over the school year.

The questions on page 183 can help you evaluate the IEP as it relates to your understanding of your child's needs. Check the "yes" boxes if you believe the issue is adequately dealt with by the IEP. Use the "no" boxes when you believe the IEP does not deal adequately with your child's needs. The "?" boxes can be used when you are uncertain and need to obtain more information before you can be sure of the answer.

These questions will help you make sure a comprehensive evaluation was completed that accurately reflects your child's needs, and that a program is designed to do everything possible to help her achieve more success in school. Once your child's needs are defined, the IEP becomes a management tool, even a contract, for spelling out what will be done. Like any contract, you want to tie down as many loose ends as possible. If you have a legitimate concern, negotiate to get it into the IEP. Verbal agreements cannot be enforced. Make sure everything the school decides to do for your child is written into the IEP.

Your involvement does not cease once the IEP is signed. You may develop concerns or questions during the course of the school year. If you think the program is not adequately meeting your child's needs, you have the right to ask the IEP committee to reconvene and review the entire program.

The school can address only educational concerns. That is appropriate and significant. Your child spends about five hours of each day in the school environment. ADHD children need a total program of intervention. So even if the study team recommends adjustments to the classroom, you will still need help and advice about how to make changes at home. Thus, an outside resource will often still be necessary, unless the district has the appropriate personnel to assign to you.

Even if you do not use the resources of your local school district at the beginning, your child's teacher will still be a vital part of the treatment plan. As I said in chapter 3, one aspect to consider in choosing an outside professional is the individual's skill and ability to work closely with the school. This means that your child's teacher is a crucial part of the intervention process.

To have maximum impact on an ADHD student, his world has to provide him with unusual amounts of structure and flexibility. Often the regular classroom is limited in the extent to which these needs can be met. The classroom places a premium on self-control

IEP Questions

yes	no	?	
❏	❏	❏	Was the evaluation comprehensive, nondiscriminatory, and multidisciplinary?
❏	❏	❏	Does the evaluation describe a full range of your child's strengths and weaknesses, including learning styles and possible disabilities?
❏	❏	❏	Does the IEP accurately and fully describe your child's present level of educational performance in all relevant developmental areas?
❏	❏	❏	Do you agree with the assessment results?
❏	❏	❏	Is more information needed to present a fair and accurate picture of your child's learning status?
❏	❏	❏	Do the goals included in the IEP accurately and adequately describe the skills, behavior, and understanding you wish your child to acquire in the next year?
❏	❏	❏	Do the goals represent all aspects of the educational experience and draw from the intellectual, social, emotional, physical, and spiritual domains that you believe are crucial for your child?
❏	❏	❏	Are the goals listed in order of priority from most to least important?
❏	❏	❏	Are the goals written so as to build on your child's strengths and present level of performance?
❏	❏	❏	Do the goals specify *what* service is to be provided, *who* will provide the service, *how* and *where* the service will be delivered, along with *how often* and *how much* service will be provided, and *when* the service will start?
❏	❏	❏	Do all the professionals who know and will work with your child agree with the components of the IEP?
❏	❏	❏	Does the IEP clearly outline the balance of time your child will spend in regular and special-education programs?
❏	❏	❏	Is there at least one annual goal and short-term objective for each type of service your child will receive?
❏	❏	❏	Are all goals and objectives written in understandable, positive, and measurable terms?
❏	❏	❏	Does the IEP include clearly defined methods for systematically (at least annually if not more often) evaluating your child's progress toward each of the goals and objectives included in the plan?
❏	❏	❏	Given everything that is included in the IEP, are you able to sign it?

and sustained attention. At the same time, consequences for failure to conform tend to be inconsistent, infrequent, and delayed. An ADHD child is drawn to events that are most stimulating and intriguing. Unfortunately, this usually means it is more fun to watch a fly on the ceiling or to pass notes to a classmate than to complete a sheet of long division.

An ADHD child will impulsively grab for attention wherever and whenever it may come his way. In most classrooms this means he will get attention for doing something wrong more often than for doing something right. Such limitations of the learning environment strongly suggest that there is need for change in the classroom if an ADHD child is going to have a better chance of survival and success.

Dr. Michael Gordon has summarized the essential needs of an ADHD child. I believe this list gives us a good overview of where we need to head in terms of changes for your child. Keep these needs in mind as you work with the school to develop programs for your child.

Essential Classroom Needs of an ADHD Child

1. Clearly specified rules, expectations, and instructions.
2. Frequent, immediate, and consistent feedback on behavior, and redirection to task.
3. Reasonable and meaningful consequences for both compliance and noncompliance.
4. Programming and adult intervention designed to compensate for the child's distractibility, limited organizational skills, and low frustration tolerance.
5. A well-integrated and functioning team of parents, teachers, administrators, and clinician who communicate often and work together to create a structured and supportive environment.

• *Strategies for classroom assistance.* Most schools will take a three-step approach to providing educational services to a child.

Step one provides modifications within the regular classroom.

This usually entails consulting with the teacher, making sure he or she is knowledgeable about ADHD, and implementing classroom management programs tailored for the mainstreamed setting.

Keeping students in the regular classroom, or mainstreaming, is the presumption of most schools. The most desirable alternative is to help the ADHD child function successfully in the regular classroom. This "least restrictive environment" principle directs schools to establish programs that allow handicapped children to interact with nonhandicapped peers as much as possible. Most school districts will err in the direction of not segregating special-needs children. Of course, this is also the least expensive of the available options.

Step two offers more intensive services through a combination of regular and resource room activities. This may entail the child leaving class for an hour or more per day in order to receive individual attention. Sometimes the resource room teacher will come into the child's class and work with him there. Additional services are added as needed for situations where the child might require special help, such as language or learning deficiencies.

Step three involves special class placement for most of the child's school day. This is required when the ADHD child has significant emotional, behavioral, or learning problems.

ADHD children require help at least at the first step and often at the second step of assistance. Often the focus of the resource room activity can be on review and organization of regular classroom assignments. This is in contrast to trying to instruct the student in skills using tasks unrelated to current classroom assignments. Frequently, ADHD children need to sit down on a one-to-one basis and go over the assignments they had trouble focusing on in class. This can be a time to make sure that all the homework assignments are understood and recorded prior to taking work home. The resource room teacher can also be a primary liaison between the school and parent, helping coordinate incentive efforts, providing daily report cards, and facilitating feedback. Of course, the resource teacher can also provide remedial help in basic skills.

There is no definite bench mark for moving from one level of intervention to the next. It boils down to the broad question of, "Is your child making satisfactory progress under the current instructional methods?" If he is not, then more resources may be needed. The simple checklist on the next page will help you look at your child's educational status.

Educational Status Checklist

Yes No

❏   ❏ 1. Is your child making satisfactory academic progress? Are his progress reports and report cards satisfactory, given his potential and ability?

❏   ❏ 2. Is your child's behavior maintaining at an appropriate level? (If he is being disciplined frequently, excluded from class, or spending lots of time in the principal's office, there is a problem.)

❏   ❏ 3. Does your child's teacher seem generally optimistic about your child and his progress?

❏   ❏ 4. Does the teacher believe s/he is able to give your child the attention he needs?

❏   ❏ 5. Is your child relatively free from being a scapegoat or marked child by either the teacher or his peers?

❏   ❏ 6. Does your child seem pleased and happy with school?

❏   ❏ 7. Are you relatively satisfied with the school program for your child?

The more "yes" responses you have, the more likely the school program is currently meeting your child's needs and the less likely you will need to pursue additional services at another level. There may always be adjustments to a treatment program, such as more time in the resource room to work on a particular problem. Maybe the student is having a harder time with long division and needs some extra help. This is the type of change that needs to be monitored closely. You don't want your child to struggle for two months in math and then get a poor report card before you hear about it for the first time. Don't be lulled into apathy out of fatigue or by the fact you haven't heard from the school for a few weeks. I know it's tempting to believe that no news is good news. You may have spent so much time working to resolve various problems with your child that you can't bear another teacher conference. Your weariness is understandable. Yet, life with an ADHD child requires vigilance and never-ending monitoring.

Choosing the Best School[3]

In this section, I want to give you some things to look for in selecting the best school for your ADHD child. You may not always have a choice in where your child attends school. However, these suggestions may help you choose among various teachers within your neighborhood school. If too many of these characteristics are missing, it may be difficult for the IEP to be carried out, and you need to question how effective the proposed location is really going to be for your child.

You may be considering private schools. If so, these characteristics can be helpful to sort past the marketing brochures and zero in on the key components of their program. Your goal is to pin down whether the overall philosophy of education, staff, instructional strategies, as well as policies and procedures, are supportive and appropriate to ADHD students.

Does the school recognize the legitimacy of ADHD?

As you talk with administrators and staff, determine what kind of training has been conducted for the teachers. How many similar students already attend the school? How are they being accommodated? What is the general attitude toward students with special needs? You don't need pat answers, promises of quick cures, or more guilt placed on your shoulders. Avoid as much of this as possible by getting a decent impression up-front.

Does the school have specific programs for dealing with ADHD and learning-disabled students?

Some private schools may be more interested in filling up classrooms than in screening students for whether the school can actually meet their needs. The prospect of small class size may sound appealing. However, ADHD students need much more than smaller classes. Avoid frustration by finding out as much as possible before you ever enroll your child. Try to talk with other parents from the school whose students have similar problems. Determine what has been done for their child and how effectively they believe the instruction has been.

Ask to see a statement of goals, purpose, and mission for the school.

Do the goals of the school match your intentions for your child? No school can meet all of your goals. Establish your priorities as a family and look for the best match possible. Remember to apply your general goals to your child's IEP. The IEP is not intended to cover the total scope of educational goals, but those goals and objectives that are included need to be within your expectations.

Ask the administrator what instructional groupings are available.

What are the average class sizes for your child's grade? Class size above twenty-eight is no different than most public schools. Are extra staff present in the room if larger class size is common? How are small groups constituted for special instruction such as reading or math help?

You might also want to know how many other special needs students are going to be in your child's classroom.

How many students will be mainstreamed or included from special-education programs? If there are more than three or four such students, determine if this begins to exceed the teacher's capacity to meet all student needs adequately.

How are students matched to teachers?

ADHD children need experienced and capable teachers. They make high demands of the teacher. Does the school have staff available who have the strength, stamina, and motivation to work with children like yours?

What kind of professional assistance is available to consult with the school about special needs and intervention?

Mental health, special-education, and medical personnel will be needed at one time or another to advise about proper management and teaching of ADHD students. The school should be willing to provide additional training as needed for teachers of ADHD and learning-disabled children. Is the school receptive to having your own psychologist, or other such professional, visit and consult with the staff? The school should be open to such consultation and not be threatened by your proposing such assistance.

If this is a private school that has limited resources, has there been a history of cooperation with public school or other private school resources?
Many ADHD students also have learning disabilities. This combination of needs can put high demands on the teacher and other school staff. Is the school capable of making these adjustments through their own or outside resources? What will be the associated costs for any additional programs? Who will pay for transportation costs if an adjunct program is used?

Has the school completed any outcome studies to demonstrate that its program works?
Can the school show you data that indicates other ADHD students have made progress? Does the data clearly indicate effects of specific school interventions as opposed to changes in medication or family dynamics? If you are going to entrust your child to a different school, try to get some idea of the effectiveness of the new program with children like yours.

Be careful about a school or program that offers quick fixes, cures, or unrealistic goals for your child.
At this point there has been no demonstrated cure for ADHD. Many interventions can be helpful. These students can be helped. But there are no guaranteed programs. Special gimmicks, high-tech equipment, or enriched teaching methods may sound good. But is there support for their efficacy? A school that markets itself with too many promises should be avoided.

Compare the cost versus the gain.
You may be considering a private school. That usually means tuition costs that would not have to be paid if your child attended public school. Prayerfully consider whether the advantages of the private school really outweigh those of the public school. The answer may be a resounding, "yes." In other situations, the differences between the two programs may be minimal. Under those conditions, would it be wiser to spend the tuition money on family enrichment items, and end up better off in the long run?

What is the school's philosophy about homework?
Many private schools expect their students to complete heavy

amounts of assignments outside of the classroom. This can be very frustrating to the ADHD student unless some accommodations are made. Does the school advocate and support necessary classroom adjustments to make your child more successful? Suppose you get a response such as, "Well, we do have standards for all of our students to meet. However, if your child really needs some adjustments, we can probably make some exceptions for a little while until s/he gets caught up and used to our way of doing things." This tells you their heart really isn't into accommodation. They simply don't understand the problems of ADHD students.

Ask about the school's policy and procedures for monitoring and dispensing medication.

You need to know how medications are handled if your child is taking any. There may also be state guidelines that must be followed. A trained person such as a nurse should dispense the pills, and a consistent record of dispensing occasions needs to be kept. Some schools may believe ADHD students do not need medication and therefore be reluctant to cooperate with you and your child's physician. Be cautious about the match for your child if this condition is true.

What kind of classrooms exist in the school?

Many innovations in education such as classroom clusters and open-concept rooms may not be ideal for your ADHD student. The expanse of classroom space, constant movement of students, and simultaneous instruction for many groups can be a disaster for your child. A traditional classroom with a minimum of transitions and interruptions is most desirable. In general, is the facility a pleasant and productive place to go to school?

If your child should demonstrate some behavior problems and get into trouble, how will s/he be treated?

What are the procedures for disciplinary action? Is corporal punishment used? What is your opinion about spanking or paddling in the school? Is there a strong redemptive and instructional focus to the school's disciplinary methods? More emphasis should be placed on regarding acceptable behavior than on punishing unacceptable behavior. Procedures, and both student and staff rights and expectations, should be available in written form. Often schools will prepare a student handbook that details these kinds of issues. Ask for a copy before registering your child.

Open communication is a must for ADHD students, their parents, and school personnel.

Does the administrator encourage parent-teacher communication? Do you feel welcome to drop in at the school? Can conferences be arranged without too much hassle? Ask to see examples of assignment sheets, organizational notebooks, academic journals, and other such tools. These are crucial to the success of your child and they should be common and routine items for the classroom your child will attend. The classroom teacher and support staff should be open to consulting with you on a regular basis. Opportunities to volunteer at school should also be available. If you can spend time in your child's classroom, you will have better communication with the teacher and a clearer understanding of the daily routine. This will help you with your son's or daughter's homework assignments and class projects. If your child has trouble acting out in impulsive and/or aggressive ways, your presence in the classroom will help you and the teacher work out beneficial management procedures to help your child.

If you are considering a Christian school, how are those values and beliefs presented?

Is there a consistent method of integrating issues of faith with daily learning? Is the same accommodation and variety of instruction available for religious education as is available for the rest of the curriculum? An ADHD student should have all of the same assistance to learn about God that s/he would have to learn about math and reading. Make sure the Bible classes, for example, offer the same level of support as other classes. Otherwise, your child may get turned off from doing the assignments in an area most crucial to the development of the whole person.

In summary, if you have the option, choose a school that best matches up with the needs of your child. If an IEP has been developed within the public school system, it can still be applied to a private or home school placement. You began the process by obtaining a comprehensive evaluation of your child's needs. In selecting the school program, you want to be equally as comprehensive in your appraisal. Use the preceding areas of inquiry to help you determine which school seems to have the most potential for helping your child.

What If the School Is Uncooperative?

Most schools try very hard to help children with special needs.

Countless teachers spend extra time and money out of their own pockets to develop materials for children in their classrooms. Many teachers will take on a strong advocacy role for a particular child when they believe supplementary services are necessary. Unfortunately, some schools and administrators will not respond to reasonable requests for special services. It's not always an issue of money, although that is the excuse most frequently given. Sometimes it's because of a particular philosophy or belief of a principal or administrator that ADHD does not exist, or that all children should receive the same services. In meeting with school officials, I have heard other opinions bordering on insanity!

The law provides several means through which you can challenge the school's decisions regarding your child. These range from meeting with various committees that oversee special-educational services to calling a due-process hearing which is presided over by an impartial judge. You can learn about these remedies by contacting your state education department or by contacting your local ADHD or Learning Disabilities Association. The addresses for the national organizations are given in Part Three.

The inclusion of ADHD in Public Law 94-142 goes a long way toward requiring schools to respond to the needs of attention deficit students. Section 504 of the Rehabilitation Act of 1973 gives you another route to follow. Your local chapter of the various support and advocacy groups offer ideas on how to draw on these laws for the benefit of your child. In reality, you have considerable legal clout, should you need it. The Legal Services Administration has an Educational Advocacy Branch which can be tapped for legal resources if your local efforts prove fruitless. There are times when parents need to be a forceful and informed presence in the school. This might mean that you become a bit of a nuisance, or that you band together with other parents to push for needed changes.

Your best bet is to remain on a cooperative basis with your school. An adversarial relationship should be avoided if at all possible. Nobody likes to be threatened or forced to provide services, and the schools are no exception. You don't want to pursue formal action until you are sure that all other avenues for negotiation have been exhausted. An extensive (and costly) legal battle to win a class adjustment for your child may leave you with such a bad taste in your mouth that you wouldn't put your child back in that program for all the tea in China. You need to establish a workable balance between active cooperation with the school and energetic insistence on change.

Once again, your clinician should be of assistance in working with the school to develop a reasonable program. I have often been part of Individual Education Program (IEP) meetings with local elementary and secondary school staffs. Sometimes there has been reluctance by administrators to provide appropriate services for a student. I will be there with data in hand to argue the child's case for whatever kind of resources I believe are appropriate. My presence can make a difference in the decision-making process. At other times, a letter from me has been sufficient to move the process along.

Remember to always keep a record of your contacts with school and other officials during the course of your efforts. It takes a bit of work, but you should keep a log of phone calls, letters written, meetings attended, promises made, and administrative no-shows. These records can be very valuable if there is ever any legal action. Make copies of all your correspondence, and don't let the originals of anything disappear into the bureaucratic paper mill.

Classroom Management of ADHD

Although you probably can't choose your child's teacher, you should think about the best kind of classroom for your child. Invariably, ADHD children perform better in a more structured setting directed by teachers who prefer defined work patterns, rather than open-ended choices, for tasks.

I recall being a part of an elementary, school-based teacher training project a number of years ago. In cooperation with the local school district, the university where I taught was establishing an open-concept, continuous-progress learning environment. It was a brand-new school building with large open classrooms built in circle-shaped clusters. The idea was to have all the children move through various teaching stations over the course of the day, utilizing the many regular teaching staff, university professors, student teachers, and aides.

All of this looked good on paper. Much of the funding was from a special grant, and many of the ideas came from the pen of a professor in the ivory tower of the university. The reality was that the school was located in a part of town where 40 percent of the school population would change during the course of the school year. Most of the children came from economically disadvantaged families. Many of the homes represented by these students had economic, emotional, and domestic turmoil, as well as problems with drugs and abuse. I'm sure many of these students would have qualified as ADHD if we had been looking for it.

Can you imagine the chaos of those first few days? Here was the cream of the district teaching staff, experienced professors, and lots of university students trying to get these hundreds of hyperactive, rambunctious, disrespectful elementary students to tolerate this unstructured environment. It was a disaster. After only a couple of days, there were hurriedly called staff meetings at each teaching level. At the beginning of the second week of school, the large folding doors dividing the rooms were pulled shut and individual classrooms were formed. Team-teaching efforts were put on hold. And what we had was a very structured, traditional set of classrooms, conducting business in a very methodical manner.

These children had no experience in unstructured settings. They needed clear directions, limits on their actions, and predictable sequences. It was just too unrealistic to expect them to handle the new system. I might add that by Christmas, things had smoothed out, and most of the team-teaching and modified open-concept classrooms were operating as designed.

Classroom Intervention for the ADHD Student

We have examined what to look for in selecting a school for the ADHD student. That gives us a general setting for education to take place. The real changes occur in the classroom. Those changes take place one day at a time, usually in gradual steps. Sometimes it will seem like three steps forward, then two steps backward. There will always be ups and downs. About the time you think things have smoothed out, a call comes from the principal saying your child just called the substitute teacher a bad name, flushed the class goldfish down the toilet, and bit the school nurse on the elbow. It obviously has been a very bad day.

Try to keep your wits about you and remember these major incidents are now happening far less frequently than last year. Keep your sense of humor (perhaps you could ask if there should be a memorial service for the goldfish), and set out to find what created all this turmoil. We do have many procedures that increase the chances of success for the inattentive, impulsive, and hyperactive student. We are not asking for the ADHD child to be coddled or excused from responsibility. However, each child does require special handling of the type described below. Here are some useful and tested guidelines for making educational interventions with your ADHD child:[4]

The classroom must be structured and predictable, but not punitive or sterile.

The student needs clear and consistent rules, but positive consequences for following those rules.

A traditional self-contained classroom works best.

Four walls and one door without panoramic views of the playground or parking lots are just fine. Open-concept classrooms with constant transitions and lots of distractions are very problematic for ADHD students.

Assignments should be clearly communicated in written form, both to assist the student and to inform the parents.

Weekly assignment sheets for each subject are encouraged. Both teacher and parents will need to see and sign assignment sheets to ensure accuracy and completion by the student.

Homework completion will need to be a team effort.

The teacher will need to take responsibility to make assignments clear, and to assist the parents in developing a strategy that includes the following components: (a) clear definition of assignments; (b) written format for communication of assignments; (c) method for student to store and transport assignments, such as a special notebook; (d) seeing that student gets assignments and necessary materials out the door and headed for home; (e) parents then take over to check for necessary homework on a daily basis and communicate with teacher if questions arise about assignments; (f) establish time and place to complete homework, and monitor to ensure compliance and successful completion of assignments; (g) make sure assignments and school materials are in child's possession and returned to school; (h) teacher makes certain there is set procedure for turning in homework.

ADHD students do much better when there are set, routine procedures for completing daily activities.

Establish formats for initial classroom activities, methods of turning in homework or seat work, and preparation and dismissal for recess and other transition times.

ADHD students need to be taught specific strategies for learning.

This helps to organize the learning process and to make it more meaningful. Examples would include use of diagrams and pictorials to help with information to be memorized; mnemonic strategies (e.g., HOMES for the Great Lakes—Huron, Ontario, Michigan, Erie, Superior); mental pictures or associations to assist in storage and retrieval of information; and emphasis of critical pieces of instruction by highlighting with color or underlining.

Extra attention may need to be given to transition times throughout the school day.

Movement from an unstructured time, such as recess or PE, to silent reading or seat work, is very hard. The teacher will need to set rules and consequences for transitions and monitor them closely until compliance is well ingrained. Whenever there is a change in schedule, such as a school assembly, close monitoring will be necessary.

Many ADHD students have trouble with long-term endeavors such as term papers or social studies projects.

Projects will need to be divided into smaller parts, with a time line for completion of those components. Close communication with parents is necessary, along with lots of reinforcement for progress along the way.

Teacher reprimands should be limited, especially in front of the class.

Comments are most effective when accompanied with a consequence, such as loss of privilege or time out. Negative emotions need to be kept at a minimum by the teacher, with a total emphasis on positive reinforcement whenever possible. Avoid lengthy reasoning with a child over misbehavior.

Try to match the ADHD student with a highly organized teacher who will model and encourage neatness, efficiency, and organization for the child.

A creative, but informal, unpredictable, and inconsistent teacher will be difficult for the ADHD child.

Directions and instructions to the student must be clear, concrete, and concise.

Give only a few directions at a time, and use as many visual, auditory, and hands-on demonstrations as possible. Direct eye contact, one instruction at a time, and requests for student feedback and understanding are very helpful in ensuring comprehension.

Distractions should be minimized for the student.

This may mean seating the student close to the teacher and away from obvious distractions such as windows, air conditioners, active classmates, gerbil cages, or pencil sharpeners. Seat the ADHD student next to students who will be positive examples.

Immediate and frequent feedback is required.

Redirection will often be necessary so that long periods of unproductive activity are minimized. Teach the student hand signals or "private signs" that can be used to remind him when not to talk, as well as when to get back on task. Mechanical and electronic devices can also be used to remind and reward.

The student needs both verbal and tangible positive consequences for attention to task and assignment completion.

Other meaningful positive and negative consequences will be needed to assist the student in learning appropriate classroom behavior. Contracts, incentive systems, self-monitoring programs, and behavior modification strategies are often used with ADHD students.

Reinforcement strategies will need to be altered from time to time.

Motivation can be enhanced with the introduction of a new method of monitoring and rewarding appropriate behavior. What may be rewarding to one student may not be interesting to another. The teacher will need to be sensitive and flexible to the need for changes over time, and for variations among students.

The curriculum needs to be adjusted to allow the student to be successful.

This is done by modifying the instruction methods to accommodate the child's difficulty in paying attention and concentrating. Some flexibility is needed to allow for the student's low frustration tolerance. Assignments may need to be shortened. Computers can be used to compensate for poor handwriting ability. Assignments might be divided into smaller parts to help the student feel successful, and to give more frequent opportunity for feedback.

Computer-assisted instruction can be useful to hold the interest of the ADHD student.

Color, sound, interactive formats, and immediate feedback keep the attention of most students. Computers can be used for reinforcement of appropriate behavior as well as for instruction and review.

Build on the strengths of the student.

The teacher should identify the child's best methods of learning, as well as areas of creativity, interest, and competency, and use those strengths for motivation, class leadership, and esteem building. Try to make sure the student has at least one task each day that s/he can do successfully.

Academic work should be tailored to the student's ability and achievement level.

The student needs to experience success and to move to new material after s/he has demonstrated competency over previous concepts and skills.

If the ADHD student also has other learning needs, such as learning disabilities, these require specific, individual educational programs to be established and implemented for all identified areas.

Make sure the IEP is relevant and comprehensive for the student's total educational needs.

High- and low-interest activities can be interspersed throughout the school day.

Long periods of uninterrupted seat work are hard for the ADHD student. Plan for times of concentration and attention to be alternated with hands-on, multimodality, high-interest learning activities.

Create learning partnerships.

A calm, capable peer is paired with the ADHD student to help him learn new concepts and/or to review and practice previously learned material.

Within a particular assignment or teaching activity, add some type of novelty to the end of the task.

Minimize repetition within assignments, and add as much activity as possible to student tasks. More behavioral disruptions will occur the longer an ADHD child is exposed to any particular setting or task.

Movement is necessary.

Allow the hyperactive student opportunities to work while standing or pace while thinking, as long as s/he learns to do so without disturbing others. Activities such as running an errand or cleaning the fish tank can be used as individual rewards for improvement and assignment completion. (Just make sure the activity doesn't prove so stimulating that it causes more problems than it solves.)

For students who have trouble waiting, give them substitute verbal or motor responses to make while waiting.

At the same time, encourage productive thinking and/or appropriate task completion while waiting for teacher attention. The teacher should attend to and reward increasing lengths of time the student is able to wait.

For students who interrupt, teach them to recognize pauses in conversations and how to hang on to ideas. Also instruct and reinforce social conventions found in contexts such as personal recognition (hello, good-bye); courtesies (thank you, please); cooperation (your turn); and compliments (good job).

The teacher will need to be sensitive to ways the ADHD student can escalate from minor irritations to major explosions.

Find ways to distract the child from a total focus on the problem of the moment and redirect attention to classroom tasks. Time-out may be used if the student becomes too aroused. Teachers should know how and when to pick a battle, and be able to back off and ignore smaller irritations.

Students need to be taught conflict resolution and problem-solving skills.

This will help them learn to resolve differences and plan cooperatively. An example is the SODA strategy mentioned on page 114.

Above all, the teacher must look for the good in each child.

The student has value for who s/he is, not for what s/he can do. Effort must be extended to affirm the worth of the ADHD student and to do everything possible to nurture the child's sense of identity, competency, and belonging.

It is crucial for the entire team of educators, mental health professionals, medical personnel, and parents to maintain continuous communication with each other.

Everyone must work together toward the common goal of ensuring the student the best educational experience possible.

The parent will usually need to maintain an advocate status with the schools.

There are many other students to take up the school personnel's time. Don't wait for the six-week progress reports. Become very familiar with the teacher and the classroom routine. Be courteous and tactful, but maintain a constant vigil on your child's behalf.

The previous suggestions can go a long way toward helping your ADHD child prosper in the classroom. Remember, no one strategy will reap all the results. It takes constant monitoring and changing of interventions to keep up with the unpredictable challenges of attention disorders. About the time you begin to relax, things are likely to slip a little. Don't look at that event as failure. It is the normal process of educating that lovable creation of God who sometimes drives you to distraction.

Implement home/school report-card system to monitor progress.

There are many ways to implement the daily or weekly report card. There are three basic components. The first is the *identification of the specific school-related behaviors* that are being monitored. There can be both "uppers" and "downers," preferably some of both, with an emphasis on the positive. Remember, "uppers" are appropriate behaviors that the child should do more often, while "downers" are inappropriate behaviors that should be happening less often. The second component is *a system of record-keeping* that is simple, yet effective, in monitoring the student's behavior on a daily basis. The third part of a card program is *a reward system* for improvement in the student's study and school-related behavior.

The form on page 201 is an example of what can be used to communicate the student's performance on a given day. It takes only a minute or two to complete.

The specific behaviors can be changed to suit the needs of your child. You can specify rewards for high-point days, as well as loss of points for poor-behavior days. Rewards can be based on weekly improvement or on the total points for a week. A response-cost arrangement can be used where a weekly reward is established. Let's say it is two dollars or two hours of TV time on the weekend. Every day the report card comes home with ones or twos, nothing is lost. However, if there are any zeros, twenty-five cents or fifteen minutes are subtracted from the reward. Each day's transaction needs to be recorded or visualized in some way.

Daily Report Card

Teacher: Please rate each behavior using a point system from the following scale:

    0 Did not have a good day.
    1 Had a good day.
    2 Had a very good day.

Child's name: _____ **Date:** _____

Behavior:
1. Completed homework   _____

2. Completed seat work   _____

3. Listened to instruction   _____

4. Cooperated with classroom rules   _____

                              Total: _____

A jar of marbles or tally marks on a paper will serve the purpose. By the end of the week, the child will receive whatever amount of reward remains. This type of strategy seems to work well with most ADHD children.

The School and Medication

The school should be informed if your child is on medication or trying new doses. The teacher will be asked to provide regular feedback on the child's classroom behavior and academic achievement. This information is crucial in determining the medication's effectiveness. The physician or clinician will provide the rating forms to be used in evaluating the student's behavior. Explain how important the accurate and timely completion of these forms is to the outcome of the decision. At the outset, you should explain the monitoring process. If a double-blind study is used, the teacher will not know which protocol is being employed. Make it clear that you need to hear from the teacher if he or she notices any alarming behaviors such as twitches or social withdrawal. Also convey to the school personnel that you are desirous of using medication if it proves beneficial, but that you know all other special-educational services are also needed. The school should not be allowed to expect that medication is going to solve all your child's problems, and thus assume that the educational program can remain unchanged.

When a child continues on medication, the teacher should continue to look for things such as in-seat activity, improvements in handwriting and organization on paper, decreased impulsiveness, and a higher frustration tolerance. Also, the teacher needs to be observant of differences in behavior at different times of day to help in dosage adjustments. It is important to report any side effects such as irritability, sadness that may approach or mimic depression, increased restlessness, and excessive talkativeness.

The teacher should also be encouraged not to make statements to the child such as, "You are having a bad afternoon. Did you forget to take your pill?" Medication does not make a child "good." Pronouncements such as, "You're such a good boy when you take your medicine," should likewise be avoided.

If a midday dosage is required, you will also have to work out the mechanics of the process. Some children are reliable enough to carry a pill in their lunch bag or pocket and take it at the appropriate time. Most need some kind of structure or reminder to maintain consistency. It might be necessary to have the school nurse dispense it, although this can be awkward for the child to have to parade up to the nurse's office every day.

For many years, school will remain a significant concern. Yet, you will gain more confidence and encouragement as you see the fruits of your efforts. It is an ongoing process, but one where you can see very definite payoff in your child's attitude, academic achievement, and relationship to teachers and classmates.

References

1. United States Department of Education, "Clarification of Policy to Address the Needs of Children with Attention Deficit Disorders within General and/or Special Education" (Washington, D.C.: Office of Special Education and Rehabilitative Services, 1991).

2. M. Gordon, *ADHD/Hyperactivity: A Consumer's Guide* (DeWitt, N.Y.: GSI Publications, 1991), 108.

3. Adapted from Grant L. Martin, *Help! My Child Isn't Learning* (Colorado Springs: Focus on the Family, 1995), 111–15. Used by permission.

4. Ibid., 116–20.

CHAPTER NINE

HOW CAN GOD HELP?
Spiritual Issues in
ADHD Treatment

A little boy with ADHD asked his mother, "Mom, why can't something be wrong with my arm and not my brain?" Then he added, "A broken arm will get better, but you can't fix my brain."

You may have had the same question, along with, "Why my child? Is this God's punishment for sins of the past?" or "Why would God allow this to happen?"

I certainly don't have the answers to these questions, any more than I would claim to understand the mind and purposes of God. However, I do believe ADHD children have every potential for creative and fulfilled lives. There is ample reason to be optimistic about their ability to mature, yield fruit in season, and prosper in whatever they do (Psalm 1:3).

Parenting is difficult with any child, and even more challenging when a child has special needs. That is why the spiritual resources available to a Christian parent can make all the difference in the world. You don't have to face this task alone or with only your own strength and understanding. You have God's promise of direction and power. If part of God's purpose is to help a parent develop patience, then blessing you with a child with attention deficit is a guaranteed way to meet that goal.

Spiritual Foundations for Parenting

If parenting any child is worth a college education, then raising an ADHD child should give you a Ph.D. The task is continuous and the challenge is great. Our spiritual foundation gives the Christian father and mother a basis to claim a victory, even when the progress reports are discouraging. In this section, I want to review our basic position between God and our children and apply it to the special needs of a child with attention deficit.

As Christians we are part of a royal priesthood (1 Peter 2:9). The priesthood of all believers means that each Christian has personal access to God. Each of us can approach God on behalf of another. We are to declare the praises of Him who called us out of darkness into light.

This has great implications for parents. We are called and ordained by God as priests for our children. This relationship involves two basic positions that we see symbolized in a liturgical form of worship. The first position is when the minister or priest faces the people, speaking to the congregation on behalf of God. The second position is when the minister or priest faces the altar, speaking to God on behalf of the people. Our responsibility to our children takes these same positions. We are called to *present God to our children* through our actions and words. We are also called to continually *present our children to God* in prayer.

One mandate for Christian parenting is found in Deuteronomy 6:4-9. This passage points out both of the positions we are to fill between God and our children.

> Hear, O Israel: The Lord our God, the Lord is one. Love the Lord your God with all your heart and with all your soul and with all your strength. These commandments that I give you today are to be upon your hearts. Impress them on your children. Talk about them when you sit at home and when you walk along the road, when you lie down and when you get up. Tie them as symbols on your hands and bind them on your foreheads. Write them on the doorframes of your houses and on your gates.

Christian parenting is based on our faith in God. We are to first love God with our whole being. The rest of the injunctions follow from that requirement. This passage suggests that we have four means of presenting God to our children, and one means of presenting our children to God.

Example

The first way we present God to our children is by our *example*. We are to "impress" our children in matters of faith and of life. We do this by action as well as word (1 Kings 9:4; 2 Chronicles 17:3; 2 Timothy 1:5). The old saying, "Do as I say, not as I do," simply does not work. A child will follow the example he sees every day much more than the lectures he hears about how and why he should act in certain ways. This tremendous influence starts with day one. If a teenager has received years of criticism from his parents, the effects are not going to disappear overnight.

Our example before our children should include the full range of human emotions. Reality tells us there will be days of sadness and anger, as well as days of happiness and joy. A child does not need to be privy to all the innermost feelings of his parents. However, he needs to see that a Christian can mourn a loss, feel anger over frustrations, and yet work through those events with the grace and strength of God. Our children need to see that victorious Christian living is not accomplished by eliminating all our problems. Rather, it is achieved by allowing God to work His wonders in spite of our problems.

The ADHD child encounters many frustrations. He knows very early that life can be difficult. The message we want to convey is that we serve a God who will show His power in spite of our weaknesses. The parallel of life to the presence of ADHD is clear: ADHD will not go away; life contains its inevitable problems. We have a chance to show our children that we do our very best to cope with life, and then learn to glorify God as He works through our weaknesses (2 Corinthians 12:9-10).

A child's image of God is greatly influenced by parental example. The way we set forth a standard of conduct, behavior, and worship toward God will guide our children toward an ability to see God in their lives. Our children begin to understand that God is real and vital when they see that God is authentic and active in our lives. We have said that an ADHD child needs repeated exposure to hands-on learning experiences with immediate feedback; he needs the same repetition of spiritual example. Our children should see and hear daily evidence of our faith in action.

Words

The second form of influence is through the *words* of our mouths. This is the *instruction* or teaching we provide. We are to "talk" about our love of God, our beliefs and values, and why they are important (Proverbs 22:6; Colossians 3:16; 2 Timothy 3:15). Deuteronomy 4:9 instructs us, "Teach them to your children and to their children after them." Our instruction is to be diligent and pervasive. Instruction is to take place whether we are walking in the park, fishing on a lake, or kneeling down for bedtime prayers. This instruction can be informal as well as formal. It occurs during the chat while riding in the pickup to the hardware store. Stories told at dinnertime can have a lasting impact, as well as the instruction given over devotions or at family meetings. Sometimes the message appears to be going in one ear and out the other. However, parental instruction, whether direct or indirect, guides many of the values, attitudes, opinions, and beliefs of our children. We should talk with them about their activities, so that they realize these are to be undertaken with care and thoughtfulness.

Symbols

Another form of presenting God to children is seen in verses 8 and 9 of Deuteronomy 6. We see that *pictures* and *symbols*, or the many nonverbal or aesthetic forms of communication and expression, are important ways to communicate truths about God. The way we decorate our homes can either intensify or dull an awareness of God and Jesus. We have many symbols in the church—the cross, a lamb, the alpha and omega, three intertwined circles, a Nativity scene, and various pictures or artistic renditions of religious themes. All of these objects communicate the importance of our faith and should have a place of prominence. Think back over your own life. How many sermon outlines do you remember? How many illustrations, stories, word pictures, or life experiences can you recall? Many of our recollections will contain pictures and scenes as the component of lasting spiritual influence. Be sure to draw on this source of influence for the benefit of your children.

Consequences

The next form of parental impact takes place through *consequences*. The commandments mentioned in Deuteronomy 6:6 were subject to the consequences of God's discipline. Likewise, parents are to exercise loving authority with their children (Proverbs 19:18; 23:13-14; 29:15, 17). In earlier chapters I have discussed many ways to apply consequences. You will need to draw on both positive and negative consequences. Remember to make more deposits in the relationship account than withdrawals.

This category of consequences is very practical and beneficial because it parallels the discipline of God. There are negative consequences for sin and there are positive fruits for obedience. We present part of the plan of God as we apply consequences to the actions of our children. Learn to do it effectively.

Prayer

The final injunction to parents is to present our children to God *in prayer*. We read about Abraham praying for Ishmael (Genesis 17:18), and David praying for the life of his child (2 Samuel 12:16) and for Solomon (1 Chronicles 29:19). The first chapter of Job tells us how Job made sacrifices and prayers for his children (Job 1:5). Scripture likewise describes New Testament parents who petitioned Christ for the benefit of their children (Matthew 17:15; Mark 7:26).

As parents we are to continually pray for our children as we present them to God. In addition, we are to teach them to pray. We are to petition God for their spiritual and physical well-being.

Types of Prayer

There are different kinds of prayers presented in Scripture:

Prayers of confession (Ezra 10:11; 2 Chronicles 7:14; 1 John 1:9; James 5:16)

As you deal with the frustrations and aggravations of raising an ADHD child, there may be times when your patience runs thin and you respond in ways that are unhealthy or destructive. Later you will feel convicted and go to God in confession and repentance. The magnificent grace of God extends to any and all errors of parenting you may make. Take your confession to Him and He will relieve the burden.

Prayers for guidance (2 Samuel 2:1; 1 Chronicles 14:14; Psalms 5:8; 143:10)

Prayers seeking God's guidance are very important. He has promised to give us direction for all aspects of our lives. This certainly includes the nurturing and correction of a child with attention deficit.

Your prayer can be like that of Jesus as He sought His Father's will—"Your will be done on earth as it is in heaven" (Matthew 6:10). For it is only God who can bring about the miracle of a transformed life. Praying for the knowledge of God's will and the power to carry it out helps you set aside selfish motives. Through prayer you can receive reassurance of God's presence and know He wants your child to lead a healthy and productive life.

Guidance will also come through reading God's Word. It is important to spend time in Scripture with the purpose of letting His truths speak to you. Scripture is a lamp to your feet (Psalm 119:105). It is food to help you grow (1 Peter 2:2). God's Word is a life-giving force (Ezekiel 37:1-14). It has the power to save (Romans 1:16). Scripture gives hope (Romans 15:4), and it will help probe and illuminate your specific needs (Hebrews 4:12). I don't believe one can spend time in Scripture with the specific intent of having God speak to you, and have that time prove fruitless. This applies to your personal life as well as to the task of parenting your child.

Prayers for wisdom (2 Chronicles 1:10; Psalm 90:12; Ephesians 1:17; Colossians 1:9)

Wisdom is more than knowledge of basic facts and principles. It is the application of understanding in prudent and thoughtful ways that reflect discernment and spiritual comprehension. It certainly requires the wisdom of Solomon to know when to correct an ADHD child for noncompliance rather than to instruct him for incompetent behavior. It takes experience with the child in order to make these distinctions, and it takes wisdom to know the best ways of communicating. Basic techniques and strategies, such as those found in this book, are helpful places to begin. However, your requests for holy insight can make all the difference in the world.

Prayers of thanksgiving (Deuteronomy 8:10; Psalm 100:4; Colossians 1:12; 1 Thessalonians 5:18)

God will answer your prayers in some form. You will see your children pass milestones of development. Seemingly insurmountable problems will be resolved. Then it is most important to thank God for His mercy and answers to your petitions.

Prayers of adoration (Psalms 21:13; 47:9; 57:11; 108:5; Acts 4:24; 16:25)

He is awesome and worthy to be praised. God is to be exalted above all things. Our children need to see and hear our praises directed to God for the blessings He bestows on all of His children.

Prayers of meditation (Psalms 4:4; 19:14; 104:34; 119:99)

These are times when we search our hearts for answers to life's vexing problems. We dwell on the Word of God and ask that it be made real and alive in our daily lives. This is the essence of meditation. We examine the precepts of God and consider His ways as they relate to coping with the demands of an ADHD child. The result is insight that transcends the mere teaching of men. Meditation and prayer open our eyes to the richness of God's teaching and direction for our lives.

Prayers of intercession on behalf of our children (Luke 22:32; John 14:16; 17:9)

Just as Jesus through the work of the Holy Spirit intercedes for us, so we petition God for the needs of our children. Sometimes our intercession is for their very salvation and eternal destiny. At other times, you may approach the throne of God for success in school or friendships for your ADHD child.

You may also need to have periods of prayer and fasting (Joel 2:12; Matthew 6:18; Acts 14:23). This is valuable when you confront serious obstacles in your child's progress toward health and maturity. It gives a time of focus and concentration for your prayers and sharpens your ability to pray for specific needs and concerns for your child.

Prayers of deliverance (2 Kings 19:19; Psalm 91:3; 2 Corinthians 1:10; 2 Timothy 4:18; 2 Peter 2:9)

Our children may fall into bondage, sin, or under demonic attack. It takes the mighty name of Jesus Christ through His shed blood on the cross and the power of Almighty God to confound and defeat the wily ways of Satan. There is no question about the eventual winner in the claim for our eternal lives. God will triumph in the battle for our children, including the struggles of an ADHD child. Yet there may be times when we need to call on the warriors of heaven and light to help us fend off the entanglements of the prince of darkness.

Short arrow prayers (Nehemiah 2:4; Ecclesiastes 5:2)

This is perfectly acceptable. In fact, God has instructed us to keep our prayers short and to the point. If we pray only to hear ourselves or to impress others, God will not hear us. Maybe you are in the process of correcting your child right in the middle of the produce section at the grocery store. Time and circumstance won't allow a bended knee or lengthy discourse with God. You simply utter a request for guidance and go on with your discipline. When we have an ongoing communion and relationship with God, we don't have to spend twenty minutes giving the spiritual passwords to gain His attention. He is there immediately whenever we need Him. Prayer is a pretty simple activity. Your prayers do not need to be wordy or complex. A simple expression of adoration for God, followed by statements of confession, need, and thankfulness, is sufficient. The Lord's Prayer is a perfect model (Matthew 6:9-13; Luke 11:2-4).

I know you may have called out to God in times of crisis and wondered if He would ever answer. Why does your child have to struggle with problems of inattention, low self-esteem, and conflict with family members? All of us have had feelings of being abandoned and ignored. Biblical heroes such as Jeremiah and David expressed the same feelings. God has made some rather remarkable promises, and He does not lie. Here are a few of those promises:

- God will answer our prayers (Mark 11:24).
- God has never failed to keep His promises (1 Kings 8:56).
- God has guaranteed to be faithful (Deuteronomy 7:9; 1 Corinthians 1:9).
- God will deliver us from afflictions (Psalms 30:5; 41:3).
- God knows our limits (Isaiah 43:2; 1 Corinthians 10:13).
- God will comfort us in hard times (Isaiah 43:2).
- God will help remove obstacles (Luke 17:6).

Biblical Principles for Structure

The ADHD child needs consistent structure. All children do. It's just that the ADHD child needs more of it, and for a longer period of time. To this end, in earlier chapters I have described many examples of structure that can apply to your child. The principles underlying these techniques are identified in Scripture.

The first principle is clarity (Matthew 5:37)

Because you are competing with a distractible and inattentive nature, you should make your instructions clear and simple. When you tell your child no, you should act accordingly. It only makes the problem worse if an ADHD child learns that if he badgers Mom long enough, she will eventually give in. Make your rules and stick to them unless there is clear reason to change. The rules, and consequences for violating those rules, should be spelled out clearly. Rewards for success should be equally clear.

The second principle is consistency (Psalm 15:4)

This verse talks about a man keeping his word. There are several types of consistency that affect an ADHD child. These were discussed earlier in chapter 5. The first is to be consistent between parents, the second is to be consistent over time, the third is consistency from place to place, and the last form of consistency is to make sure all of a child's caretakers are following the same procedures.

Avoid making promises you aren't sure you can keep. It may be better not to say anything about a future event if you aren't sure it will happen. For example, you may want to take your child to the indoor playground that just opened near the shopping center. If Dad doesn't have to work overtime this coming Saturday, the family can probably go. It's better to wait until you know for sure that Dad is available before telling your child. Otherwise, you will have to deal with the overreactive outburst of feelings when Dad calls and says he has to work Saturday.

Regularity is the third principle we see in Scripture that applies to the ADHD child (2 Timothy 1:5)

Just as Paul saw sincere faith in Timothy's mother and grandmother, so parents today are to be diligent, persistent, and regular. ADHD children are demanding. Patience will run out. Cross words will be spoken, and grace must be extended again and again. Repeatedly *tell* your child you love him, and then *show* it on a regular and continuing basis.

Another idea we see in Scripture is the importance of enforceability (Ecclesiastes 8:11)

Consequences, whether positive or negative, need to be applied immediately for the best effect. Parents should not make idle threats. If you can't carry out a threat, don't make it (Proverbs 29:20). I have heard of statements like, "Behave yourself or I'll kick you out of the car and make you walk home." There is no way a responsible parent is going to make a six-year-old child walk the busy streets or a lonely country road back to his house. Hasty comments are generally harmful comments. ADHD children have trouble using rules and abstract values to control their behavior. They are more governed by the immediate. So parents need to enforce rules immediately. Do not say, "Wait till your father gets home." The child will have forgotten what the consequence was all about, and the effect will be lost.

Finally, we see the principle of fairness (Genesis 25:28; 37:3)

These Old Testament references show the human resentment that comes when a child perceives he isn't being treated fairly. Granted, children often confuse fairness and equality. Fairness occurs when your expectations match the abilities of your child. Parents need to discuss their mutual expectations for their ADHD child. These expectations should correspond with both developmental considerations and known ADHD features.

Consider the differences between *unwilling* and *unable* described earlier. It is unfair to reprimand or punish a child for doing something that is out of his control. With ADHD children, it's certainly not easy to make the distinction. But that is where experience and prayerful discernment come into action to help you "know" when to lower the boom and when to back off.

Trusting God

Being a Christian doesn't take the hard work out of raising an ADHD child. It does give you the spiritual resources to cope with the frustrations. Another key ingredient in the process is your ability to trust God for the future of your children. This task of trusting is certainly challenged by the daily drain of coping with a child who doesn't pay attention and seems to overreact to everything in his world.

"Trust in the Lord with all your heart and lean not on your own understanding; in all your ways acknowledge Him, and He will make your paths straight" (Proverbs 3:5-6). These verses capture the essence of your need to trust. Your finite understanding can only lead to incomplete efforts to manage yourself and your family. Trusting in God demands an affirmative decision. You must move through the veil of denial which shuts out the light of God. Your path will be illuminated and made straight by choosing to let God be your guide.

Trust happens with experience and grows over time. At this point you may be able to give God responsibility for only part of your life. That's OK. Give Him what you can. As you see His faithfulness in some things, you will be able to hand over more aspects of your life and your ability to parent.

Abraham is listed in the Hebrews 11 roll call of the heroes of faith. His faith did not develop overnight. Abraham was one of the Bible's greatest worriers. He worried that foreign kings would covet his beautiful wife and kill him to get her (Genesis 12:12-13; 20:11). He worried about shortages of grazing land for his animals (Genesis 13:6-8), about retaliation (Genesis 15:1), about a lack of an heir (Genesis 15:2-3), about God's possible inability to honor His covenant (Genesis 17:17-18), and about God's intent to destroy Sodom and Gomorrah (Genesis 18:23-33).

In spite of God's promises, Abraham worried that he and Sarah were too old to bear children. After the birth of Isaac, Abraham worried that God wouldn't know which of his two sons to use in fulfilling the promise of many descendants (Genesis 21:11).

It took time and experience for Abraham to become a man of faith. He grew from his experiences, just as we can. There were times Abraham took matters into his own hands, with disastrous results, just as we do. However, God was patient. Abraham became obedient and learned to trust God. You can experience the same steps to belief. Be patient with yourself; yet continue to be diligent in moving toward that greater understanding of the love and mercy of the Lord.

The role of the church in the total intervention process for ADHD children

There are several ways the church can be a resource for you and your child. The first is for the community of believers to be a source of support and encouragement for you as parents. Through Bible study groups, home meetings, and corporate fellowship, your needs for spiritual and social inspiration can be met. Take the risk to share your burden with others in the church, so they can help carry the load (Galatians 6:2).

There are practical ways your church should be able to help— baby-sitting, referral recommendations, respite care while Mom and Dad take a break, safe and secure day care, and guidance from church staff for the spiritual training of your child. Also, corporate prayer can be very important.

Ideally, the Christian education program of your church should provide a structured opportunity for your child to gain exposure to the principles of Christian living and biblical truths. The very same ideas presented earlier for classroom teachers may need to be applied to the Sunday School classroom. Your child may have been a disruptive force there before the ADHD assessment was administered and the treatment process was started. With your current understanding, take these techniques to the church context so your child is able to profit from the spiritual training offered there. Perhaps you will need to take the initiative to see that appropriate in-service training is provided to your child's teachers. The materials described in the resource section are appropriate to use. A Sunday School teacher or youth leader needs to have the same understanding about *unable* versus *unwilling* that you and the schoolteacher have acquired. Make sure the church staff have an opportunity to learn about the special characteristics and needs of a child with attention deficit. Your goal should be to have your child experience *at least* the same amount of loving concern and appropriate structure from his church learning environment as he receives from his classroom teacher.

CHAPTER TEN

COULD I ALSO HAVE ADHD?
Adult Attention
Deficit Disorder

This chapter is for those parents of attention deficit children who might wonder if this cluster of problems with attention and self-control might also apply to adults. The answer is a definite "yes."

This chapter is written to stand alone as a more complete summary of adult ADHD. There will be some overlap with the material presented earlier in the book. However, I wanted all of the information to be readily available for the person who may not take the time to read the earlier chapters. Additional information can be found by consulting the materials located in the resource section.

Introduction
Joe can't sit still in church or meetings. He squirms his way through movies and TV watching, clicking from one channel to another. He can't stand waiting for anybody or anything, and avoids lines like the plague. Read a book? Are you kidding? Joe's mind wanders so far and so fast he has no recall of what he has read.

Jim's friends call him the absent-minded professor. While Jim is obviously quite bright, he is very forgetful and disorganized. He has a hard time finishing whatever he starts and will tend to switch from task to task in a haphazard way.

Sally is known for her three D's—Disorganized, Distractible, and Discombobulated. She is distracted by the smallest event. She has trouble finishing even routine tasks. She tries to pay attention, but her mind wanders even while attempting to listen in one-on-one conversations. Sally also will erupt into a rage over small frustrations or irritations.

Do these adults have some type of diagnosable disorder, or are they just hassled and frazzled citizens living in a frenzied world? While we can't tell from these brief descriptions, we do know that the features of distractibility, restlessness, and impulsiveness are key characteristics of Attention-Deficit/Hyperactivity Disorder (ADHD). These are the same characteristics described earlier for children.

As we saw earlier, attention-deficit/hyperactivity disorder is used to describe persons who have chronic impairments in their thinking ability that affects their capacity to function in school, work, and social relationships. Persons with ADHD have more problems getting organized for work-related assignments. They have trouble attending to details and in sustaining attention and effort for assigned tasks. They may also have difficulty ignoring distractions, in keeping track of things, and in remembering what they are doing. Some adults with ADHD are chronically impulsive and hyperactive, but many will have difficulties primarily in the area of inattention and distractibility.

Research suggests that 6 to 8 percent of elementary school-age children have some type of ADHD. However, attention disorder is not just a problem of childhood. Recent studies indicate that about 50 to 80 percent of ADHD children continue to experience problems with ADHD impairments in adolescence and adulthood. There may be 5 million adults with ADHD. The features that show up in adults are quite similar to those in ADHD children. There is some tendency for hyperactive children to lose some degree of their hyperactive characteristics as they move into adulthood. However, the inattentive, forgetful, and distractible features tend to persist.

ADHD adults are at greater risk for a variety of problems. Studies have shown that individuals with ADHD are more likely to have problems with school functioning, thinking skills, social skills, substance abuse, legal difficulties, and even things like speeding tickets and auto accidents.

Symptoms and Signs of ADHD

There are three categories of primary symptoms of ADHD: inattention, hyperactivity, and impulsivity.

Inattentive features would include having difficulty with details or a tendency to make careless mistakes, sustaining attention, listening, finishing tasks, organization, sustaining mental effort, losing things, being easily distracted, and being forgetful.

Hyperactive characteristics include being fidgety, having a hard time remaining seated or staying in one place, feeling restless, difficulty completing activities that require quiet, feeling tense or driven, and talking too much.

Impulsive symptoms include blurting out answers, difficulty awaiting turns, and often interrupting or intruding on others.

There are numerous other secondary symptoms of ADHD that are often seen by counselors who work with attention deficit adults. These include a chronic sense of underachievement, low self-esteem, frequent procrastination, and the starting of many projects but trouble with follow-through. Also seen is a tendency to be easily bored, a high need for thrill-seeking or constant stimulation, the tendency to be impatient, and a low tolerance for frustration. Many adults with attention disorder also display mood swings, depression, and a tendency toward addictive behavior. In addition, they often have family histories with ADHD symptoms, or the presence of addictive behaviors, or other problems with impulse control or mood.

It should also be pointed out that most ADHD adults are creative, intuitive, talented, or intelligent in many ways. Even if disorganized and distractible, many of these persons have gifts and abilities that are worthy of cultivation and affirmation.

Causes of ADHD

The exact causes of attention disorder are not fully understood. However, with the large effort being put forth to discover its origin, we have begun to gather convincing evidence of numerous factors associated with ADHD. The first category includes various agents that can lead to brain injury or abnormal brain development. This can include trauma, disease, fetal exposure to alcohol and tobacco, and early exposure to high levels of lead.

Diet has been proposed by some as a factor in attention disorder. However, there is no consistent scientific evidence that sugar in any form, additives, preservatives, or the presence or absence of vitamins or minerals are a significant cause of ADHD symptoms. What we eat is a major factor in our health and well-being. Some children and adults may have definite negative reactions to certain elements in their diet. If so, this information should be used to guide their eating habits. Yet, at this time, there is no persuasive evidence regarding diet as a significant source for ADHD.

The major evidence points to diminished activity in certain brain regions and heredity as the most likely causes of most forms of attention disorder. From the available research on the brain, ADHD is essentially a problem with "putting on the brakes." When you step on the brake pedal of your car, that action is transmitted, by means of brake fluid flowing through the brake lines, to each of the wheels of your car. The increased pressure of the brake fluid then activates the braking mechanism on the wheels, and you begin to slow down. However, if you are low on brake fluid, or have a leak in the system, the brakes may not respond precisely the way you want. You may want to stop or slow down, step on the brakes, but nothing happens. This is roughly what happens in the brain of a person with ADHD.

The cause of ADHD is understood to be dysregulation of certain neurotransmitters in the brain which make it harder for a person to sort out or regulate certain internal and external stimuli. These deficits in brain neurochemistry make it harder to concentrate and focus. Several neurotransmitters, including dopamine and norepinephrine, probably affect the production, use, and regulation of other neurotransmitters, as well as the functioning of some brain structures. These problems with regulation of certain brain functions seem to be centralized in the frontal lobes, which makes it more difficult for an ADHD person to control input from other parts of the brain. The frontal region of the brain, which is just behind the forehead, is said to control the "executive functions" of our behavior. The executive function is responsible for memory, organization, inhibiting behavior, sustaining attention, initiating self-control, and planning for the future. Without enough dopamine and related neurotransmitters, the frontal lobes are understimulated and unable to perform their complex functions effectively.

Distractibility and inattention, from a brain-function perspective, are the failure to "stop" or tune out unwanted internal thoughts or outside stimuli, such as a voice in the other room, or a bird outside the window. Rapid mood changes and hypersensitivity are the results of the brain having more difficulty moderating those parts of the brain which regulate motor movements and emotional responses. Finally, an ADHD person's difficulty with hyperactivity and impulsive behavior may stem from frontal lobe deficiencies which make it hard to wait, delay gratification, and inhibit actions. All of these characteristics can then interfere with a person's memory and ability to learn and efficiently process information.

Whatever the exact nature of the brain structure or chemistry behind ADHD, there appears to be a strong genetic basis for its occurrence. Studies show that between 20 and 30 percent of all ADHD children have at least one parent with attention disorder. Studies of identical and fraternal twins have found a significantly higher incidence of ADHD in identical rather than fraternal twins. This strongly suggests a genetic predisposition to the disorder. Studies in molecular biology also support the idea that ADHD is an inherited condition.

The scientific support for the fact that ADHD is a genetically based neurobiological disorder can be a great help to adults with attention disorder who have previously believed they were lazy, stupid, or careless. These symptoms we have described are not just a result of poor parenting, faulty education, lack of self-control, insufficient motivation, or lack of trying. While each of these factors can intensify or complicate the problems associated with attention disorder, they are not the basic causes for the condition. This fact can be a great source of empowerment and liberation for the adult who has struggled with self-blame and shame for years. Attention disorder is a neurobiological problem that has significant impact in the daily life of the ADHD adult. It is not his fault, yet we can offer hope because of the many strategies available to help him cope with this disorder.

ADHD and Individual Responsibility

Having touched on the neurobiological causes of ADHD, we still need to emphasize the place for individual responsibility. Once an attention disorder has been diagnosed, each person must be accountable to learn how to deal effectively with the problems associated with ADHD. The presence of the disorder should not be an excuse for irresponsibility. "I'm sorry I was late and forgot to pick you up. You'll have to excuse me because I have an attention disorder," might be the plea of some ADHD adults. This is not the proper perspective.

For example, it is not a person's fault that he has become near-sighted and requires correction for adequate vision. It is his responsibility to wear his glasses so that he has adequate vision, especially when driving, so that he is not a danger to others. This principle also applies to adults with ADHD. It is not their fault they have the condition, but it is their job to learn how to cope and accommodate in the most effective manner possible. This not only brings a greater level of personal accomplishment and satisfaction, it also contributes to harmony and trust among the ADHD adult's family and friends.

Diagnosis of ADHD

In spite of the increased knowledge about attention disorder, the accurate diagnosis of this condition remains somewhat difficult and subjective. There is no single test for an attention disorder. The process will involve tracing patterns of behavior through childhood and adolescence, as well as evaluating the person's current emotional, social, and intellectual problems. All of this should be completed by a professional trained in the area of diagnosis and treatment of ADHD. We should remember that attention disorder is relatively uncommon and affects only about 2 to 5 percent of the adult population. While it is a very real condition that accounts for distress in many adults, it is important to be cautious and thorough in coming to a final diagnosis.

Generally, the diagnostic process should include the following areas of assessment:

The first is a review of the person's childhood with the purpose of identifying the defining characteristics of attention disorder. This includes the features of inattention and/or impulsivity and hyperactivity. Even if the person was never identified as having ADHD, the process will endeavor to determine if some of the features were present but never diagnosed. Old report cards, teacher evaluations, past test results, self-descriptions, background information forms, and descriptions from family members may be used.

The second component is to identify if there are current ADHD symptoms present in the day-to-day functioning of the adult. This part of the evaluation will look for both the primary and secondary signs and symptoms described earlier. Clinical interviews, rating scales, selective tests, job evaluations, and corroborative descriptions by family, friends, or work associates are used here.

The third aspect of the diagnosis is to confirm that these symptoms are producing impairment in many areas of the person's life, such as on the job, in school, social acceptance, daily responsibilities, relationships, marriage, and emotional adjustment. The same methods of interview, review of past documentation, and rating forms as used previously will be applied to this diagnostic feature.

The final aspect of the assessment process is to identify other medical or emotional conditions that might masquerade as attention disorder or may be occurring along with the ADHD. This would include screening for alcohol and related substance abuse problems. A thorough medical and psychological history, along with specific tests, will be used to help determine the most effective course of treatment for the person's particular constellation of symptoms. Many persons with attention disorder also have some type of learning disability. Consequently, tests of learning potential and achievement may be given to identify the role of learning in a person's difficulties.

If you suspect you may have ADHD, discuss the idea with your medical doctor. If you are seeing a mental health professional, ask his or her opinion. If it seems appropriate, ask your doctor for a referral to someone with expertise in the diagnostic procedure. Another way to find a professional trained in diagnosing adult attention disorder is to check with a local chapter of CH.A.D.D. (Children and Adults with Attention Deficit Disorder, 499 NW 70th Avenue, Suite 109, Plantation, FL 33317; phone 305-587-3700; web site www.chadd.org). They may be able to help you find an experienced professional in your area. You may also know others who have attention disorder and who have gone through the process. Ask them who they used and their degree of satisfaction with the resource.

In selecting a professional, you will want to know his or her level of training and experience in working with adult ADHD. Ask about the nature and cost of the assessment, as well as the possible progression and components of treatment. To be successful, your care provider should be personable and concerned about your situation. He or she should be able to communicate and explain things to you in an open and understandable manner, as well as respond to your questions in a favorable way. Your provider should also be open to family involvement in your treatment, as well as to other aspects of a multidisciplinary or team effort on your behalf.

As a Christian, you will also be looking for a professional who has a sensitivity and ability to deal with spiritual issues, and is one who can relate faith and practice to your needs. Your pastor may be a source of referral for Christian professionals. You may also want to look up Christian counseling centers in your area and ask if they have a person on staff who specializes in adult ADHD. Remember, just because a person is a Christian doesn't mean he or she has the other qualifications you need. Be sure to ask the various questions described earlier.

Treatment of Adult ADHD

Approximately 70 to 90 percent of adults with attention disorder find their symptoms improve with medication. These persons are more able to concentrate on formerly difficult material or tasks. They are able to maintain more self-control, and they are able to calm those restless behaviors.

As helpful as medication can be, it is not a cure or a panacea for all the problems associated with ADHD. There are some for whom medication does not work. And even for those who find benefits from medication, there is usually a host of associated features that require continual treatment in the form of therapy, training, or education.

Medication

Because medication has proven helpful with a vast majority of ADHD adults, drug therapy has become a chief element in the treatment process. Two types of drugs have been proven to be most effective in treating attention disorder—stimulants and antidepressants. Stimulants, such as Ritalin, Dexedrine, and Adderall, are believed to increase the amount of dopamine available to the brain. In some way these medications increase the braking power of the brain over behavior. The result is often improved ability to concentrate, sustain attention, and maintain effort on a task.

Sometimes other medications prove helpful. These include antidepressants such as Tofranil, Norpramin, Elavil, and Prozac. These drugs were developed to treat depression, but they have been found to be helpful with many of the symptoms of attention disorder. Apparently, these drugs increase the amount of norepinephrine and serotonin, as well as dopamine, available for work within the brain, especially in the frontal lobe region. They restore a proper balance of neurotransmitters to the brain, which allows messages about concentration and behavior to be more efficiently processed. These medications can also be used along with stimulants when there are accompanying problems with moods, such as depression, anxiety, and panic reactions, or problems with sleeping. The results may include less irritability, fewer temper outbursts, elevation of mood, and less anxiety or worry.

There can be side effects with any of these medications. These can include difficulty sleeping, decreased appetite, irritability, headaches, stomachaches, dizziness, dry mouth, diarrhea, and anxiety. How you will be affected depends on many factors. Which drug or combination of medications will work best for any given individual depends on his own particular brain chemistry and constellation of symptoms. The process of finding the correct medication and the appropriate dosage is often a process of trial and error, so you will need to take a patient and persistent approach to the process (not easy when you have ADHD!). The good news is that the majority of people with attention disorder report that coping with the side effects and/or having to try several different medications or dosages is a small price to pay for the benefits medication eventually provides. Each person has to make his own decision about the relative merits and disadvantages of medication.

Additional aspects of treatment

There are numerous components to a comprehensive treatment plan for attention disorders. These can include education about ADHD, individual and family counseling, career counseling and planning, skill building in time management and organization, support groups, coaching, and treatment for addictive behaviors.

Usually, if drug or alcohol abuse or other serious addictions are present, the first order of business is to start a treatment program for these issues. Work on the ADHD features will not be effective if the person is actively caught up in an addictive cycle.

The educational process begins with the diagnostic process and continues when a positive diagnosis is reached. Now the person needs complete information about ADHD and how it affects his or her life. Books, tapes, classes, seminars, and support groups can play an important part in fulfilling the educational component of treatment.

Counseling will often be an important part of learning to deal with the emotional, relational, spiritual, and practical aspects of attention disorder. Traditional insight-oriented psychotherapy generally has not proved effective for dealing with ADHD symptoms.

However, a lifetime of frustration and failure can leave some adults with a need for the healing of emotional and psychological wounds. For them, individual therapy will be helpful. Others will choose to focus on behavior strategies and skill building for concerns such as time management, procrastination, money management, and memory assistance, which will help them accommodate or compensate for their attentional deficits.

Memory problems are frequently a cognitive deficit experienced by many persons with ADHD. Working with a counselor or consultant, ADHD adults can learn compensatory memory systems. These can include written memory devices such as a daily planner, electronic systems such as a pocket computer, auditory reminders such as a tape recorder or electronic timer, and task-specific aids such as a pill alarm or melodic key-finder.

Marriage and family counseling can be an opportunity for family members to be educated about the realities of ADHD and how problem-solving, conflict resolution, parenting, communication skills, and teamwork can be applied to the situation.

It will be important to set realistic goals and then devise appropriate, but manageable, plans and sequences of objectives to achieve those goals. Sometimes, the ADHD adult may need to hire a consultant for specific projects, such as organizing his home or office, and then monitoring his progress so that the organization can be maintained.

Career counseling and planning can be very helpful. Many ADHD adults are mismatched to their jobs. They may be very good at meeting people, for example, so they go into sales. However, when required to complete the paperwork attached to client follow-up, many persons with attention disorder run into problems. Career counseling can help identify personal strengths and match them to the best work environment.

The concept of coaching has been applied to the process of learning more effective ways to cope with the problems associated with ADHD. A coach is someone, usually not a family member, who is willing to communicate with the ADHD adult several times each week for several months. Either by phone or in person, the person communicates with his or her coach and they review goals and plans necessary to implement desired changes. This accountability relationship provides ongoing feedback, encouragement, and instruction which makes movement toward established goals more successful. For the Christian, it is also a format in which prayer and fellowship can be used to nurture a person toward greater spiritual fulfillment.

Attention-Deficit/Hyperactivity Disorder is a reality affecting millions of adults. While there is no cure, a great deal of knowledge can be applied to the processes of diagnosing and treating this disorder. There is every reason to be hopeful. May God bless as you take this information and apply it to yourself or to someone you love.

References

Children and Adults with Attention Deficit Disorders (CH.A.D.D.) *ADD & Adults: Strategies for Success from CH.A.D.D.* (Plantation, Fla.: CH.A.D.D., 1997).

Sam Goldstein, *Managing Attention and Learning Disorders in Late Adolescence & Adulthood: A Guide for Practitioners* (New York: John Wiley, 1997).

Edward Hallowell & John Ratey, *Driven to Distraction* (New York: Pantheon Press, 1994).

Kate Kelly & Peggy Ramundo, *You Mean I'm Not Lazy, Stupid Or Crazy?* (Cincinnati: Tyrell & Jerem Press, 1993).

Kevin Murphy, *Out of the Fog. Treatment Options and Coping Strategies for Adult Attention Deficit Disorder* (New York: Skylight Press, 1995).

Kathleen Nadeau (ed.), *A Comprehensive Guide to Attention Deficit Disorders in Adults* (New York: Brunner/Mazel, 1995).

Thomas Whiteman & Michele Novotni, *Adult ADD* (Colorado Springs: Pinon Press, 1995).

PART THREE

Resources for ADHD

"So do not fear, for I am with you; do not be dismayed, for I am your God. I will strengthen you and help you; I will uphold you with My righteous right hand."

Isaiah 41:10

Resources

Books for Parents and Teachers

Alexander-Roberts, C., *The ADHD Parenting Handbook* (Dallas: Taylor Publishing, 1994).

Alexander-Roberts, C., *ADHD & Teens* (Dallas: Taylor Publishing, 1995).

Bain, L.J., *Attention Deficit Disorders* (New York: Dell Publishing, 1991).

Barkley, R.A., *Taking Charge of ADHD* (New York: Guilford Press, 1995).

CH.A.D.D., *ADD and Adolescence: Strategies for Success from CH.A.D.D.* (Plantation, Fla.: CH.A.D.D., 1996).

Conners, C.K., *Feeding the Brain: How Foods Affect Children* (New York: Plenum Press, 1989).

Copeland, E., & Love, V., *Attention Please!* (Plantation, Fla.: Specialty Press, 1995).

Dendy, C.A., *Teenagers with ADD: A Parent's Guide* (Rockville, Md.: Woodbine House, 1995).

Dobson, J.C., *Solid Answers* (Wheaton, Ill.: Tyndale House, 1997).

Flick, G.L., *Power Parenting for Children with ADD/ADHD* (West Nyack, N.Y.: The Center for Applied Research in Education, 1996).

Fowler, M.C. *CHADD Educators Manual* (Plantation, Fla.: CASET Associates, 1992).

Fowler, M.C., *Maybe You Know My Kid* (New York: Birch Lane Press, 1990).

Garber, S.W., Garber, M.D., & Spizman, R.F., *If Your Child Is Hyperactive, Inattentive, Impulsive, Distractible . . . Helping the ADD Hyperactive Child* (New York: Villard Books, 1990).

Goldstein, S., & Goldstein, M., *Hyperactivity: Why Won't My Child Pay Attention?* (New York: John Wiley, 1992).

Goldstein, S., & Goldstein, M., *Parent's Guide: Attention-Deficit Hyperactivity Disorder* (Salt Lake City: Neurology, Learning & Behavior Center, 1990).

Gordon, M., *ADHD/Hyperactivity: A Consumer's Guide* (DeWitt, N.Y.: GSI Publications, 1991).

Hartman, T., *Attention Deficit Disorder: A Different Perception* (Penn Valley, Calif.: Underwood Books, 1993).

Ingersoll, B., & Goldstein, S., *Attention Deficit Disorder and Learning Disabilities: Realities, Myths, and Controversial Treatments* (New York: Doubleday, 1993).

Juern J., *A Christian Educator's Guide to the Attention Deficit Disorders* (Milwaukee: Kremer Publications, 1995).

Kelley, M.L., *School-Home Notes: Promoting Children's Classroom Success* (New York: Guilford Press, 1990).

Martin, G.L., *Help! My Child Isn't Learning* (Colorado Springs: Focus on the Family, 1995).

Maxey, D.W., *How to Own and Operate an Attention-Deficit Kid* (Charlottesville, Va.: HAAD, 106 South St., Suite 207, Charlottesville, VA 22901, 1989).

McCarney, S.B., & Bauer, A.M., *The Parent's Guide to Attention-Deficit Disorders* (Columbia: Hawthorne, 1990).

McCarney, S.B., *The Attention Deficit Disorders Intervention Manual-School Version* (Columbia, Mo.: Hawthorne, 1989).

McEwan, E.K., *Attention Deficit Disorder* (Wheaton, Ill.: Harold Shaw, 1995).

Moss, R.A., *Why Johnny Can't Concentrate: Coping with Attention-Deficit Problems* (New York: Bantam Books, 1990).

Parker, H.C., *The ADD Hyperactivity Handbook for Schools* (Plantation, Fla.: Impact Publications, 1991).

Parker, H.C., *ADAPT: Attention Deficit Accommodation Plan for Teaching* (Plantation, Fla.: Specialty Press, 1992).

Parker, H., & Gordon, M., *Teaching the Child with Attention Deficit Disorders: A Slide Program for In-Service Teacher Training* (DeWitt, N.Y.: GSI Publications, 1992).

Pierangelo, R., & Jacoby, R., *Parents' Complete Special Education Guide: Tips, Techniques, & Materials for Helping Your Child Succeed in*

School and Life (West Nyack, N.Y.: The Center for Applied Research in Education, 1996).

Rief, S.F., *How to Reach and Teach ADD/ADHD Children* (West Nyack, N.Y.: The Center for Applied Research in Education, 1993).

Severson, R.W., *Can't You Sit Still? Adoption and Attention Deficit Hyperactivity Disorder* (Dallas: House of Tomorrow Productions, 1992).

Silver, L.B., *Dr. Larry Silver's Advice to Parents on Attention-Deficit Hyperactivity Disorder* (Washington, D.C.: American Psychiatric Press, 1993).

Taylor, J.F., *Helping Your Hyperactive Child* (Rocklin, Calif.: Prima Publishing & Communications, 1990).

Warren, P., & Capehart, J., *You & Your A.D.D. Child* (Nashville: Thomas Nelson, 1995).

Weiss, L., *Give Your ADD Teen a Chance* (Colorado Springs: Pinon Press, 1996).

Zeigler Dendy, C.A., *Teenagers with ADD: A Parent's Guide* (Rockville, Md.: Woodbine House, 1995).

Books for Adult ADHD

Children and Adults with Attention Deficit Disorders (CH.A.D.D.), *ADD & Adults: Strategies for Success from CH.A.D.D.* (Plantation, Fla.: CH.A.D.D., 1997).

Fowler, Rick, & Fowler, Jerilyn, *"Honey Are You Listening?" : How Attention Deficit Disorder Could Be Affecting Your Marriage* (Nashville: Thomas Nelson, 1995).

Goldstein, Sam, *Managing Attention and Learning Disorders in Late Adolescence & Adulthood: A Guide for Practitioners* (New York: John Wiley, 1997).

Gordon, M., & McClure, F.D., *The Down and Dirty Guide to Adult Attention Deficit Disorder* (DeWitt, N.Y.: GSI Publications, 1995).

Hallowell, Edward, & Ratey, John, *Driven to Distraction* (New York: Pantheon Press, 1994).

Kelly, Kate, & Ramundo, Peggy, *You Mean I'm Not Lazy, Stupid or Crazy?!* (Cincinnati: Tyrell & Jerem Press, 1993).

Latham, Peter S., & Latham, Patricia H., *Succeeding in the Workplace. Attention Deficit Disorder and Learning Disabilities in the Workplace: A Guide for Success* (Washington, D.C.: JKL Communications, 1994).

Latham, Peter S., & Latham, Patricia H., *Attention Deficit Disorder and the Law: A Guide for Advocates* (Washington, D.C.: JKL Communications, 1992).

Murphy, Kevin, *Out of the Fog. Treatment Options and Coping Strategies for Adult Attention Deficit Disorder* (New York: Skylight Press, 1995).

Nadeau, Kathleen, *A User-Friendly Guide to Understanding Adult*

ADD (New York: Brunner/Mazel, 1996).

Nadeau, Kathleen (ed.), *A Comprehensive Guide to Attention Deficit Disorders in Adults* (New York: Brunner/Mazel, 1995).

Nadeau, Kathleen, *College Survival Guide for Students with ADD or LD* (New York: Brunner/Mazel, 1994).

Quinn, Patricia (ed.), *ADD and the College Student* (New York: Brunner/Mazel, 1993).

Weiss, Lynn, *Attention Deficit Disorder in Adults* (Dallas: Taylor Publishing, 1992).

Weiss, Lynn, *Attention Deficit Disorder in Adults Workbook* (Dallas: Taylor Publishing, 1994).

Whiteman, Thomas, & Novotni, Michele, *Adult ADD* (Colorado Springs: Pinon Press, 1995).

Books for Children

Bauer, K., *Active Andy: An Elementary School Child's Guide to Understanding ADHD* (Wauwatosa, Wisc.: IMDW Publications, 1993).

Corman, C., & Trevino, E., *Eukee the Jumpy Jumpy Elephant* (Plantation, Fla.: Specialty Press, 1995).

Frank, K., & Smith, S.J., *Getting a Grip on ADD: A Kid's Guide to Understanding and Coping with Attention Disorders* (Minneapolis: Educational Media Corporation, 1994).

Galvin, M., *Otto Learns about His Medicine. A Story about Medication for Hyperactive Children* (New York: Magination Press, 1988).

Gehret, J., *Eagle Eyes. A Child's View of Attention-Deficit Disorder* (Fairport, N.Y.: Verbal Images Press, 1991).

Gordon, M., *I Would If I Could: A Teenager's Guide to ADHD/Hyperactivity* (DeWitt, N.Y.: GSI Publications, 1992).

Gordon, M., *Jumpin' Johnny. Get Back to Work. A Child's Guide to ADHD/Hyperactivity* (DeWitt, N.Y.: GSI Publications, 1991).

Gordon, M., *My Brother's a World-Class Pain: A Sibling's Guide to ADHD* (DeWitt, N.Y.: GSI Publications, 1991).

Moss, D.M., *Shelley, the Hyperactive Turtle* (Rockville, Md.: Woodbine House, 1989).

Nadeau, K.G., & Dixon, E.B., *Learning to Slow Down and Pay Attention* (Annandale, Va.: Chesapeake Psychological Services, 1991).

Parker, R.N., *Making the Grade: An Adolescent's Struggle with ADD* (Plantation, Fla.: Impact Publications, 1992).

Parker, R.N., *Slam Dunk: A Young Boy's Struggle with ADD* (Plantation, Fla.: Impact Publications, 1995).

Quinn, P.O., & Stern, J., *Putting on the Brakes* (New York: Magination Press, 1992).

Shapiro, L., *Jumpin' Jake Settle Down: A Workbook to Help Impulsive Children Learn to Think Before They Act* (King of Prussia, Pa.: The

Center for Applied Psychology, 1994).

Shapiro, L., *Sometimes I Drive My Mom Crazy. But I Know She's Crazy About Me* (King of Prussia, Pa.: The Center for Applied Psychology, 1993).

Books for Professionals

Barkley, R.A., *Attention Deficit Hyperactivity Disorder. A Handbook for Diagnosis and Treatment* (New York: Guilford Press, 1990).

Barkley, R.A., *Defiant Children: A Clinician's Manual for Assessment and Parent Training (2nd ed.)* (New York: Guilford Press, 1997).

Copeland, E.D., *Medications for Attention Disorders (ADHD/ADD) and Related Medical Problems* (Atlanta: SPI Press, 1991).

DuPaul, G. L., & Stoner, G., *ADHD in the Schools: Assessment and Intervention Strategies* (New York: Guilford Press, 1994).

Goldstein, S., *Understanding and Managing Children's Classroom Behavior* (New York: John Wiley, 1995).

Goldstein, S., & Goldstein, M., *Managing Attention Disorders in Children* (New York: John Wiley & Sons, 1990).

Gordon, M., & Irwin, M., *The Diagnosis & Treatment of ADD/ADHD: A No-Nonsense Guide for Primary Care Physicians* (DeWitt, N.Y.: GSI Publications, 1997).

Robin, A.L., & Foster, S.L., *Negotiating Parent-Adolescent Conflict: A Behavioral Family Systems Approach* (New York: Guilford Press, 1989).

Silver, L.B., *Attention Deficit Hyperactivity Disorder. A Clinical Guide to Diagnosis and Treatment* (Washington, D.C.: American Psychiatric Press, 1994).

Weiss, G., & Hechtman, L.T., *Hyperactive Children Grown Up (2nd ed.)* (New York: Guilford Press, 1995).

Wender, P.H., *Attention-Deficit Hyperactivity Disorder in Adults* (New York: Oxford University Press, 1995).

Werry, J., & Aman, M., *Practitioner's Guide to Psychoactive Drugs for Children and Adolescents* (New York: Plenum Press, 1993).

Resources for Teaching Social Skills

Most of these materials can be obtained from the A.D.D. WareHouse (800) 233-9273 or from Childswork/Childsplay (800) 962-1141. Obtain their catalogs for a complete description of these and other materials that can be used for teaching social skills, self-control, and study skills.

Camp, B.W., & Bash, M.A., *Think Aloud. Increasing Social and Cognitive Skills: A Problem-Solving Program for Children* (Champaign, Ill.: Research Press, 1985).

Berg, B., *The Self-Control Game* (Cognitive-Behavioral Resources,

265 Canterbury Dr., Dayton, OH 45429). Other titles include: *The Anger Control Game, The Social Skills Game,* and *The Self-Concept Game.*

Braswell, L., & Bloomquist, M.L., *Cognitive-Behavioral Therapy with ADHD Children* (New York: Guilford Press, 1991).

Drew, Naomi (ed.), *Learning the Skills of Peacemaking* (Minneapolis: Free Spirit Press, 1997).

Duke, M., & Nowicki, S., *Helping the Child Who Doesn't Fit In* (Atlanta: Peachtree, 1993).

Elardo, P., & Cooper, M., *AWARE: Activities for Social Development* (Menlo Park, Calif.: Addison-Wesley, 1977).

Goldstein, A.P., *The Prepare Curriculum: Teaching Prosocial Competencies* (Champaign, Ill.: Research Press, 1988).

Hazel, J.S., Bragg Schumaker, J., Sherman, J.A., & Sheldon-Wildgen, J., *Asset: A Social Skills Program for Adolescents,* video program, (Champaign, Ill.: Research Press, 1981).

Huggins, P., *Helping Kids Handle Anger. Teaching Self-Control* (Longmont, Colo.: Sopris West, Inc., 1990).

Kendall, P.C., *Stop and Think Workbook* (238 Meeting House Lane, Merion Station, PA 19066, 1988).

McGinnis, E., & Goldstein, A.P., *Skillstreaming in Early Childhood* (Champaign, Ill.: Research Press, 1990).

McGinnis, E., & Goldstein, A.P., *Skillstreaming the Elementary School Child* (Champaign, Ill.: Research Press, 1997).

McGinnis, E., & Goldstein, A.P., *Skillstreaming the Adolescent* (Champaign, Ill.: Research Press, 1997).

Shure, M.B., *I Can Problem Solve (ICPS), Preschool, Kindergarten-Primary, Intermediate Elementary* (Champaign, Ill.: Research Press, 1992).

Stanfield, James, *Be Cool,* video program to teach how to manage conflict, anger and emotions, available for lower and upper elementary, middle/jr. high, and high school levels (Santa Barbara, Calif.: James Stanfield Co., 1994–97), (800) 421-6534.

The Fourth Street Company, *Stop, Relax and Think Game.* Available from Childswork/Childsplay.

Walker, H.M., Todis, B., Holmes, D., & Horton, G., *The Walker Social Skills Curriculum: The ACCESS Program* (Austin, Texas: Pro-Ed, 1988).

Resources for Building Study Skills

Crutsinger, C., *Thinking Smarter: Skills for Academic Success,* Student and Teacher editions (Carrollton, Texas: Brainworks, 1992).

Davis, L., & Sirotowitz, S., *Study Strategies Made Easy: A Practical Plan for Success* (Plantation, Fla.: Specialty Press, 1996).

DeBrueys, M.T. (Project Coordinator), *125 Ways to Be a Better Student: A Program for Study Skill Success* (Moline, Ill.: LinguiSystems,

1986).

Ellis, D.B., *Becoming a Master Student (7th ed.)* (Boston: Houghton Mifflin, 1994).

Lazzari, A.M., *Help for Memory* (Moline, Ill.: LinguiSystems, 1996).

Rooney, K., *Independent Strategies for Efficient Study* (J.R. Enterprises, 211 Willowick Lane, Richmond, VA 23233, 1990).

Scheiber, B., & Talpers, J., *Unlocking Potential: College and Other Choices for Learning Disabled People* (New York: Adler & Adler, 1987).

Study Smart. A board game that is not intended to teach study skills, but rather to reinforce the use of study skills in a highly motivating way. Useful from age 10 through adolescence. Available from Childswork/Childsplay.

Videotapes

Barkley, R.A., *ADHD: What Do We Know?, ADHD: What Can We Do? ADHD in the Classroom, and ADHD in Adults* (New York: Guilford Press, 1993, 1994).

Copeland, E.D., *Understanding Attention Disorders* (Atlanta: 3 C's of Childhood, 1989).

Goldstein, S., & Goldstein, M., *Why Won't My Child Pay Attention?* A video guide for parents (Salt Lake City: Neurology, Learning and Behavior Center, 1989).

Goldstein, S., & Goldstein, M., *Educating Inattentive Children.* A video guide for teachers (Salt Lake City: Neurology, Learning and Behavior Center, 1990).

Goldstein, S., & Goldstein, M., *It's Just Attention Disorder.* A video guide for kids (Salt Lake City: Neurology, Learning and Behavior Center, 1991).

Goodman, J.F., & Hoban, S., *Around the Clock: Parenting the Delayed ADHD Child* (New York: Guilford Press, 1994).

Phelan, T.W., *All about Attention Deficit Disorder, 1—2—3—Magic, Medication for Attention Deficit Disorder* (Carol Stream, Ill.: Child Management, 1989, 1984, 1994).

Reif, S., *ADHD Inclusive Instruction and Collaborative Practices* (New York: National Professional Resources, 1993).

Robin, A., *ADHD in Adolescence: The Next Step: A Video Guide for Clinical Description, Diagnosis and Treatment of Adolescents with ADHD* (Worcester, Mass.: Madison Avenue Marketing, 1993).

Sources of Materials

A complete listing of books, tests, scales, and programs for ADHD children is available from *A.D.D. WareHouse,* 300 Northwest 70th Avenue, Suite 102, Plantation, FL 33317. (800) 233-9273. Web site:

www.addwarehouse.com.

Another mail-order supply source for ADHD materials as well as other useful supplies for working with children is *Childswork/Childsplay*, c/o Genesis Direct, 100 Plaza Drive, Secaucus, NJ 07094. (800) 962-1141. Web site: www.Childswork.com.

Organizations

American Coaching Association, P.O. Box 353, Lafayette Hill, PA 19444. (610) 825-4505.

Attention-Deficit Disorder Association (ADDA), 9930 Johnnycake Ridge Road, Suite 3E, Mentor, OH 44060. (800) 487-2282 or (216) 350-9595. Web site: www.add.org.

Adult ADD Association, 1225 East Sunset Drive, No. 640, Bellingham, WA 98226. (360) 647-6681.

Associates for Coaching with HOPE, 4150 Channelview Drive, Vicksburg, MI 49097. (616) 649-1005.

Children with Attention-Deficit Disorders (CH.A.D.D.), National Headquarters, 499 Northwest 70th Ave., Suite 109, Plantation, FL 33317. (305) 587-3700 or (800) 233-4050. Web site: www.chadd.org.

CH.A.D.D. Canada, #214-1376 Bank Street, Ottawa, ON, Canada K1H 1B3. (613) 731-1209.

Clearinghouse on Disability Information, U.S. Department of Education, Switzer Building, 330 C Street SW, Rm 3132, Washington, DC 20202-2524. (202) 732-1723 or 732-1241.

Council for Exceptional Children, 1920 Association Dr., Reston, VA 22091. (703) 620-3660. Web site: www.cec.sped.org.

Council for Learning Disabilities, P.O. Box 40303, Overland Park, KS 66204. (913) 492-3840.

Christian Council on Persons with Disabilities, P.O. Box 458, Lake Geneva, WI 53147. (414) 275-6131.

Dyslexia Research Institute, 4745 Centerville Rd., Tallahasse, FL 32308. (904) 893-2216.

Equal Employment Opportunity Commission, 1801 L Street, NW, Washington, DC 20507. (202) 663-4900 or (800) 800-3302.

Foundation for Attentional Disorders, 57 Pinecrest Road, Toronto, ON, Canada M0P 3G6. (416) 341-1515.

Learning Disabilities Association of America (LDAA), 4156 Library Road, Pittsburgh, PA 15234. (412) 341-1515 or 341-8077. Web site: www.ldanatl.org.

National Center for Learning Disabilities, 381 Park Ave., Suite 1420, New York, NY 10016. (212) 545-7510 or (888) 575-7373. Web site: www.ncld.org.

National ADDA, 9930 Johnnycake Ridge Road, Suite 3E, Mentor, OH 44060. (800) 487-2282 or (216) 350-9595. Web site: www.add.org.

Office of Civil Rights, U.S. Department of Education, 400 Maryland Avenue, SW, Washington, DC 20202-4135. (202) 401-3020.

Tourette's Syndrome Association, 42-40 Bell Blvd., Bayside, NY 11361-2861. (800) 237-0717 or (718) 224-2999.

Periodicals

Adult Challenge, P.O. Box 2277, West Peabody, MA 01960-7277. (800) 233-2322.

ADDult News, ADDult Support Network, 2620 Ivy Place, Toledo, OH 43613. (419) 866-9183.

The ADHD Report, Guilford Press, 72 Spring St., New York, NY 10012. (800) 365-7006.

Attention!, CHADD, 449 N.W. 70th Ave., Suite 208, Plantation, FL 33317. (305) 587-3700 or (800) 233-4050.

Brakes: The Interactive Newsletter for Kids with ADD, Magination Press, 19 Union Square West, New York, NY 10003. (800) 825-3089.

CHADD Newsletter, CHADD, 449 N.W. 70th Ave., Suite 208, Plantation, FL 33317. (305) 587-3700 or (800) 233-4050.

Challenge: A Newsletter on ADHD, P.O. Box 2001, West Newbury, MA 01985. (508) 462-0495.

Journal of Attention Disorders, edited by C. Keith Conners, Multi-Health Systems, Inc., 908 Niagara Falls Blvd, North Tonawanda, NY 14120. (800) 456-3003.

ADHD children are high maintenance.
the constant advocacy
attention to details &
remediation efforts
takes your concentration & patience